TWAYNE'S WORLD AUTHORS SERIES

A Survey of the World's Literature

Sylvia E. Bowman, Indiana University

GENERAL EDITOR

ITALY

Carlo Golino, University of Massachusetts

EDITOR

Alessandro Manzoni

TWAS 411

Alessandro Manzoni

ALESSANDRO MANZONI

By GIAN PIERO BARRICELLI

University of California, Riverside

TWAYNE PUBLISHERS

A DIVISION OF G. K. HALL & CO., BOSTON

Library of Congress Cataloging in Publication Data

Barricelli, Jean Pierre.
Alessandro Manzoni.

(Twayne's world authors series; TWAS 411)
Bibliography: p. 185–88.
Includes index.
1.   Manzoni, Alessandro, 1785–1873.   I.   Title.
PQ4715.B34   853'.7   76-16481
ISBN 0-8057-6251-5

To

MARCO, LAURA, & FRANCA

who in their own way
also rinsed their clothes
in the Arno.

Contents

About the Author

Preface

Chronology

1. With Things Human   13
2. That Faith Which Pierces Every Veil   22
3. To Feel and to Meditate   39
4. Provident Ill-Fortune   55
5. Upright Heart and Perfectioned Mind   84
6. That Branch of Lake Como   111
7. Right and Wrong Never Neatly Divided   118
8. Those Words One After the Other   140
9. Angelic Goodness and Diabolic Machinations   148
10. The Juice of the Whole Tale   157

Notes and References   165

Selected Bibliography   185

Index   189

About the Author

Gian Piero Barricelli is Professor of Romance Languages and Comparative Literature at the University of California at Riverside. He was born in Cleveland, Ohio in 1924, and received a B.A., M.A., and Ph.D. from Harvard (1947, 1948, and 1953 respectively). He taught at Harvard and Brandeis before going to California in 1963, as well as at the University of Bergen and the School of Business Administration in Norway. Among the honors he has received are: Phi Beta Kappa, Harvard Humanities Award, two Fulbright Awards, a University of California Humanities Institute Award, and his campus' Distinguished Teaching Award. He is also a professional musician, having taught music and composed various instrumental sonatas, a piano concerto, art songs, a scherzo for orchestra, and a mass for mixed chorus; in addition, he conducted the Waltham Symphony Orchestra and the Cafarelli Opera Company of Cleveland for five seasons. He has published studies on Balzac, Leopardi, Diderot, Dante and Calderón, Mazzini, Chekhov, Chausson, Zweig, Pound, Boccaccio and others, in addition to his own poetry, and has translated works by various authors like Virgil, Wergeland, Machiavelli, and Leopardi. He works primarily in the areas of Romanticism and Renaissance, and has made a specialty of the interrelationships between literature and music. He is past editor of the *Italian Quarterly*, and currently edits the American Comparative Literature Association's newsletter on literature and the other arts, *The Heliconian*. At UCR he has been chairman of Comparative Literature and now chairs the Department of Literatures and Languages.

Preface

Alessandro Manzoni is not, as the ancient Romans used to say, a *magni nominis umbra,* a shadow of a great name, either on the European Continent or in England. Yet this outstanding nineteenth-century artist and thinker, included in the Harvard Classics and hailed outside of his native Italy by such personalities as Goethe, Scott, and Sainte-Beuve among others, has suffered from the neglect of American critics and litterati. Perhaps he was too unassuming a man who shied away from the polemics of Romanticism and Nationalism; perhaps he was too many things simultaneously—poet, tragedian, novelist, religious writer, historian, literary critic, philologist, and philosopher, not to mention agronomist. Whatever the case, many writers of lesser stature are better known in the United States. It is hoped, therefore, that the present study will help to bring Manzoni to the attention of a broader spectrum of students and professionals of literature and intellectual history, for he is the kind of author whom one does not simply discover, but whom one keeps discovering. It is hoped too that the present study, which, by bringing together many critical points of view is not intended exclusively as an introduction to Manzoni, will contribute toward a rethinking among scholars of a number of problems connected with his works.

To this end, I have considered Manzoni's pertinent biography before and after his conversion in 1810 (Chapters 1 and 2), his poetry before and after this year (Chapter 3), his two tragedies (Chapter 4), and most of his essays, for it is here that the immense scope of the man's intellect proves itself—in his religious, historical, critical, linguistic, and philosophical speculations (Chapter 5). There is much to be said about his later poetry and his second tragedy, and many of his essays stem from a depth of intellectual consciousness which establishes them readily as significant pieces of work. In this study, then, I have paid special attention to these writings, and to substantiate my point of view I have relied heavily throughout on Manzoni's correspondence as the most sincere gauge of his innermost attitudes and beliefs.

As if preplanned in a very rational way, and with much more total coherence than one might expect, all culminates in *I promessi sposi* (The Betrothed). His one novel is his greatest achievement, of course, and, as it should be, his best-known publication. Hence my discussion of it occupies well over a third of the present volume. As with any great work, there are many dimensions to be considered, beginning with the genesis of the novel to its philosophical meaning. In between, I have attempted to treat questions relating to the historical novel, the problem of oratory and of Jansenism (Chapter 6), the characters and their psychology (Chapter 7), the style and the matters of dialogue, humor, and irony (Chapter 8), the structure and how word and imagistic symbolism define meaning (Chapter 9), and finally the application of the labels of Romanticism and Realism to a novel which both in manner and in message transcends all classifications (Chapter 10).

I should add here, as I have stated in the notes, that all translations in this volume, whether from primary or secondary sources, are my own. I should add, too, that from the University of California I received a Humanities Institute Award which enabled me to complete much reading and research in connection with this book, and I am therefore grateful to this institution for its awareness of Manzoni, and for its willingness to utter with him that "Di libri basta uno per volta. . . ." Indeed, "One book at a time is enough . . ." Perhaps it was time for this one.

G. P. Barricelli

Riverside, California

Chronology

1785   Alessandro Manzoni born March 7 in Milan, via San Damiano.

1791–   Education in various religious schools.
1801

1792   Father and mother legally separated.

1795   Mother goes to London, then Paris, with Carlo Imbonati.

1801–   Manzoni leaves school and lives in Milan, Venice, and
1807   Lecco, travels in Switzerland, Piedmont, and Lombardy.

1801–   First poems, including "Il trionfo della libertà," "A Fran-
1809   cesco Lomonaco," the *Sermoni*, "L'Adda," "In morte di Carlo Imbonati," and "Urania."

1805   Moves to Paris with his mother and Imbonati, who dies there.

1807   Father dies, leaving him heir to the estate (he had also inherited some wealth from Imbonati).

1808   Marries Enrichetta Blondel in Milan in a Calvinist rite.

1810   Marriage celebrated in a Catholic rite; nervous crisis in Paris following fear of loss of wife in a crowd; conversion to Catholicism of both Enrichetta and Manzoni; return to Italy.

1811–   Religious poetry, including the *Inni sacri*, excluding "La
1815   Pentecoste" (1822).

1815   Nervous crisis at news of Napoleon's defeat.

1819   *Osservazioni sulla morale cattolica.*

1820   Publication of *Il Conte di Carmagnola.*

1821   Begins novel, writes "Il cinque maggio" and "Marzo, 1821."

1822   Publishes *Adelchi* and *Discorso sopra alcuni punti della storia longobardica in Italia.*

1823   *Lettre à M. Chauvet sur l'unité de temps et de lieu dans la tragédie* and *Lettera sul Romanticismo*, finishes first version of *Fermo e Lucia.*

1827   First edition of *I promessi sposi;* leaves for Florence to polish the novel linguistically.

1829   *Lettre à Victor Cousin.*

1833   Wife Enrichetta dies.

1837   Marries Teresa Borri, widow Stampa.

1840–1842   Final edition of *I promessi sposi*.

1841   Mother dies.

1842   *Storia della colonna infame*.

1845   *Discorso sul romanzo storico* and *Del sistema che fonda la morale sull'utilità*.

1850   *Dell'invenzione* and *Sulla lingua italiana*.

1859   Victor Emanuel II assigns him a life-pension of 12,000 lire annually.

1860   Named Senator of the Kingdom.

1861   Wife Teresa dies.

1868   *Intorno al vocabolario* and *Dell'unità della lingua e dei mezzi di diffonderla*.

1872   Granted Roman citizenship.

1873   Dies in Milan, May 22; solemn funeral on May 29; Giuseppe Verdi resumes work on his *Messa da Requiem*, dedicated to Manzoni and performed May 22, 1874 in the church of San Marco (Milan).

1889   *Saggio comparativo su la rivoluzione francese del 1789 e la rivoluzione italiana del 1859*.

1923   *Sentir Messa*.

CHAPTER 1

With Things Human

L IKE that of his French counterpart Victor Hugo, the life of the main figure in Italian literary Romanticism and most admired writer of his day spanned most of the nineteenth century. The analogy, however, ends here. For Alessandro Manzoni's life, which extended from before the French Revolution to after the Italian Unification, was relatively tranquil: it avoided the stridencies of social and political reform and literary pomp, and the show of self-imposed exile. Manzoni did not see himself as an *éco sonore* (*sonorous echo*), as Hugo did. His life appears fairly closed, stolidly intellectual, and unassumingly reserved, the life of a man of quiet meditation who nonetheless advised his century on its religious, political, historical, moral, and aesthetic problems. His passionate dedication to them shaped the major part of his intimate existence, the part that "died with him"[1] and that we can only surmise by weighing the uneventfulness of his life against the abundance of his literary, critical, and philosophical productiveness. Indeed, even his conversion, normally a dramatic event in any biography, yields to the biographer little factual material and continues to be shrouded in not much more than scholarly hypotheses.

The Italy into which Manzoni was born had already received the promptings of independence and unification, well ahead of the revolutionary explosion in France. While progressive reformism had yielded in many quarters to reaction, new ideas inflamed Jacobin clubs in many a city. By 1796, Napoleon controlled most of Lombardy, from where a strong movement for liberty, democracy, and unity aimed against the Austrians spread to the rest of the peninsula, at least among the intellectuals, the middle class, and many artisans. A purely literary term at first, *risorgimento*, or rebirth, was given political currency by Vittorio Alfieri. Dissension or disinterest, however, kept twisting the libertarian goal off target, for

13

many Italians opposed the French and the Jacobins; the nobility was uninterested, the clergy hostile, and the peasantry ignorant. This situation enabled the Austrians to return without much difficulty, until again Napoleon, now First Consul of France, recaptured a good part of the North in 1801, a year before this general area was named The Italian Republic and three years before he crowned himself Emperor of France—which also meant King of Italy. Here he appointed Eugène de Beauharnais his viceroy.[2]

By this time, any attempt by the French at "democratic" rule in Northern Italy had to be abandoned; though the peninsula remained completely dependent upon France and French interests, its political reality was that of a police state serving at best an enlightened despotism. True, Italians administered their own government and even possessed a Kingdom's army, but the fact remains that such an arrangement served French interests in opposition to the Austrian menace. And as the ups and downs, hopes and defeats, of the struggle were to indicate until the missions of Cavour, Mazzini, and Garibaldi finally achieved success, it also served French (and Papal) interests not to unify Italy lest, to quote Napoleon himself, the Italians become stronger than the French and gain control of the Mediterranean. Still, contrasted with the oppressive reactionary policies of Austria—and Metternich's takeover after Waterloo quickly proved that—Napoleon, as associated with his Revolutionary background of political liberalism, to say nothing of his Italian blood, remained Italy's only hope, and he was so regarded by all Italian patriots and intellectuals. As might be expected, the latter took great stock in their Classical, Roman, and Medieval past, Italian traditions of local autonomy, and eighteenth-century liberalism, while the taste of unification in the form of the Napoleonic Kingdom of Italy whetted their appetites.

Italian Romanticism developed in a political atmosphere charged with aspirations, frustrations, and extraordinary examples of both heroism and martyrdom. It was the atmosphere of the reviews, *Il Conciliatore* and *Antologia*, of the secret, conspiratorial society of the Carbonari, with its Freemasonic rituals and its Romantic seductiveness which lured any number of non-Italians, like Byron and Stendhal, to its cause, and of Mazzini's activist revolutionary club La Giovane Italia, a prelude to La Giovane Europa. Hardly a literary utterance in Italy was devoid of moral or civic overtones, a fact which colored the Risorgimento with idealistic hues of an artistic nature perhaps unmatched in political movements anywhere. For Italian literary Romanticism sought to achieve national independence by combating the servitude and passivity to which the population had become unhappily accustomed after centuries of foreign domination. The country needed a new artistic affirmation alongside the spiritual (political) education of the people. Across the Alps, Hugo had said it succinctly: "Great revolutions march together!" Italian Romanticism's credo was summarized in Giovanni Berchet's *Lettera semiseria di Grisostomo* of 1816, in which the need for "a common literary fatherland" was linked with that for "a common political fatherland." In retrospect, Mazzini was to comment that for Italians, independence in matters of literature was but the first step toward a much greater independence. About this, every Romantic author who wrote during Manzoni's lifetime—Monti, Foscolo, Berchet, Porta, Pellico, Giusti, Grossi, D'Azeglio, Settembrini, Nievo, Guerrazzi, Aleardi, Praga, even Leopardi—was exaltingly conscious and almost feverishly sensitive. But of all of them, no voice became at once as retiring and respected and significant as that of Alessandro Manzoni.

He was born in Milan on March 7, 1785, of Count Pietro Manzoni and Giulia Beccaria,[3] the daughter of the famous criminologist and economist, Cesare Beccaria, author of *Dei delitti e delle pene* (*On Crimes and Punishments*). The family was of recent nobility. His early years were not happy ones; they were marked by spiritual privation and the normal confusion that arises in the mind of a sensitive child before an impassive father and a carefree mother who did not get along. The incompatible parents separated in February, 1792, leaving Alessandro estranged from his father and with a deep sense of longing for his "tender mother."[4] To remove him from the unhappy domestic surrounding, for which the beautiful open air of Lecco did not compensate, he had been sent to study in religious schools, first in Merate and Lugano from 1791 to 1798 under the Somaschi brothers, then in Magenta and Milan until 1801 under the Barnabites. But these experiences were not invigorating. Introverted and shy by nature as well as nervously troubled (Lombroso later noted a near psychopathic sensibility), he fell easy prey to the bullying of his fellow students. He developed a strong reserve and a dislike for crowds, and one of his biographers notes how he had difficulty in writing, would isolate himself for long periods of time, felt voids opening up before him when he had to cross a street, and according to stories told about him weighed his clothes often and resented birds in the trees under his windows.[5] There were no dramatic displays or tantrums, however. As he grew, he reacted sharply against his religious education, believing himself an atheist and favoring those French Revolutionary ideas that were in the air which abetted his youthful radicalism, republican interests, and admiration of Parini and Alfieri. Parini taught him great sympathy for the hard-working peasant at the beck of the superficial aristocrat, while Alfieri fired his revulsion for absolute government and tyranny. The combination of Alessandro's views, temperament, and situation was not conducive to an orderly pursuit of a formal education. It is not surprising that it stopped at the age of sixteen.

In Milan, an aunt and ex-nun introduced him to the frivolous pleasures of upper society, into which he stepped without bothering about the Parinian contradiction. In fact, for a short while he even gambled at the Ridotto of La Scala and savored dissipation in Venice. Milan provided his first flirtation with love in the person of Luigina, and Venice his second—if we are to believe a passing confession to his friend Giambattista Pagani in which he declared having tasted in that city "the herbs/of the Epicurean garden."[6] Despite her being thirty, twelve years older than he, he loved her with a passion and offered to marry her, to which she responded: "At your age one thinks of going to school, not of making love."[7] At that time, Alessandro was living out his Voltairian rationalism, through which it was not difficult to blend libertarian ideas with worldly attractions. Beginning in 1799, his association in Milan with the poet Vincenzo Monti channeled his interests along more intellectual lines, particularly in the direction of the literary neo-Classicism that characterized the Napoleonic era. His first poem, "Il trionfo della libertà," written after the peace at Lunéville, is Jacobin inspired and dates from this period (1801).[8] So do the idyll "L'Adda" (1803), with its rich texture of mythological adornments, and the four satirical *Sermoni* (1801–1804). "A Francesco Lomonaco" (1802) rings with patriotism. Another friend, the historian Vincenzo Cuoco, who had fled Bourbon Naples, further contributed to his revolutionary leanings and introduced him to historical studies.

Meanwhile, his mother had run off to London, then Paris, in 1795 and in 1796, with her lover, the great Milanese banker Carlo Imbonati, an event that buzzed with the charm of scandal throughout the Lombard city's salons. In 1805, the couple invited Alessandro to join them, but just as he arrived, Imbonati died, leaving the twenty-year old youth considerable property.[9] His mother's questionable tie with the banker did not seem to bother Alessandro, as far as we can determine from the record we have; in fact, he composed an elegy to his benefactor's memory one year later, which he dedicated to his mother: the *Carme* "In morte di Carlo Imbonati,"[10] and regretted that he had never had the opportunity "to assure him orally of the deep respect and affection he had for him."[11] After his conversion in 1810, however, he discarded the elegy from among his collected works out of moral scruples, just as he discarded the heavily classical and mythological poem "Urania" (1809) out of aesthetic scruples, describing both of them as *"delicta juventutis."*[12]

Through his mother, Alessandro was ushered into the society of the French Directorate. The period between 1805 and 1810 turned out to be one of the most important periods in his intellectual formation, one in which he met many writers and philosophers, reading their works and discussing them at length at the salons of Mme. Helvétius, Mme. Cabanis, Mme. de Condorcet, and elsewhere. Not that these experiences constituted his first contact with French literature and thought; it would be unreasonable to suppose this, given the intellectual climate of the whole of Europe at that time, as well as the precocious intellect of Alessandro. But it is one thing to read about the salon environment at a time when deism was on the wane and skepticism on the rise, and quite another to touch it. One of his first acquaintances, who became a lifetime friend, was historian Claude Fauriel, who lived with Mme. de Condorcet, and at whose home many Ideologues met, supported by Mme. de Staël in her opposition to Napoleon. Fauriel, himself a disciple of Cabanis and Condorcet, brought the young Italian in touch not only with politicians like Constant, historians like Guizot, and poets like Pyndare Lebrun, but also with Cabanis himself (Helvétius and Condorcet having died in 1771 and 1794 respectively) and his ideas relating the physical to the moral in man, with Volney and his aesthetic morality, with Maine de Biran as he expounded on the difference between sensations and perceptions, with Garat and his materialistic physiology, with Destutt de Tracy and his views of how ideas are analyzed into sensory elements. And to keep up with this kind of company, Alessandro surely must have renewed his acquaintance with Condillac's theory of sensations with reference to the formation of ideas and the origin of language, with Helvétius' relation of psychology to sensationist premises, and with Condorcet's argument about the mathematical basis of the moral and political sciences. While concrete evidence of such influences is lacking, it is legitimate to speculate that conversations around these topics took place, simply because it is impossible that they did not. When in 1806 he penned the phrase in a letter: "the horrible figure of a priest"[13] (a phrase he regretted later), is it vain to speculate that somewhere in his mind during these preconversion days floated the notion popularized by D'Holbach that religion is a sly invention of priests?

Influences notwithstanding,[14] Alessandro never became aggressive in expressing his ideas, and in no way, despite his sympathies, could he be called a revolutionary. He was by nature always gentle, even delicate, and the reserve that characterized his mature years and his art was in evidence in his youth. He had learned early the wisdom in the words he had put in Imbonati's mouth: "with things human/experiment only so much as you need/not to care for them."[15] The philosophers' arguments he inhaled: they formed part of an atmosphere of libertarian thinking that characterized the turn of the century. But the budding poet focused on something more central for him, and not simply because toward the end of the first decade of the new century the dominance of the Ideologues was being supplanted by the rise of more spiritually-oriented philosophers. Besides, in Paris he developed a fundamental love and admiration for French letters and the French language which he learned to write and speak fluently, and if he ever was at all outspoken, it was in regard to this. In his conversations with Fauriel and subsequent correspondence, he revealed that his primary concerns at that time centered less around sensationistic and materialistic philosophies than around literature and the problems of art, of writing, of the Italian language, of poetry which should spring from the heart and which by so doing engenders its own style of versification. Poetry, in a sense not a "thing human" for being born of feeling, occupied the spotlight, conceived in the Romantic manner of his friend Fauriel: "I agree with you more than ever about poetry; it must be drawn from the bottom of the heart; one must feel, and know how to express one's feelings sincerely; I could not state it any other way."[16] The French experience, then, was important because

it helped sharpen Alessandro's literary thinking by bringing together questions of aesthetics and language, morality and religion,
psychology and historicity, his finest attributes as the writer he was
to become.

Around "divine Paris"[17] centers another important event in Alessandro's early years. He met there a young lady of Calvinist (reformed evangelical), Genevan background in 1808 and married her
in Milan according to Evangelical rite. Henriette Blondel was only
sixteen; "besides, she is Protestant, in short, a treasure," as he
exclaimed to Fauriel, "an angelic creature."[18] Enrichetta, as she
then became known, did not belie Alessandro's epithet. She was in
every sense "very sweet, very proper,"[19] an uncommonly loving
and gentle person of deep religious sentiments, a veritable inspiration particularly to someone of his sensibilities. There can be no
doubt that, plunged as he was in pensive questioning and intimate
deliberations in the midst of the capital's intellectual fermentation,
he benefited by her suavity and mansuetude which had the effect of
tacitly urging him in the direction of increased spiritual awareness.

Alessandro guarded closely the secret of his conversion—that is,
of his reconversion to Catholicism. Because of the importance of
such an awareness in his later works, critics and biographers for
years have attempted not only to reconstruct his motivations but
also to piece together even the slightest clues which might contribute a thought, however tenuous, toward an explanation of that culminating event of 1810. It suffices, for instance, because three
years before this Manzoni had expressed concern over corruption in
his native land, that therefore his statement can be construed as an
indication of the change slowly taking place within him. But whatever the antecedents, there are a number of reasonable conjectures
which may be noted, apart from what may have been the pious
example, perhaps even the promptings, of Enrichetta.

First of all, there is the report by his stepson,[20] Stefano Stampa,
who suggested that Alessandro first felt the divine intervention lis-
tening to sacred music in the church of Saint Roch, into which he
had wandered one day in April, 1810 (during a public celebration of
Napoleon's marriage to Marie Louise), dizzy and nervous, having
lost his wife in the crowd, and desperately asking God to give him
proof of His existence. Illumination supposedly came at this time.
Years later, in responding to a related query of his daughter Vittoria,

he chose merely to ask her to thank God who had taken pity on him that day, the same God who had revealed Himself to St. Paul on the road to Damascus.

Then there is the probable influence of Jansenist thought which he encountered frequently in Paris, of Pascal (who, too, had converted, though more dramatically than Alessandro), author of the spiritually stimulating *Pensées* and the anti-Jesuitic *Lettres provinciales* (no mention is made of Jesuits in *I promessi sposi*, we might interject, though they were at the acme of their influence and power in the seventeenth century, the time of the novel's action[21]). As Galletti has pointed out so convincingly, and Pellizzari more recently, notable was the influence on Enrichetta as well as on her husband of Jansenist thinkers like Eustachio Dègola in Paris,[22] and Luigi Tosi who took over Dègola's spiritual counseling in Milan.[23]

And finally, as has also been frequently conjectured, we may surmise a need and a search for inner peace on Alessandro's part, a desire for a more traditional environment for his family (his daughter Giulia Claudia, who was born in Paris around Christmas, had to be registered at baptism as belonging outside the Church), and a desire to sort things out generally. He had been disturbed by the contradiction between the dissemination of death by Napoleon's armies and the expectation of a freer life for all nations in its wake; the aesthetic Christianity of Chateaubriand had made some impression on him, and he had noted the return by the very circles which once had encouraged his skepticism to more conservative attitudes. In February, 1810, his marriage to Enrichetta was recelebrated, this time according to Catholic cermony.[24] Three months later, Enrichetta left the Protestant faith for Catholicism, a shift which moved her parents to "most immoderate anger,"[25] and Donna Giulia herself converted. By year's end, Manzoni was fully within the fold.

Momigliano makes as good a statement as any regarding the conversion:

Manzoni's religious conversion is the definitive settlement of his moral conscience, the moment in which his scrupulous honesty finds an unwavering basis. He already believed in God—he must have been an atheist for a very short time—, he already felt a deep aversion for every act and every feeling which was less than noble; but all these were instincts, sensations, thoughts which lacked a unifying principle or a sanction. To convert was for Manzoni a clarification of his morality, a warming of it by the flames of a strong and accurate feeling. The deist becomes theist, and his humanitarian morality becomes Catholic morality. The step is not great, but it is certainly accompanied by an intense toil which escapes us. . . . His return to the faith gathered all his forces around a single point, moved him to seek the moral ideal of Catholicism in every one of his activities. Hence, in life: modesty, love of meditative solitude, charity, a reluctance to speak ill of his neighbor, and an acute and indulgent penetration into the motivations for human actions; in art: the portrayal of these and similar virtues, and of the opposite defects, so rendered as to induce approval of the former and revulsion of the latter; in criticism: the struggle against poetry that is of no use to the loftiest interests of the soul.[26]

The real reasons for profound and genuine conversions, like Manzoni's or Pascal's, always "escape us": they are always unfathomable, and in any event do not stand out ultimately as significantly as the results. In the case of Manzoni, it is evident that his literary, philosophical, and critical production took on broader spiritual dimensions from 1810 onward. The neo-Classical modes gave way to more Romantic utterances which were not of the mystical and Germanic variety but of Christian and Latin inspiration. Artistically, morally, and intellectually, a definitive corner had been turned.

CHAPTER 2

That Faith Which Pierces Every Veil

A NY account of Manzoni's postconversion years becomes largely a matter of intellectual biography. Even those episodes which might otherwise emerge as distressing, such as the neurasthenic attacks from which he suffered[1] ever since he lost Enrichetta in the celebrant crowd, or the premature deaths of nine children and two wives, do not stand out in any way in the generally unagitated picture we have of his existence. In the first place, he rarely wandered away from his native Milan or from his country retreats in Brusuglio and Lesa; there was a Parisian parenthesis in 1819–1820, a visit to Genoa in 1842, and two trips to Florence in 1827 and 1856 (including Viareggio). In the second place, his great sense of reserve—some would call it timidity or shyness—did not permit him to seek any form of visibility beyond what his writings conferred upon him, and even the honors he received he accepted with some embarrassment. He had "resolved to enter into literary associations in no way,"[2] much less to participate in literary polemics, which he never felt applied to him anyway, since, as he wrote to Fauriel, he saw Romanticism (through its mouthpiece *Il Conciliatore*) insufficiently imbued with positive moral concerns and continuously engaging in "negative discussions."[3] Besides, he felt "an extreme aversion, like a kind of terror, to express judgment on literary matters, particularly in writing."[4] There is no escaping the fact that Manzoni's was an introverted life; his writings may have animated and incited others, but his own visible profile as a human being remained at all times contemplative and meditative, studious and humble. In addition, he was devoted to his family. Tommaseo left a good description in a letter to a friend: "I met Manzoni; an adorable man! His modesty expands his greatness a thousand times. Not that I could get close to him. He is too withdrawn in his studies and his love for his family; he does not want new people around. It took all my typical imprudence to get all the way to him."[5] If there is one word

22

which characterizes all aspects of his existence, particularly that of his mind, it is "equilibrium," the equilibrium that comes from a reasoned and circumspect assessment of all that occurs around us and an aversion for the loud display of enthusiasms. Equilibrium engenders dispassion, and dispassion does not make for startling biography.

In matters of the intellect, Manzoni's conversion did not imply a renunciation of the Enlightenment, just as his Romanticism did not rebelliously shun Classical norms. Throughout his mature life, in his consistent attempts to reconcile opposites, he maintained a serene balance between the most polarized points of view, such as skepticism and materialism on the one hand and mysticism and idealism on the other. He could be an intimate friend of the Masons without becoming one himself; when he had been anticlerical and atheist, he still had never abandoned a deeply-rooted moral and spiritual attitude toward life,[6] and now that he was Catholic, he could not forsake the spirit of his former libertarian principles. Unlike so many authors in other countries, and to a greater extent than many in his own (Grossi, Foscolo, D'Azeglio, Berchet, and Pellico), Manzoni did not allow Chateaubriand, Mme. de Staël, Lamartine, Hugo, and Lamennais to supplant Voltaire, Montesquieu, and Diderot while granting a passing nod to Rousseau. Rather, he saw the latter group complementing the former. For the mind still keen with Beccaria's humanitarianism and Alfieri's patriotically Italian utterances on liberty, country, equality, and the rights of man could not discard those ideals under the pressure of any orthodoxy.

Indeed, it was orthodoxy that was to be tempered. The posture of Manzoni's newly rediscovered Catholicism vis-à-vis the eighteenth century contrasted with that of the Jesuits who at that time found it proper to deny the godless Age of Reason. His Catholicism could best be described as a pure and original form of Christianity; it was evangelical. Even a cursory reading of his *Osservazioni sulla morale cattolica* reveals a humanization and naturalization of dogma, not inconsistent in the long run with the spirit of the thought of the *philosophes*, except for the fact that the substance is lyricized and poetically rendered. The lost Christ is found again inside us; Providence returns to earth by working itself out within us through the cultivation of hope and prayer, pardon and peace. Manzoni's religious conscience and his vast readings shaped his awareness of the sorrow of all earthly forces and of God's eventual synthesis of all

human events. More than that, they inculcated in him the absolute
need for spiritual serenity, and given his artistic predisposition, it
was art that could provide it. We might say, then, that, like Christianity, political Romanticism was for Manzoni a matter of faith, and
like Romanticism Christianity was a motive for art. His Horatian
goal stressed the useful along with the beautiful.

It was in this frame of mind that, after returning to Italy from
Paris in 1810 (he had grown less and less fond of the French capital),[7] he wrote his first religious poetry, the *Inni sacri*, between 1812
and 1813. The poems—"La Risurrezione," "Il nome di Maria," "Il
Natale"—were not well received in 1815 when they were published
together with another religious poem, "La Passione." This was
Catholicism filtered through the liberal webbing of the French Revolution, said those who were uneasy at their fervor, or who did not
understand the reconciling mind of their author. Seven years later,
he added a fifth, "La Pentecoste," but he never completed the
series, which was to contain at least twelve poems. He never composed "L'Epifania," "Ognissanti" (except for fourteen verses),
"L'Ascensione," "Il corpo del Signore," "La cattedra di San Pietro,"
"L'Assunzione," and "I morti."[8] Collectively, the *Inni* had an
evangelical purpose: to imbue religion once more with those noble
and human sentiments that are basic to it and without which religion
simply would not be. But adverse reaction may have steered Manzoni in the direction of prose as a vehicle to try for the expression of
religious thoughts. Whatever the case, we know that Monsignor
Tosi pushed him into writing the *Osservazioni* in 1819 in response to
Sismondi's *Histoire des républiques italiennes du moyen âge* (1807–
1818), in which the Swiss author implicates Catholicism causally
with the corruption in Italian life. This charge made no sense to
Manzoni, who saw more Christianity in the word "Catholicism"
than Sismondi with his pragmatic optics. The latter admitted subsequently that he and Manzoni were talking about different things.
For the *Osservazioni* once again made common cause of patriotism,
religion, and art in the form of an aesthetic Christianity. Not feeling
he had said all there was to be said on the subject and with an eye to
elaboration, Manzoni reworked it later, and in 1855 published a
second version, this one including a fragmentary second part.

After this intensely religious period, Manzoni engaged literature
proper more directly and brought his political consciousness more
earnestly into play. By this we mean that both in his readings and in

his writings he became more deeply concerned than ever before in questions of language and form and in the desirability of making religion and politics serve each other simultaneously and organically in a single literary work. He believed that content dictates form—advisedly, to be sure—from within, like an intellectual fermentation that ends by shaping its own formal configurations. In so stating, he clearly outlined the profile of his Romanticism. Manzoni was "Romantic" in his own terms before much of Europe could be described as being fully within the swing of Romanticism. It was not, however, a spontaneous Romanticism, the kind any liberal and sentimental humanitarian would have acquired simply by breathing the air of the 1820s. His was measured and cautious, even diffident and at times severely self-critical: he did not conceal his dislike for its lack of careful historicity, its wallowing in sweet vagueness, its hollow spiritual rhetoric, its egocentric *moi*, and its morbid *mal du siècle* (century's disease). These are qualities we are wont to associate with Chateaubriand or Senancour or Wackenroder or even Novalis, or with later and more militant Romantic temperaments; they do not describe Manzoni.

Just a few disparate examples may serve as illustrations. To begin with, he never counted many friends in the intimate sense inside his wide circle of acquaintances ("I must bemoan the fact that I know extremely few people"[9]); among the Romantics, he only had one who could be called close, one with whom he could discuss dispassionately all phases of human history and not only the latest Romantic events. This was Claude Fauriel: "Your judgment . . . for me is the highest authority."[10] Then, too, after his conversion, his sense of humility ran so deep that he thought of not using the first person singular, even in speech, because "I" exhibited pride and pretentiousness; his use of the plural might be termed a case of spiritual grammar.[11] Related to this verbal idiosyncrasy is his much more significant dismissal of fame, or glory, as "a proud pain," something with emptiness and bitterness inside forever betraying its vanity. Again, he saw in history the vehicle to blend religion and patriotism, but this history, artistically used, had to shun Romantic indeterminateness and represent fundamental truths in order for its moral content to become useful and therefore beautiful. And finally, his love of nature and solitude sprang genuinely from innate demands of his personality rather than from cultivated inclinations, of which we may justifiably suspect a number of his contemporaries; he practiced his convictions, to the point of envisaging the merchant as valuable as the poet, and of describing the poetic life as inseparable from the practical life of duties, which in turn offered the mind its best education.[12] He said this in his famous letter to Marco Coen. He also practiced these convictions by seeking, whenever possible, the solitude of Brusuglio in particular, not alone for the purpose of retiring to his study there, but of getting involved with plants and agriculture, to see things grow and care for nature rather than just write about it. In the words of a specialist, "his vast mind . . . embraced all there is to be known about agriculture."[13] His organic world view related as much to his Schlegelian ideas about novelistic structure, as Peer has pointed out,[14] as to his experience with plants; like Providence, they all grow from within. These disconnected examples suggest how, on the biographical, verbal, and intellectual levels, Manzoni instinctively counterpoised the ideas, attitudes, and behavior of many of his ebullient Romantic contemporaries.

If we follow him in his readings, we cannot fail to be impressed by the fact that they appear to constitute less a random accumulation of information gathered by an inquisitive mind than a program for the orderly education of that mind. He was not a fast reader, nor was he trying to gain a learning of Rabelaisian, pyrotechnical brilliance. Reading for him was a form of meditation. During the decade 1817–1827, which culminated in his great novel, he frequently asked Fauriel to send him books he was interested in, including books on agriculture (Olivier de Serre's *Théâtre d'agriculture*, for example), of course returning the favor by sending his correspondent many he had come across himself, especially on Romanticism. In this manner, a host of foreign authors reached Manzoni's study, their works often translated into French: Schlegel, especially the *Vorlesungen über dramatische Kunst und Literatur*, Lessing and his *Laokoon*, Shakespeare (Le Tourneur translations), Plato (probably the Victor Cousin translations), Aristotle, Plutarch, Hegewisch through his history of Charlemagne, Littleton in Guénée's translation (the *Preuves de la mission divine de St-Paul*), much of Goethe and Schiller, Locke, Kant by way of Villers' studies, Sterne, Scott, etc., as well as innumerable French authors, including Voltaire through his tragedies and his commentaries on Corneille and Racine, Mme. de Staël and her *De l'Allemagne*, Crébillon *père*, Rousseau, Molière, Corneille, Racine, Boileau (especially the funeral sermons), Ducis, Cousin, Descartes, Nicole, Bourdaloue,

Abbadie (his *Traité de la religion chrétienne*), De Luc, Bergier (*Certitude des preuves du christianisme*), Paschoud, Say, De Bonald, Lamartine, Hugo, and others. And needless to say, his Italian shelves were well stocked not only with the Dantes, Machiavellis, and Vicos or with the Horaces and Virgils, but with many authors to whom we tend to pay less attention today: Galluppi, Galiani, Genovesi, Verri, Gioia, Romagnosi, Vida, etc. Many books not obtainable in Milan he received from his Italian friends like Gaetano Cattaneo, Carlo Morbio, and the person in Italy he most admired, like Fauriel, intellectually and humanly, the celebrated philosopher Antonio Rosmini.

The result was a sharpened sense in his thinking of the interrelationships between historico-political and ethico-religious elements. Years later, he was still able to assert to young Edmondo De Amicis: "Religion and Fatherland are two great truths, in fact, in varying degrees, two holy truths."[15] His ode of 1821 on the death of Napoleon on Saint Helena, *Il cinque maggio*, gives an historical and religious interpretation of the Napoleonic phenomenon, following, not surprisingly, no partisan line. The poem brought him international fame; it appeared in twenty-two languages, including a German translation by Goethe and a later English one by Gladstone. Manzoni viewed the Emperor with what may be paradoxically termed dispassionate enthusiasm. Responding to the burning liberalism of Alfieri and Parini, Napoleon was for him the child of the Revolution who could bring about Italian independence and not the warring monarch who laid waste the plains of Europe. As early as 1800 he had seen him at Milan's La Scala, and had never forgotten the piercing power of his gaze. Understandably, the news of Waterloo had sent the young patriot into convulsions. But in 1821, his poem made an objective assessment, leaving unanswered the question: "Was his true glory?" For it was not long after Waterloo that the Austrians occupied Northern Italy, and Milan became even more the hotbed of nationalistic activity so admired by Stendhal and Byron. Manzoni, who had had his passports for travel to Paris denied him in 1817, signed an appeal for assembling an electoral college; he supported the *Conciliatore* and almost took part in the Carbonari conspiracy of 1821. Another poem written this same year, though not actually published until he wrote the last stanza in 1848, "Marzo 1821," made Manzoni a leading voice in the assertion of Italian unification. But this was as far as his "actions" went.

We must always put Manzoni's patriotism into perspective. It is significant that he did not complete a poem of incandescent patriotism in 1815, "Il Proclama di Rimini," based on Gioacchino Murat's (King of Naples) promise of freedom and independence for the Italians; the events surrounding Murat unfolded too fast, to be sure, but the poem's inspiration, too, rang with excessive activism. The "leading voice" was not a leader; the meditator on political ideals was not a man of action, much less did he go and seek causes in which to participate. And he was aware of his limitations. An often quoted letter written to refuse election to the Board of the College of Arona alludes to his lack of a practical sense, to his inability to discern "where the desirable meets the feasible" in such a way as to sacrifice the former, and to his further inability to propose the desirable anyway because, while he could chat about it with friends, he could not deliberate about it formally without getting confused with doubts and unclarities.[16] He referred to himself often as insufficient and hesitant,[17] even inconclusive and stammering.[18] He recognized that he was so constituted as to be able to help his fellow man only through his writings, that however much he admired him who could behave according to practical norms, especially in turbulent moments of great national need, he was by nature too Christian to brandish a sword himself. For to brandish a sword implies some hatred, and whatever the righteousness of the cause, Manzoni could not hate even the Napoleon who ravaged Europe and caused the death of so many of its youth. The evangelical beauty of "Catholic morality" remained indelibly etched in all his thinking, and what counted ultimately was more the similarity among men than the diversity among nations.

From religious and patriotic verses to historical and ethical plays the step was not only short but logical. As Manzoni matured artistically, he chose ever broader forms to give shape to ever broader physical and intellectual settings. History provided the receptacle in which the moral, artistic, political, and religious could blend under the heading of truth, and he selected events in Italian history of the eighth, fifteenth, and seventeenth centuries for his two tragedies and his novel through which he could reflect by analogy his country's deep-seated aspiration for national independence. Intermittently, from 1816 to 1819, he worked on his first verse tragedy, *Il Conte di Carmagnola*, dedicated to Fauriel. So basic in his mind appeared the relationship between truth and poetry if any work was to be both beautiful and useful, that he preceded its publication, early in 1820, with a "Preface" on the aesthetics (the unities) and usefulness of the theater, together with historical notes on the *condottiere* Carmagnola, lest the reader not be able to sift verity from invention. The story concerns the rivalry and war, lamentable to all those who harbored the ideal of a united Italy, between two Italian States from 1425 to 1432, the Duchy of Milan and the Republic of Venice. For this as well as for his next historical tragedy, *Adelchi*, composed between 1820 and 1822 and dedicated to Enrichetta, Manzoni steeped himself in historical readings. *Adelchi* too is preceded by "Historical Notes" to identify the hero and to acquaint the reader with the period of 772–774 A.D., which saw the end of the Longobard and the beginning of the Frankish domination of Northern Italy under Charlemagne. Italian liberty can never be attained under foreign rule, however well intended that rule is. When the faithful and admiring Fauriel had translations of both tragedies published in France in 1823, he included a critical piece by his friend, written three years previously and directed to the French critic Chauvet who had made unfavorable statements about the plays. As the title suggests, however, the *Lettre à M. C*** sur l'unité de temps et de lieu dans la tragédie* was prompted less by patriotic sentiments than by anti-Aristotelian aesthetic arguments based on a respect for historical subjects, and as such it assumes considerable importance in the evolution of Romantic drama. Also related to these concerns and even more to the historical point through its analysis of the relationship between the Longobard and Italian peoples was the *Discorso sopra alcuni punti della storia longobardica in Italia* (1822–1845).

The vigorous hope that underlay "Marzo 1821" was shattered that same year, with many of Manzoni's friends either exiled or imprisoned for political reasons by the Austrians. The *Conciliatore's* opposition turned out to be short-lived, and Manzoni, who had taken to having friends visit him regularly in his Milanese home in Via Morone, suddenly found so few of them left undispersed that he dejectedly abandoned the city for Brusuglio. It was here that, still absorbed in the meaning of his tragedies, and impelled further by readings of Muratori's *Annali d'Italia*, Ripamonti's Milanese stories, Gioia's treatises on economics, and the novels of Sir Walter Scott, he decided to broaden the setting of the tragedies and write a historical novel centering in seventeenth century Lombardy. All Monsignor Tosi's inducements to keep writing Catholic apologetics could not deter Manzoni from his new literary purpose. Here too he proposed to show the hunger, pestilence, and devastation occasioned by mercenaries and foreign occupation, but he expanded the dimensions of his previous works by illustrating more poignantly the suffering of the innocent and the providential ways in which God's will ultimately curbs human aberrations. He wrote the novel before arguing its theory, namely, the possibility of reconciling aesthetically the actual facts and events of history with the superimposition of artistic invention. This critical argument he brought forth only in 1845, for in the meanwhile historiography had developed into a precise science which militated against the aesthetic reconciliation. It is unlikely that the novel could have followed the arguments we find in *Del romanzo storico e in genere dei componimenti misti di storia e d'invenzione*, and the question has been raised of whether Manzoni would have attempted a "historical novel" at all if he had theorized before creating. But in the 1820s he did not think in such strict historical terms. The novel's first version, relatively undistinguished because of its many Romantic commonplaces, occupied him from 1821 to 1823 and bore the title *Fermo e Lucia*. Thoroughly self-conscious artist that he was, and unattracted by the cheaper Romantic demands of his day, he spent most of 1825 to 1827 refashioning it under the projected title of *Gli sposi promessi* which finally became *I promessi sposi*. Manzoni's concern with language took him to Florence in 1827, where the best Italian was spoken and where, according to his famous phrase, he went "to rinse his clothes in the Arno," and for many years—in fact, until 1842, the year of the novel's second edition—he polished and repolished the work linguistically. The novel, as we know, was a success. (Two thousand copies were sold immediately; originally published in Milan, it was reprinted in Leghorn, Lugano, Florence, Naples, Paris, twice in Turin, and by 1839 had undergone 53 editions—Manzoni usually unaware of them; German editions of Lessmann's and Bülow's translations came out four times; French translations by Rey-Dusseuil, Gosselin, and Montrand appeared seven times; English, Spanish, and Swedish translations also came on the market; all together, some seventy editions appeared, without much financial benefit to the author.)

Whether the earlier or the final version, *I promessi sposi* was received with patriotic fervor by the dean of Italian critics, Giordani, who saw it as "something superb and divine to assist the minds of the people," and who wanted it "preached in all the churches and inns, learned by heart . . . as the book of the people, as a cate-chism."[19] With a different vocabulary of enthusiasm, Eckermann quoted Goethe's opinion: "*I promessi sposi* surpasses what we have in its genre. . . . This book makes us pass continuously from ten-derness to admiration and from admiration to tenderness, in such a way that we never leave these two great emotions. I do not think one can reach greater heights. . . . Manzoni's . . . manner of treat-ing subjects is clear and beautiful, like the sky of his Italy."[20] Most of Europe applauded the artistic feat ("it has taken Europe by storm," wrote his daughter Giulietta to Fauriel[21]), and so, even, did Sis-mondi, who at one point might have wished to be spared a second novel by Manzoni, but who finally had to admit his "great talent."[22] Lamartine spoke of one of the best books he had ever read, and Poe, who admired the episodes of the Nun of Monza and the plague, saw in it a new style in novel writing. But the most quoted accolade came from Walter Scott himself who, when apprised by Manzoni that his historical novels had provided the models, is supposed to have exclaimed: "in this case, *I promessi sposi* is my best work."

There were, of course, the critics, from those like Don Bosco who deemed it irreligious and immoral to those like Carducci who smelled the "sacristy" in it, or like Settembrini who detected slav-ery, negation of patriotism, submissiveness, and reaction. Others considered it dangerous because the peasants look better than the nobles; or, being temperamentally different from Manzoni, still others (like Stendhal and Leopardi) received it coolly. And the En-glish *Quarterly Review* dubbed it an "indifferent novel," though written with "no inconsiderable portion of talent"—in fact it au-gured well, of all things, for a future conversion of all Italians to Protestantism.[23] Whatever the reaction, however, *I promessi sposi* was destined to become immediately a landmark in world literature.

In Florence, Manzoni made a few new friendships (Giovan Pietro Vieusseux, Pietro Giordani, Giovanni Battista Niccolini, Giacomo Leopardi, among others), to add to the few of Milan (Tommaso Grossi, Giovanni Torti, Ermes Visconti, Luigi Rossari, etc.), but his most salient reason for the visit was linguistic. For a long time, and particularly as a result of his French experience, he had held that the Italian language was poor and that the legacy of Dante had deteriorated through lack of a consistent verbal tradition underpinned by a habit of discussing moral and philosophical questions orally. Only this way could it become a living language. Reversing the direction of Du Bellay in the Renaissance, who had suggested that French be enriched through Italian and Classical languages, Manzoni wrote to Fauriel that his own compatriots should read foreign works, especially those written in French, with its unquestioned virtue of clarity. Too much abstruseness prevailed, fostered by the pompous Academies, and of all the Italic tongues which could lend themselves to euphony and clarity, Tuscan stood out most prominently, favored as it was by a noble literary tradition as well as by an unmatched suavity of rhythm. His going to Tuscany, then, stimulated him to handle better the instrument of style, for "to write a novel well in Italian is one of the most difficult things."[24] It also stimulated him to continue Dante's legacy by unifying the language, by demonstrating a stylistic standard which the whole peninsula could recognize. Even in this matter, Manzoni abetted the unification of Italy, for the strength of provincialisms notwithstanding, through *I promessi sposi* he converted the whole of Italy to Tuscan Italian.

Linguistic matters never ceased to occupy Manzoni's mind; he saw in language a crucible for unity, based on an equation identifying philological concerns with political desires. Whether in the tranquility of Brusuglio or the turmoil of Milan, he meditated extensively on the ideological as well as artistic connotations of the problem, which became part and parcel of his concept of Romanticism. The ingredients may have been distinguishable, but not separable. Indeed, he envisaged a book on the subject, *Della lingua italiana*, which he never composed. However, we know his thoughts in detailed fashion: he left a number of separate pieces, written for different occasions, all of which bore on the same problem. *Sentir Messa* he must have written before 1850, though it was not edited until 1923; *Sulla lingua italiana* is a critical letter of 1850 directed at Giacinto Carena, the author of a dictionary of common terms; another critical letter, *Intorno al vocabolario*, directed at Ruggero Bonghi, carried forth the Carena conversation in 1868, the same year he responded to the request by Minister of Education Broglio (who had named Manzoni president of a commission to investigate the problem) with his report *Dell'unità della lingua e dei mezzi di diffonderla*. In 1869 Manzoni published an appendix to this report to rebut the opposing arguments adduced by Raffaello Lambruschini.[25] Manzoni's point of view remained consistent throughout. In one way or another, he always maintained that language must have an organic homogeneity, be derived from usage, and that this usage reflect directly the educated Florentine "dialect," rejecting any distinction between the literary and the spoken tongue. Manzoni's perceptiveness in this debate makes him a forerunner of many linguistic principles discussed in the twentieth century.

The last forty years of his life were beset with sorrow. Even to a man of such sincere faith, the death of the beloved Enrichetta in 1833 must have been wrenching; he called it "a great and irreparable misfortune."[26] Remembering that before their marriage, he had tended to be an acid judge of his contemporaries and that immediately after it his serenity and confidence in life had become his most pronounced personal characteristics, and remembering, too, that he derived from her his conviction that the underpinnings of morality can be found only in a solid religious faith, we cannot minimize the importance of this angelic young lady in his biography. To her mansuetude his conscience owed its tranquility, and it is not too much to speculate that his artistic genius and creative powers might not have flourished as they did in the absence of her cherished inspiration. We need but look at *Adelchi*'s gentle Ermengarda, or at *I promessi sposi*'s pious Lucia, to understand that in giving them life Manzoni was not adopting Romantic conceptions of heroines but was indeed externalizing a warm personal experience. Raffaello Barbiera, the author of the well-known work of cultural history entitled *Il salotto della contessa Maffei*, recounted the following touching anecdote:

I saw in the garden of Manzoni's villa in Brusuglio two withering acacias, on which Manzoni's sweetest and most sorrowful memories of love are joined. On that side of his garden which looks out to the mountains, the poet had planted two young acacias. One night shortly after his marriage, he stood there with his Enrichetta conversing in the midst of that greenery and peace. She approached the two acacias, and with her hands twisted one around the other, telling her spouse: "So our lives shall live!" And the acacias grew together, strong and entwined. When Enrichetta died, Manzoni, almost stifled with sighs, walked over to the two acacias and carved a cross on their trunk with a knife; and for a long time he wanted to cultivate himself a flower-bed around those plants.[27]

To the loss of Enrichetta must be added the loss of many of his children, only two of whom, Enrico and Vittoria, survived him.

Before her death, two had already passed away, Luigia M. Vittorina the same year of her birth, in 1811, and Clara in 1823. Then came an uncommonly sad string of deaths: his first born Giulia (who married the writer Massimo D'Azeglio) in 1834, Cristina in 1841, Sofia in 1845 along with another daughter who died at birth, Matilde in 1856, Filippo in 1868, and Pietro in 1873. And as if this were not sufficiently painful to bear, his closest friend Rosmini died in 1855, his second wife—Teresa Borri Stampa—whom he had married in 1837 died in 1861, and his son-in-law D'Azeglio died in 1866.[28]

It may be understandable that during the last half of his lifetime Manzoni did not again attempt creative writing, other than in the form of retouching up until 1842 the earlier version of his novel. He knew that he worked slowly, but he also must have known to what extent his youthful energies had dwindled and how unlikely it was that he could carry through successfully a sustained creative effort. To Louise Collet he declared in 1860 that "all that is left in me now is the capacity to appreciate [not write] poetry—I mean that poetry which, stemming from the heart, filters through a brilliant, fecund imagination"; poetry no longer sought him out, rather he caught himself panting after it, and this was no good.[29] His health remained "weak and capricious, often and for long intervals prohibiting me the use of my pen";[30] after several hours of morning work, he experienced "lassitude, enough to keep me from thinking"—even days of it.[31] One month he enjoyed "only five or six useful days [due to] almost total incapacity."[32] His condition demanded a relaxed life-style.

Accordingly, he spent considerable time between 1846 and 1856 in Lesa, on Lake Maggiore; the sojourns kept him away from Austrian atrocities and close to Stresa where he frequently visited "our great and dear Rosmini."[33] Next to his relationship with Fauriel, this relationship with the philosopher-educator-statesman turned out the most constructive of all. Manzoni followed closely the arguments of the "incomparable man"[34] on being and intellectual perception, politics and education, ethics and God; in turn, Rosmini, like Tosi, encouraged him to add to the *Osservazioni* and felt particularly rewarded in his esteem for him as a philosopher when, in 1845, Manzoni published *Del sistema che fonde la morale dell'utilità* as an appendix on utilitarianism to the *Osservazioni*. Though Manzoni never considered himself a philosopher in the formal sense of the word, Rosmini regarded him in this light and refused to believe that his friend's Parisian years, followed in 1829–1830 by a sharp critique of Cousin's eclecticism (*Lettre à Victor Cousin*), did not rank Manzoni among the philosophers. In fact, the dialogue *Dell'invenzione* of 1850, so full of Rosminian idealism in its postulation of artistic excellence in the reality of ideas whose ultimate manifestation is the idea of God, can easily invite our agreement. The accessibility of Rosmini (at least up to 1855) and his own primarily meditative spirit make the final pages of his biography a superb—but for the mournings one might be tempted to say enviable—example of the meditative life plunged in philosophy, philology, history, and criticism.

With the final version of *I promessi sposi* went a narrative reconstruction of the trial of some unctioners of 1630, *Storia della colonna infame*, heavily moralistic in purpose, but even more heavily historical in presentation, carefully adherent to facts and to the extant juridical documents which inspired it. An even more important essay, which dated as far back as 1823 but whose definitive publication came in 1871, was his letter to Marquis Cesare D'Azeglio entitled *Sul romanticismo* (*in Italia*), one of the signal documents in which his lucid assessment of the strengths and weaknesses of Classicism vis-à-vis Romanticism, though not a comprehensive study of the latter movement, singles him out not simply as the circumspect moderator which he was but more significantly as an important theoretician of the movement itself, inside and outside of Italy. In addition to his linguistic and philosophical writings, we must finally mention another comparative essay, this one also historical in nature, published posthumously because unfinished, the *Saggio comparativo su la rivoluzione francese del 1789 e la rivoluzione italiana del 1859*, perhaps the best document through which to measure the final evolution of his early Jacobin attitudes. Through all these letters and essays, it would be difficult to detect the kind of lapses or unevennesses we might expect from a man who was ill and almost perpetually in a state of mourning. On the contrary, what we note is continuous clarity and balance of judgment, consistency, and unwavering attachment to truthfulness and logic.

No doubt, the philosophical serenity which had become his *modus cogitandi* (manner of thinking) had also become his *modus vivendi* (manner of living), something which enabled him to face repeated grief if not with stoic fortitude at least with Christian equanimity: "Resignation, or better, full and natural consent to the

Lord's will, and its attendant serenity. . . ."[35] His fame had grown with the years; he had become an institution, a national (and international) monument, receiving visits by Italians in pilgrimage as well as by noted foreigners like Gladstone, Longfellow, Minister John H. Newman, Emperor Pedro II of Brazil, and Balzac. He had more than responded to the encouragement he had received as a young man from Goethe. For Leopardi he was "a man full of amiability, and worthy of his fame"; for Giordani "a most amiable and modest person, revered and loved by all. . . ."[36] Countess Maffei referred to him as "our holy man"; in the public gardens crowds shouted his name and brought him their children to bless. Lamartine put it aptly, asking a friend to remember him to Manzoni: "Bring him my greetings—which is always a tribute, when it is intended for a man like him."[37]

Indeed, there was something sacerdotal about him personally, but more accurately about the role he played in the world of politics and letters. In his own withdrawn way, he had shaped a national conscience,[38] from 1814 when he joined others in refusing to ask the Gallic Eugène de Beauharnais to become king of Italy, to 1838 when he did not participate in the Milanese celebrations for the despotic Bourbon Ferdinand I and refused Austrian honors, to his being counted among those dissatisfied with Austrian rule who signed the document by Lombard moderates asking Carlo Alberto (who declared war on Austria on March 23)[39] to intervene from Piedmont-Sardinia in 1848, to 1858 when he was sick and did not respond to the foreigner Archduke Maximilian's visit to his villa. He refused the French king's offer (urged by Victor Cousin) of the Legion of Honor in 1840, as he had refused the Grand Duke of Tuscany's offer of the Order of Merit six years before.[40] He also refused to sit as deputy in the Piedmontese Chamber.[41] By Victor Emanuel II (who in 1859 had assigned him a life-pension of 12,000 lire annually) he was made Senator of the Kingdom in 1860, in which capacity one year later he voted in favor of the bill to transfer the Italian capital from Florence to Rome, and in 1872 was named Honorary Citizen of the new capital. He was eighty-eight when he died in Milan on May 22, 1873, less than a month after seeing his son Pietro laid to rest. All of Italy mourned at the news of his death, which inspired Giuseppe Verdi to return to work on the *Messa da Requiem* he had begun to write for the death of Rossini five years before. Even the solemn funeral orations delivered on May 29 were outdone by the remarkable *Requiem,* which was performed one year later in Milan's church of San Marco to commemorate the day of May 22.

Bernard Wall has given us a verbal portrait of Manzoni: "In the Manzoni of the creative period we see a man not unhandsome, with rough greying hair and a hint of muttonchop whiskers. His eyes have a calm gaze of awareness, but above all it is his mouth that is expressive, a timid and good-tempered mouth yet with irony playing about the edges." The same critic goes on to describe the last photograph of Manzoni in old age: "His alertness, his poise and his irony seem to have disappeared, the face is narrow and shrivelled between the now swollen muttonchops, and the whole air is that of someone worried and almost furtive."[42] All of his mature life was a composite of these different qualities: the indulgence that comes from a keen awareness of men, the irony that comes from an alert penetration into their motivations, and the fear that in varying degrees inhabits us all, that in his case was a natural outgrowth of perhaps excessive prudence, reserve, and lofty idealism, and that was abetted by experiences both sad and jarring and by a recurrent nervous condition. All of these qualities adduced a love for the comfort and security of isolation, of "my obscurity."[43] If on the one hand he was a man of doubt and hesitation ("Doubt is killing me," he had said to Cousin), he was also a man of temperance and impartiality, one who could bear his ills without their affecting his view of others and who, therefore, enjoyed a measured confidence in himself. In the long run, his doubts and hesitations stemmed from modesty and scrupulousness rather than from lack of perspicaciousness, from circumspection rather than from weakness of judgment. If he understood the meaning of fear, he understood even more the value of faith, "that faith which pierces every veil,"[44] that pillar which supported over sixty years of his existence. Through it his view of people became a view of human nature, of mankind, but on its basis he never thought or wrote theology or divine history. His field was human history, in the most pervasive sense of the universality of man's conscience. No one can doubt that his knowledge of man was extraordinary, and that, given its dimensions, it could stimulate worry and irony along with compassion. The fact was that Manzoni's early scientific skepticism never abandoned him, and one could say that his characteristic serenity was more a virtue of his feelings than a quality of his thought. He was too attuned to the complexity of human conduct through its relation to class and economic circumstances, environment and education, pressures and the historical moment, to regard it with suave simplicity.

Whatever the importance of his other works, it is *I promessi sposi* which remains his finest legacy, for it is in this novel that all his best qualities are represented. The historian, philosopher, moralist, philologist, critic, linguist, and patriot was foremost an artist. As his English translator Colquhoun has written, the novel

has gone into over 500 editions, and been translated into every major language, including Chinese; two operas, three films, a ballet, and at least seven plays have been based on it; commentaries on it make up a good-sized library at the Centre of Manzoni Studies, the Casa del Manzoni, his old home in Milan. . . . Children in Italian Government schools now begin studying it at the age of nine. Tuscan peasants quote pages of it by heart. It is rarely that one opens an Italian . . . newspaper without seeing some phrase or theme from the book, often unacknowledged, so much it has passed into current language. It has furnished arguments for various historic political debates. On one occasion it was quoted by Cavour in the Turin Parliament, and counter quoted by the Opposition. In 1948 it was quoted by the head of the Italian Trade Unions during the debate in the Chamber after the attempt on Togliatti's life. An episode from it was even used to illustrate the rights and wrongs of the Korean war. To Italians the book is still very much alive. . . .[45]

It is part of the Harvard Classics, though in the United States it has not been rewarded with the recognition it deserves, and discussions of Romanticism or the novel as a genre are more likely to omit *I promessi sposi* than include it. Yet nineteenth-century Europe did not produce a finer work artistically nor one that was more perceptively human. It alone would grant distinction to any biography. And in this particular case one need not finally delve into prolonged biographical queries, for this novel *is* Manzoni.

CHAPTER 3

To Feel and to Meditate

L IKE every budding poet, the young Manzoni drew from his
formal sources of inspiration: Virgil and Ovid, whom he translated in fragments at the early age of nine. These Latin poets, who
combined sublimity of style, elegance, acuteness of aesthetic judgment, and artistic self-awareness, were bound to hold the admiration of someone born into a neo-Classical culture in which the written, literary "word" signified excellence and elevation of thought.
Not surprisingly, the quest for the correct vocabulary, the proper
inversions, and the fitting mythological references were too conscious at the outset; these devices of postrevolutionary neo-
Classicism adorned his first attempts at versification. What strikes
us, however, is not so much his choice of poetry as the most likely
genre for artistic expression (poetry still enjoyed that quality of
essentialness that we detect to be Dante's message in the first Canto
of the *Commedia*, and for Manzoni poetry and life formed an indissoluble unit) as his immediate concern with moral and civic problems. He yielded to no purely lyrical or autobiographical inclinations; he aimed at the issues of his day, engaging them instantly.
And he did so with the vigor of his young age, which quenched its
ardor in intemperate verses against the Church, tyrants, poetasters,
the viceful rich, unworthy teachers, and dissolute ladies. The times
had favored such a manner; Lombard society in particular entered
the new century, like the French society it reflected in so many
ways, by passing from confident pronouncements on justice, genius,
reason, man's dignity, human rights, social renewal, the value of art
and culture, and the writer's civic duty, to the crumbling of these
same ideals in practice, with an attendant resentful pessimism.

Much was buzzing through Manzoni's mind at this time, aesthetic
aspirations with philosophical uncertainties. His revolutionary, al-

39

most vitriolic comments against society, or his Voltairian invectives against religion, appear only as attempts to break down the perplexities his young mind could not yet cope with, and seek out values that would satisfy its exuberance. Behind the borrowed and conventional, neo-Classical structures, Varano, Parini, Alfieri, Foscolo, and Monti (the patriotic, revolutionary-minded Monti) people the background of his early efforts, though every now and then something with a genuinely personal ring comes through. Manzoni, we must insist, never was an imitator; to be himself was a constant and conscious concern. An early sonnet of 1802, "Alla Musa," whose thoughts were reiterated later in the *Carme* to Imbonati, bids the deity to show him "new paths," and in the event of failure, of falling from the Ascran hill, "May it yet be said: on his own footmarks does he lie."

"Il trionfo della libertà," ("The Triumph of Liberty") written in eleven-syllable tercets at the age of fifteen, is weighted with the unoriginal pomp of ancient heroes and myths and slanted with youthful intemperances; but then there is the interesting shadow of the French general Desaix, whose sacrifice for the independence of an indifferent land amounted to nothing more than the way he ended: a "barbarian . . . foreign corpse." Liberty must grow from within, moans Manzoni, she is not imposed from without. But more profoundly, Liberty's "triumph" is limited, for the crimes committed in her name suggest the melancholy conclusion that she alone cannot cure society's ills. The same pessimism, which characterizes his early mental attitude, pervades the political sonnet of 1802 "A Francesco Lomonaco," another hero-martyr for liberty, the Neapolitan patriot exiled, like Dante from Florence five hundred years before, after the disturbances and repressions of 1799. The liberal soil of Italy does not prize her best sons, so that "by barbarians oppressed you oppress your own . . . ; repentant always and never changed." Echoes of Foscolo reverberate.[1]

Perhaps one must look elsewhere. Perhaps beauty represents the noblest ideal of them all? Does not a woman of moral and spiritual perfection encompass all that is meant by beauty? Manzoni engages a traditional view, akin to that of the poets of the Dolce Stil Nuovo, though somewhat more erotically or with a more Petrarchan urge. Ought we not look at her "whose sweet mouth conceals a pure smile wherein speaks the soul" and who dominates all from her Cynthusian summit with "her contenance, . . . the movement of her eyes

. . . , and her suave voice"? This Virgilian ode ("Qual su le cinzie cime") is one of Manzoni's most impressive early poetic attempts, and we might surmise, one which up to a point reflects a less troubled mood—broken, however, in the ninth stanza when he introduces an incongruous reference to blood-stained Italy. The possibility of looking elsewhere by breaking out onto the untainted pastures of beauty did not materialize.

Manzoni's usual pessimistic and morally bitter bent reclaimed him in the *Sermoni*: "A Delia," "Contro i poetastri," "A G. B. Pagani," and "Panegirico a Trimalcione." His preaching explodes more truculently than Parini's or Gozzi's, who wrote in a century of professed optimism; rather than blame the institutions, young Manzoni blames the men and women for their sins of corruption. Through them, society is marred with foul behavior, with girls who become the playthings of lust and parlor games which prelude erotic conquests. The dethroned lover shifts through the streets in search of "incautious virgins," the inept poet holds the stage with mindless words and "hard verses," and rich Trimalchio's (from Petronius' *Satyricon*) vulgar ostentation and "occupied mouth" stands as the cultural symbol of the society.

This was the mood of the young poet who went to Paris in 1805, at a time when the same immorality he had sermonized against stained his own life through the flightiness of his parent. We cannot say from other evidence that his mother's relationship with Imbonati really revolted Alessandro—not someone whose mind in those turn of the century years, was filled with the materialistic philosophies and amoral rationalisms of the 1700s, and not, certainly, in the mind of a young intellectual who was still groping for values to which he could dedicate his total being. The tone of the *Carme* ("In morte di Carlo Imbonati" of 1805–1806 exhibits for the most part an elevation and detachment which cannot be considered an indignant invective against corruption. Yet it contains much that would have given the satirical *Sermoni* a greater moral ring if the experiences which prompted them had related to more personal circumstances. The *Carme* does inveigh, in its own cautious manner, against the commonly accepted social mores in the name of a higher moral and political authority. And the polished, traditional language does betray deeper, inner resonances which draw the mind's attention in such a way as to remind us that it is Manzoni— albeit a young Manzoni—whom we are reading:

> To feel, he rejoined, and to meditate; with little
> be content; never bend your eyes
> from your goal; with things human
> experiment only so much as you need
> to care not for them; never become slave;
> with the base never make peace; never betray
> the holy Truth; nor proffer ever a word
> that applauds vice, or virtue derides.

These precepts (a remarkable program of behavior for a twenty-year old), voiced in the poem by Imbonati with paternal solicitude, are preceded by warm words defending the cohabitation, founded on pure love, against which the acid words on the degeneracy of contemporary society seem to pale.

If the *Carme* does anything, it indicates how Manzoni's poetic manner was changing from the aggressiveness of the *Sermoni* to a more reasoned meditation, eschewing the polemic mode as much as possible in favor of an attitude that enjoyed at once greater detachment and greater intellectual depth. This is not to suggest, as some have tried,[2] that we may trace a consistent evolution in his poetry, that his poetry has a "history," in both form and content. "Urania" of 1809 shows no progression or departures; it proposes to celebrate the moral and utilitarian virtue of poetry, and to do this the lure of neo-Classical expressions, not to speak of Jacobin anti-Christian views, proved too attractive. The oratory of exclamation points, interrogation marks, and inverted syntax, coupled with the stereotyped subject matter, made Manzoni describe the poem later to Fauriel as "hateful"—too harsh a term, really, for a piece of considerable craftsmanship, but understandable from the pen of the sensitive artist he was about to become, seeking spiritual elevation in every word he wrote. "Urania," a mythologico-philosophical poem with Montian neo-Classical, anti-Cartesian, Enlightenment overtones, remains a good literary exercise in favor of beauty in poetry.

We may say the same for his last preconversion poem. The occasion of the Danish poet Emanuel Baggesen's "Parthenais" (as Fauriel had translated it when bringing the two poets together) prompted a courteous response in kind by Manzoni: "A Parteneide" is again a poem of exaltation, this one of aspiration toward poetic beauty through the symbolic Virgin Goddess:

> And when, intoxicated
> with that godly beauty and her kindly
> gesture, I attempted to approach her
> with my wings of mind, if I but knew
> how one speaks in heaven, limply weary
> I dropped my wings of mind, and to my gaze
> the vision beauteous fell silent.

The poem closes the period of Manzoni's early lyrics, hinting through these very verses that perhaps neo-Classicism was not up to the spiritual task the poet was now setting for himself, a task toward which the unproductiveness of indignant resentments and violent satire, and the rhetorical chase after beauty, had nothing to offer. The line of "evolution" runs awry with poems such as "Urania" and "A Parteneide," written at the end of the first decade of the new century and after the *Carme*, so that Sansone is correct in speaking not of "a birth of poetry" throughout this period but rather "of a spontaneous growth of inner motifs pushing toward poetry, . . . which in fact originates not just when the tonality of a poetic nature is announced from a distance but when it becomes conscious of itself . . . , and abandons itself entirely to inspiration, bringing to it the fullness of the personality."[3]

In a letter to Mme. Adélaïde de Montgolfier, the daughter of the famed inventor of the hot-air-filled balloon, Manzoni expressed some new views on poetry which confirm the critic's words and which serve as a background to the religious poems of his postconversion period: verse, he wrote, is "a form which above all likes to express what each one of us can find inside himself, but that no one has yet thought of saying, and which is capable only of rendering those thoughts that develop along with it, and mold themselves on it, as it were, as they are born. . . ."[4] It is not that the *Inni sacri* as a whole, which celebrate Manzoni's return to the fold and to the sense of confidence and security which accompanied it, represent an apogee in nineteenth-century poetry; Goethe's admiration notwithstanding, they are uneven in quality and in tone more didactic than the poet himself would have wished. But the poetic "tonality" is conscious of itself, the inspiration genuine, and they provide not a few prefigurations of the modes and the personality which were to be revealed later in Manzoni's most important work, his novel. His previous civic and moral inclinations become transubstantiated—to use a term apposite to the content of these lyrics—into universal ethical views on society.

The times generally, as well as Manzoni personally, were ready for the *Inni* (the first four hymns were published in 1815, the last in 1822).[5] After the welter of revolution and its subsequent disillusions, expressed earlier so keenly by Alfieri and stolidly by the chameleonic Monti, the same need for a refuge in faith and in the rehabilitation of some traditional values which operated in Europe operated in Manzoni. The *Génie du christianisme* signaled spiritually what the Restoration signaled politically. The pessimism that followed the bankruptcy of rational progressivism was tempered with the hope provided by the Christian outlook toward nature and society; with Manzoni, both were now newly imbued with universality, meaning that they could not be considered from the particularized perspective of the individual, but rather from the broader perspective of the collectivity, the human family. In this sense, Manzoni's Romanticism is a Christian Romanticism, centrifugally oriented toward society, not centripetally toward the ego: "Every individual movement becomes translated into a collective relationship, metaphysical in nature, between individual and society, man and God. In Manzoni, the human 'personage' is never alone. Every human tendency represents a 'value'; man in his complexity and richness vibrates everywhere. The individual is mirrored in history, and history in the judgment of God."[6]

As De Sanctis phrased it, the *Inni* are an evangelized version of the triad of liberty, equality, and fraternity. And their tone, so pervasively biblical, lends itself to the didascalic purpose. We should note, too, that this purpose was sanctioned by Manzoni's previously stated belief in the sacerdotal function of the poet. While on the one hand, various allusions in the *Carme* "In morte di Carlo Imbonati" and in the poem "Contro i poetastri" in the *Sermoni* suggest that the poet is artistically a craftsman and humanly an ordinary man, on the other he did regard him as a purveyor of truth and revealer of the religious (or national) conscience who absorbs and reshapes the voices of ordinary humans in a revelatory outpouring. Manzoni would have denied that the function of the poet is to educate, and in this sense he would dethrone him from the royalty accorded him by Parini, Alfieri, Foscolo, and later Hugo; in fact, Manzoni never exhorts in their manner. But if the useful must join the beautiful, the didactics enter tacitly and the panegyrics follow closely. Nonetheless, it is only fair to say that his "didascalic" purpose was to reveal rather than to inculcate.

The *Inni sacri* are penetrated with what T. S. Eliot might call a sense of liturgy, at once humanly and mystically felt: that is, liturgy as both social and beautiful. The overall tonality, however, derives from Revelation. Every stanza is seeded with poetic transcriptions of mainly New Testament passages, to the point where any explication would appear like a long listing of John, Matthew, Isaiah, Corinthians, Psalms, Acts, Proverbs, Luke, Job, etc., with a liberal sprinkling of Dante and Virgil. It is fitting that chronologically the first hymn was "La Risurrezione," written between April and the end of June, 1812, for the basis of Christian faith, as Goethe asserted, echoing St. Paul (Cor. I, 105:17), lies in the dogma of the Resurrection. The sense of liturgy is immediately apparent: three solemn questions in the first stanza are followed by three majestic answers in the second (as in the third and fourth stanzas of another hymn, "La Passione"):

> He has risen: the holy head
> No longer rests inside the shroud;
> He has risen: on one side
> Of the solitary sepulcher
> Lies the capstone overthrown:
> Like a strong man exhilerated
> The Lord has reawakened.

As this stanza illustrates, the poem has more optical than meditational virtues—something De Sanctis also noted about "Il Natale." The angel's coming appearance by the abandoned sepulcher is no less pictorial. Six octosyllabic lines capped by a final heptasyllabic line give each stanza a slow, biblical gait which is accordingly firm and steady, as befits the victory over sin and death, and the rapture—not explosive but measured—over the miracle through which the Gospel was illumined with divine truth in fulfillment of Daniel's prophesy. With slightly more enthusiasm than accuracy, one critic has put it this way: "It is the cry of the castaway who reaches shore, of the man who has seen his own life in all its wretched nakedness, who has felt himself die and now feels he is living again."[7] Indeed, the fact that the poet makes himself the messenger of the incomparable truth of the event, and the final note of consolation and hope for humankind struck through the Christian

feast, may provide a healthy impression of a new life. Another critic
has even ventured a differentiating comparison between the reserved and unmelancholy, Christian "gaudeamus" of this poem and
the open and melancholy, Pagan hedonism of Lorenzo de' Medici's
"Trionfo di Bacco ed Arianna."[8] But the poem errs too frequently: as
has been pointed out, the emphasis in the triple definition of Christ
(stanza 6), the questionable image of a dry leaf whisked away by a
pilgrim to depict the way the Lord threw open the tombstone (stanzas 3 and 4), the naive and folkloric rhythm of the thirteenth stanza,
and the brusque passage in stanza eleven from evangelical narration
to dramatic representation, mar its otherwise undeniable and truly
inspired assets.

Between November, 1812, and April, 1813, Manzoni composed
"Il nome di Maria"—not a hymn to rival Petrarch's or Dante's culminating prayers to the Virgin Mary at the end of the *Canzoniere*
and the *Commedia*, but one which distinguishes itself through its
fluent musicality. After an uneasy beginning, the verses flow delicately and easily: three endecasyllables and one heptasyllable per
stanza in alternate rhyme. A diffused sense of the *Magnificat* glows
throughout,[9] as if to extol the greatness of God which could give rise
to such glory as Mary's. The dissonantly hard ending, in which,
"Glorious like the sun," she is suddenly also described as
"fearsome/Like a host deployed on field of battle," has rightly disturbed many critics, but the bulk of the tribute runs with compelling sweetness or force:

> In the fears of his dark waking
> The child names You; and to You, trembling,
> When with a roar Fate swells,
> The sailor finds his recourse. . . .

Momigliano distrusts this deceptive sweetness: "often in that music
there is little fantasy and little feeling."[10] But are fantasy and feeling
the only stuff of which poetry is made? Though with less elevation
than solemnity, Manzoni keeps in mind, as usual, human miseries,
and fears, and needs.[11]

What if Christ had not come to redeem man in his tenebrous
existence? Man before Christ and man after the consoling promises
of Christ: "Il Natale," which came next, between July and September, 1813, offers an answer. In this hymn, Manzoni again varied

the metrical scheme: this time the seven verses measure 8-7-8-7-7-7-6 syllables, with rhymes on 2 and 4, 5 and 6, and 7 of one stanza with 7 of the next:

> Sleep, Celestial One: the people
> Know not the child who's been born;
> But will come the day that they'll be
> Nobly to your lineage sworn;
> For in that humble repose,
> For inside that dust inclosed,
> They'll recognize their King.

One of the key words is "humble," the humble people, a hallmark round which centers Manzoni's view of the world, as exemplified by his novel. However unsuitably and even coldly expressed, there is love for the humble in this hymn, and the background of this love gives a flaming, explosive power to the action of the angels who rend the night to sing of the holy nativity. The biblical reminiscences may not blend adequately in the poem, but the way the excellence of the birth is hidden under its own humility—the child who is concealed under the fact that He is King—compensates, at least in the final stanza, for the inadequacies. Petronio speaks of a human meaning which turns theological and transcendental.[12] And we should mention, too, that the criticism about the failure of the hymn's ponderous opening to relate to the unearthliness of the rest of the poem may not be as well founded as generally accepted. The well-known initial metaphor, the boulder which loosens from its niche and goes plunging down into the valley, is not out of character with the later development of the poem where the author speaks of the angels' gladsome song and the firmament, the high clouds and the rising, sacred song. Rather, by a forceful process of contrast, the hymn rises, as a hymn should, from material weightiness in the valleys to spiritual loftiness in the heavens. Structurally speaking, the poem remains one of Manzoni's most successful.

The sacred, oratorical devices return in "La Passione," at which Manzoni worked over an extended period, from March, 1814, to October, 1815. Noticeable once again is the different syllabic scheme: an octain composed of two groups of 10-10-10-9 (abacbddc). The monotony is abetted by certain symmetrical structures, such as the adjective-noun combination ending most of the verses in stanza

8. Perhaps the least accomplished of the hymns, though the most compact, "La Passione" alludes too sermonically to biblical prophecies regarding the coming of the Messiah and the latter's sacrifice for the sins of man. Strong images there are, but weak rhythms dilute their force. Every now and then, however, the poetry rings with intimate tones, as when a choral prayer invokes God's forgiveness for those who trespassed against Jesus:

> Oh great Father! for Him who self-sacrifices,
> Cease now your tremendous anger;
> And to better turn the insane word
> Of the blind, Oh Lord most merciful.
> Yes, may that Blood descend all over them;
> May it be but a rain of mild bathing:
> We all erred; and may that sacrosanct
> Blood cancel every error.

An article in the *Conciliatore* complained about the "scant clamor" elicited by these first *Inni*;[13] not so with Goethe, however, who in *Über Kunst und Alterthum* received them with high praise for their author's "new" poetic manner, his "simplicity of feeling" coupled with "boldness of genius, metaphors, transitions," and his way of being "Christian without fanaticism, Roman Catholic without sanctimoniousness, zealous without hardness."[14]

"La Pentecoste," his last completed hymn of the series, is fine poetry. But it gave Manzoni his longest period of gestatory torment; the time-span lasted from the end of June, 1817, to September, 1822, and even so the final version was not put together, totally revised, until March, 1855.[15] There are more extant drafts of this effort than of any other, and perhaps on this basis it is not wrong to imagine why the poet never completed his sacred series of hymns.[16] Whatever the case, "La Pentecoste" gives inspiring evidence of that transubstantiation by which moral and civic concerns are elevated to a metaphysical "collective relationship," and the religious man becomes poet. The question raised by one critic about another hymn—"Is this the hymn of a man of letters or the hymn of a pure *vir religiosus*? is it 'religious' literature or literature in the freely expressive sense of the word?"[17]—is resolved. Like St. John of the Cross, the distinction between literature and theology is obfuscated by the spontaneous emergence of accomplished poetry through which the religious meaning derives its vitality.

Among other reminiscences, the early drafts show that of Bossuet's *Sermons pour le jour de la Pentecôte* the final version leaves commitment aside and engages in pure feeling and meditation, just as this final version sheds the obviousness of the biblical references in the preceding hymns and translates concept into image with lyrical intensity. Manzoni's verses are precise, permitting no sacrifice of clarity to lyricism in an emotional gradation that reaches from trepidation and marvel to the joy of the birth of the Church under the flames of the Holy Spirit, from misery to endless serenity. In Momigliano's words, the poem exhibits "a compact poetic world, human and divine."[18] Elsewhere he says that it exhibits "the way in which Manzoni intuits his human and divine world."[19]

The reason is a skillful fusion of various elements: the atmosphere of fable or myth which enhances the spiritual intention, the "democratic" inspiration (as De Sanctis first pointed out) which makes all men equal and brothers and reproves the oppressors while investing the oppressed with glory, and the suffused idealism which breathes throughout. Many are the humans passed in review: Christians, Pagans, brides, slaves, the poor and the wretched, the young and the old, children, the wicked and the humble. We cannot add to the comment of the nineteenth-century critic Tommaseo, who saw the foundation of a renovative society as the hymn's central idea.[20]

Just as the speedy ray of light
Rains on one and yet one thing,
And draws out the various colors
Where'er it may come to rest;
So then resounded manifold
The voice of the Holy Ghost:
Arab, Parthian, Syrian
Received it in his tongue.
. . . .

Oh Spirit! in supplication
Before your solemn altars;
Alone through inauspicious woods;
Wandering o'er desert seas;
From Andes chilled to Lebanon,
From Eire to bristling Haiti;
Scattered over every shore,
Through You, singlehearted,

We implore you. . . .
. . . .

Breathe inside the ineffable
Smiling lips of our children. . . .

Moderate the confident minds
Of our daring fearless youth. . . .
Shine inside the errant gaze
Of him who dies in hope.

A variation on the versification scheme of "Il Natale," the octanes measure 8-7-8-7-8-7-7-6 syllables, rhyming 2 and 4, 6 and 7, and 8 with the 8 of the following stanza. The impressive thing is that the language is consistently poetic, and it is a new and clear language, not only for Manzoni but for Italian poetry, now about to abandon (with a helping hand from Leopardi) the traditional furrows of Petrarch, Tasso, and the Arcadians. With a characteristic touch of earthly pessimism, Manzoni uses it here not to inspire confidence in the human lot on earth but to offer the comfort of resignation to reality in this world, given the universally understood Pentecostal word. He departs from St. Luke's vision of the polyglot Apostles and adopts the one whereby their single language needed no interpreter. And through its clarity and inspiration, his own language aspires to communicate the universal message. In this poem particularly, Manzoni has not converted his moral inspiration into representational verses evolving eventually into oratory (as Russo claims), but has lifted ethics to religiosity and religiosity to a form of transcendent idealism.

Manzoni could not speak violence; if he could arouse, he could not instigate. And he could not hate. His great patriotic and political poems of 1821 continue to bear the transcendent stamp, that blend of humanitarianism and Christianity which associates all nations and individuals fraternally in the common experience of suffering. "Marzo, 1812" is a case in point, written at that time when the news circulated that a group of Piedmontese patriots, sworn to death, were about to cross the Ticino River and come to the aid of the freedom-seeking Lombards. The poem is dedicated not to an Italian but "To the illustrious memory of Theodor Koerner, poet and soldier for German independence, who died on the battlefield of Leipzig on October 18, 1813, a name endeared to all peoples who fight to defend or to reconquer a fatherland."[21] The poem contains an effective image of a humiliated Lombard, symbolic of Italian servility to the Austrian foe:

> With that visage defied and dejected,
> With that look uncertain and humbled
> Of a mendicant standing by mercy
> Tolerated and on foreign soil,
> So the Lombard had to stand on his land;
> Law for him was the other man's wish;
> His destiny the other man's secret;
> His role was to serve and stay silent.

But a people animated by righteous insurrection cannot be suppressed.

> Oh foreigners, now Italy returns
> To her own heritage, reclaims her soil;
> Oh foreigners, asunder strike your tents
> From a land which is not mother to you.

History irresistibly sanctions the Christian word:

> Beloved Italy, where'er the cry
> Sorrowful was heard of your long bondage;
> Where for this human lineage
> Hope has yet not been extinguished;
> Where freedom blossomed years ago,
> Where still in secret it matures,
> Where now a high misfortune sheds man's tears
> There is no heart that does not pulse for you.

The deep feeling is followed by meditation and confidence in the historical process, a Christian process, wherein the oppressor is not challenged with hatred, imprecation, or invective. If exhortation there is in these verses, it is calmly and serenely directed toward international harmony and justice. Carducci said that Italy needed something less solemn and less Christian. The hortatory Berchet comes to mind. But Carducci misunderstood here the poet of the *Inni sacri*, who like Pellico in *Le mie prigioni* preferred to make universal love his answer to the horrors of the Spielberg dungeons.

Perhaps Manzoni's greatest poem, of nobler and more solemn inspiration, is the political ode "Il cinque maggio"—the day Napoleon died. Goethe reacted enthusiastically to it, providing an immediate translation for his review *Über Kunst und Alterthum*. The opening registers the astonishment which struck the world when the report was issued from St. Helena:

He has been. As the mindless
Corpse, having yielded its final
Mortal sigh, lay immobile,
Deprived of a soul so great,
So striken and astonished
Lies the earth at the news,

Mutely thinking of the last
Hour of the fated man.

Before such stature as Napoleon possessed, moral judgment is impossible; therefore, the Christian poet looks to history for serene assessment, history which evolves through Providential guidance. Manzoni refused to imitate in any way his numerous poet-contemporaries in Europe who sang the praise of the Emperor while he enjoyed success, or shouted diatribes when he finally failed. Neither Kleist's wolverine attack nor Wergeland's dizzy encomium is called for. But if the reality of history cannot be changed by expressions of hate or love, the central query remains, to be answered at a later date:

Was his true glory? For posterity
Waits the complex judgment: we
Bow our heads to the Supreme
Maker, who wished to brand
Him with a grander mark
Of His creative spirit.

For Napoleon's life contained multitudes:

He tasted all: triumph
Ever greater after peril,
Flight and victory,
Sovereignty and sad exile:
Twice low in the dust,
Twice high on the altar.

But more significantly: destiny made him straddle two centuries and two eras, the pre-Revolutionary and the Revolutionary, like a symbol of a superior Will, though self-appointed, to settle the chaotic turmoils:

> He named himself: two centuries
> One against the other armed,
> . . . .
> Silence he imposed, and arbiter
> He sat between them.

The ode intensifies as the warring despot of Europe turns into the sorrowed prisoner on St. Helena, who tried to recount his own story but felt too weary to hold a pen. A dialectical opposition develops in these verses. The fallen warrior views with heavy heart the former man in a series of images flashing through the mind as rapidly as his demise:

> And he vanished. . . .
> . . . .
> As the wave wraps and weighs
> On the shipwrecked sailor's head,
> The wave o'er which in vain,
> Though taut and forward, flowed
> The gaze of the wretched man
> To spot a distant shore;
>
> So on that soul descended
> A heap of memories!
> . . . .
> And he thought back of the moving
> Tents, and the quaking valleys,
> And the flashing of arms,
> And the wave of horses,
> And the sudden command,
> And the swift obedience.

The ephemeralness of things human makes the Emperor a tragic figure who ultimately faces the hollowness of temporal glory. The poem borders on becoming a religious meditation on human vanity, betraying the bitterness of this realization in the person of an imposing hero who has now reached the edge of despair. But a higher force terminates his earthly venture:

> And he despaired; but from the sky
> Came an effective hand
> And merciful carried him
> Into air more fit to breathe;

And it sent him forth,
Through florid paths of hope,
To the eternal fields, to the prize
That furthers desires,
Where in shadows and silence lies
The glory that had passed.
. . . .
The God Who smites and raises,
Who troubles and Who consoles
On the deserted bedding
He placed next to himself.

Thus the ode ends with the image of the crucifix. An epic tonality lends it grandeur and enhances its structure, which proceeds from contemplative immobility to the movement of turmoil and anguish, to final repose in serenity and light. Though in isolated parts the poem may be picked apart critically, Croce is correct in stating that in its totality it affords a very moving experience. For the successions of lyrical and reflective passages, whereby Manzoni's historical view becomes poetic vision, betray not irregularities of presentation, much less indecisions of inspiration; rather, they constitute the ode's breathing mechanism, like a printed demonstration of the poet's own alternating creative pattern: to feel and to meditate.[22]

CHAPTER 4

Provident Ill-Fortune

"THE idea of a performance of my things gives me apprehension together with an insurmountable aversion; if, in my two poor tragedies which you deign to look upon so indulgently, I went contrary to the general taste and experienced the displeasure of hearing myself screamed at [by those who read them], I would at least find comfort in the thought that, given their strangeness, they would never appear on the stage. Indeed, you see for yourself how they are put together, without any concern for stage effects, uses, or conventions; there is a multiplicity of characters, excessive length, speeches inhuman for the lungs to bear—and even more so for the ears; there are varied and disconnected scenes, and very little of what one commonly means by action, which moves along slowly, obliquely, and in spurts. In short, all those things that can make a performance difficult and boring are gathered there, as if to compile a single study of them. Therefore, concerning those points on which you deign to seek my advice, I must tell you candidly that I have none, nor would I be able to propose anything at all—let alone anything which would be better than what you have yourself proposed, for this could not be possible. . . . Allow me, then, to enjoy the sweet thought of your friendly intention, without my having to witness too risky an effect. And I am not speaking for myself alone—for whom, I must confess, the sound of a hiss would be more bitter than that of a thousand applauses would be welcome; and, as you see, I am imagining an event much more favorable than reason dictates. I am not speaking for those two poor dramas which, if they find just enough air to breathe inside a book, could, if tested on stage, die a violent death; no, I am speaking also for Art, and for those who handle it much better than I."[1]

So Manzoni responded to the proposal by the Supervisor of Theater of the city of Florence to produce *Il Conte di Carmagnola* and

55

Adelchi. As he also stated in the letter, his intention had been "to write for readers and nothing more," a kind of armchair theater *à la* Seneca or Musset. We know that *Carmagnola* was performed in Florence in August, 1828, and *Adelchi* in Turin in June, 1843 (neither with scintillating success), but both times Manzoni stayed home. For him, drama was poetry, and tragedy a form of religious art, as it had been originally—which meant a form of meditation, best experienced in the intimacy of one's study instead of in crowded, noisy theaters. Hence the logical transition in his literary output from poetry to drama, to dramas which have always been considered more part of his lyrical production than as a separate genre, and which, even in their most rending moments, deny us the normal use of the word "dramatic." Again, as in the *Inni*, a sense of the human collectivity permeates the atmosphere, and of this collectivity in history, thus renewing our awareness of the basic ties between history and poetry. Orioli suggests that Manzoni's interest stems from the common search for truth which characterizes both pursuits: history as the succession of events and their causes, poetry as the penetration into the secret passions and motives of those who act them out.[2] The preface to *Carmagnola* speaks of a "dialogued poem" which obviates the need for performance, and the *Lettre à M. Chauvet* speaks of tragedy as "explaining what men have felt, wanted, and suffered through their acts," as a recreation of historical moral truth.

Apart from the *Inni* (especially "La Pentecoste"), the tragedies remind us of motifs in "Marzo 1821" and "Il cinque maggio," of the former's appeal to the Italic community "of arms, of tongue, of altar, / Of memories, of blood and of heart" to cleanse itself of internal conflict and rid itself of foreign masters, and of the latter's philosophy of triumph and death, the recognition of the vanity of human ambition, and the solace of faith. Historical drama afforded Manzoni a broader canvas than poetry for the representation of human reality, for the psychological portrayal of the actions of men in time; if his readings of Goethe and Schiller, Corneille and Racine, Metastasio and Calderón, and above all Shakespeare, had taught him anything they had taught him this. Furthermore, Italy presented a natural backdrop for drama. He lived in a tragic country, whose history since the disappearance of the Roman Empire read like a graveyard's inventory: death by plundering invasions, internecine discordances, political ineptness, death by occupational atrocities, servility, in short, death by ill-fortune. In the adventures and misadventures of his homeland, whose intellectual and moral greatness was systematically strangulated by suffering and corruption, were to be found many subjects worthy of the best writers. Of all the modern tragedians, Shakespeare most felt the tragic pathos of human life and best knew how to dramatize history poetically. Manzoni always retained a keen sensitivity for the mystery of the one and the complexity of the other, so that his attraction to the author of *Coriolanus, Richard II,* and *Henry IV* is easily understood.

Poetry, of course, means style. By virtue of its truth, tragedy moves the reader, but it fails if the characters do not speak "truly," that is, if they speak in the artificial rhetoric of the past. Manzoni clearly is conscious of doing something new for Italian theater, so subserviently bound to the manner of Alfieri. Even if *Carmagnola* reflects the historically-centered models of Goethe's *Egmont* and Schiller's *Wallenstein* trilogy, in what concerns the play's linguistic manner Manzoni does innovate, in opposition to his illustrious compatriot:

I hope to finish a tragedy that I began with great ardor and hope to do at least something new in this country. . . . After having read Shakespeare well, and things that have been written lately about the theater, and after having thought about them, my ideas have really changed regarding certain reputations: I dare not say more. . . . But what pains people have taken to do poorly! . . . What care to make men speak neither as they speak normally nor as they could speak, to separate prose from poetry, and to replace it with the coldest rhetorical language least apt to elicit sympathetic responses![3]

In his quest for subject matter, he came upon the story in Sismondi's *Républiques italiennes* (end of Book 7) of the fifteenth-century *condottiere*, Count Carmagnola (a plebeian who became a soldier of fortune), who left the service of Duke Filippo Maria Visconti of Milan, whose dominions he had reconquered and amplified, disgruntled at the Duke's shabby treatment of him, and entered that of his Venetian enemies, whose armies he led victoriously against the former master, only to be suspected of treason by the Doge and the Senators, condemned and executed. The fated life of one man, whom Manzoni deemed innocent (though modern historians disagree), and the fratricidal history of a people—these elements shaped Manzoni's inspiration. The Count's innocence coupled with the sharp contrast between his courageous loyalty and the petty distrust of those wielding political power seemed good material for tragedy—for national tragedy, since the destruction wrought by such egoism paved the way for the country's unhappy future. It is significant that the historical tableau reveals what one critic calls "the Italy of the *quattrocento* with her grandeurless discords, passionless wars, crafty politics devoid of daring or magnanimous ambition."[4] This kind of realism was typical of Manzoni's peculiar brand of Romanticism.

How did he construct his play? He did so not only by opposing Alfieri's classical lexicon but also by discarding the unities of time and place, and by considering unity of action not in the Racinian sense of all events leading to and evolving from a central crisis but in the "historical" sense of the events surrounding the life of one man during a single and self-contained period. In the Preface, Manzoni analyzes five objections to the unities; the most succinctly stated is the fifth: "Finally, these rules stand in the way of much beauty and cause many inconveniences." And that says it all. In its five acts, *Il Conte di Carmagnola* moves about readily from the Hall of the Senate in Venice to the Count's house to the Duke of Milan's camp, the Count's tent in the opposite camp, and the Hall of the Chieftains again in Venice, back to the Count's tent, then to his house, and finally to his prison, and all of this takes place in over six years of history (1425–1432). The author thus gave the unities "a hard slap in the face."[5]

The play opens with Francesco Foscari, Doge of Venice, discussing with his Senate the Florentine Republic's offer to join forces and wage war against the Duke of Milan. The Doge favors the war, particularly now that he can employ the services of one who had served the Milanese well but who had fled the Duchy when Visconti had attempted to have him murdered. This person is, of course, Carmagnola, who is introduced into the Senate chamber to state his views. Hortatory and eloquent, Carmagnola confidently promises victory.

> . . . of an open enemy
> The open enemy am I now. I shall serve
> Your interests, but do so frankly and with purpose
> Stated, as one who is certain
> That he undertakes a just cause. . . .
> Now is the time to beat him: seize
> This moment: boldness now is prudence.

Upon his leaving, Marino, one of the Chiefs of the Council of Ten, expresses diffidence of the Count, who could turn against Venice just as easily as he now proposes to turn against Milan. But Marino's counsel of prudence, through which the Machiavellian consciousness of Venetian political life is revealed, is opposed by Senator Marco's praise of Carmagnola; as his friend, he can vouch for the Count's integrity. His remarks carry, the Doge's desires are voted, and Marco personally bears the news to Carmagnola's home. The Count joyfully anticipates his revenge over Visconti, despite his friend's admonition to proceed cautiously, since not all Venetians look upon him favorably:

> This is the day that destiny
> Seals my life; for since this holy earth
> In her ancient glorious bosom
> Has welcomed me, and named me her son,
> This will I to be forever, and I consecrate
> This sword forever both to its defense
> And greatness.

The second act is a study in contrast, rising from microcosm to macrocosm, and ending lyrically in a lament over Italian disharmony. First we note the discordance in the Milanese camp among the various mercenary captains (Angelo della Pergola, Guido Torello, Niccolò Piccinino, Francesco Sforza, among others) concerning the feasibility of doing battle, finally resolved by their leader Carlo Malatesti's decision to attack. Then we are taken to Carmagnola's camp where, under his persuasive leadership, all receive without controversy the news of the deployment of Visconti's forces on the plains of Maclodio. In the end, the Chorus intervenes to forecast the Venetian victory, and above all to deprecate fratricidal warfare, thus coloring the old historical story with new political and humanitarian shades:

> Of one land are they all, one tongue
> Do they all speak; the foreigner
> Calls them brothers. . . .
> Oh ill-fortune! Have these foolish warriors
> No wives, have they no mothers? . . .
> Oh ill-fortune! ill-fortune! ill-fortune!
> With dead the land is now already covered. . . .
> As in the air the grain is spread
> From the fully turning airing blade,

> So all about the vast terrain
> The beaten warriors all lie scattered. . . .
> The brothers have killed the brothers. . . .
> Meanwhile from the circling Alps
> The foreigner turns his gaze downward:
> He sees the strong who bite the dirt,
> And counts them each with cruel joy. . . .
> The foreigner descends; and he is here.
> Victors! Are you weak and few?
> But this is why he comes to challenge you,
> And eagerly awaits you on those fields
> Where your brother perished. . . .
> All made in the image of a single One,
> All children of a single Redemption,
> In any hour, on any portion of the land
> That we go through this mortal life,
> We are brothers, tightly bounded in a pact;
> Cursed he who breaks it,
> Who rises up above the weeping weak,
> Who grieves a soul immortal!

In the third act, in which Carmagnola's soldiers free a number of prisoners and he defends their gesture ("This is a custom of war, as well you know") to two objecting Commissioners of the Venetian Republic, the Count's fortunes begin to wane. His unwillingness to pursue mercilessly the vanquished Milanese and his magnanimity with the prisoners are misinterpreted, and suspicion over his behavior with the foe is heightened when he is seen in polite conversation with those who in former times had ridden by his side. The Commissioners return to Venice to inform the Senate of Carmagnola's suspected treason.

Act IV takes place some years later, during which time the Count, despite several military mishaps, has been able to maintain his proud, sometimes haughty, posture. But the opposition between Marino and Marco erupts when the latter is charged by the former with guilty indulgence toward his friend and patriotic negligence toward the Republic, and when Marco protests his faithfulness to Venice, he is made to prove it by signing an agreement to leave the city to fight the Turks at Thessalonica, without warning the Count who is to be lured back to Venice deceptively and face trial for treason. Marco feels trapped and signs; later he analyzes his action along with his conscience with a fine psychological awareness matched only by his distress and feeling of impotence:

                              . . . Before today
I knew not myself! . . . Oh what a secret
I came upon today! . . .
. . . in witness I have summoned heaven
Of my odious cowardice . . . its sentence
I have underwritten. . . . I too have my share
In his blood! Oh what did I do! . . . I let myself
Be thus terrified? . . . This life? . . . Well, often times
It can't be spared without a crime:
Did I not know it? Why then did I promise?
For whom did I fear? for me? for me? for this
Dishonored head? . . . or for my friend?
My refusal would have hastened the blow,
But not deterred it. Oh my God, Who all discern,
Unto me reveal Your heart: that I might see at least
Into which abyss I now have fallen, if I've been
More foolish or more craven or ill-fortuned. . . .
                    . . . I extended him my hand;
He shook it, gallant man, and at this moment that he sleeps,
And the foe's upon him, I withdrew it;
He awakens, seeks me out, and I have fled!
He scorns me, then he dies! . . .
                    . . . And I am yet
But at the edge of precipice; I see this,
And I can withdraw. . . . Can I not find
A way? . . .
Oh impious ones, in what a net abominable
You have webbed me! Now there is for me
No noble counsel; whatever I choose, I'm guilty.
Oh atrocious doubt! . . . But I do thank them: they have
Established me a destiny: along a single way
They have shoved me, and I hasten there; at least
I'm favored that I never chose it; I choose nothing, and whate'er
I do derives from force and will of others.

Carmagnola receives the Senate invitation. His friend Giovanni Francesco Gonzaga warns him to be on his guard, but in typical fashion the Count, apart from his desire to be reunited with his wife Antonietta and his daughter Matilde, trusts in his own sense of loyalty and in his friend Marco. He returns happily to Venice: "Yet entirely happy / I cannot be: for who could tell me / If I shall ever see so fine a camp again?"

The final act is the most intense of the play. It takes place at night, in the chamber of the Council of the Ten, where the Doge speaks in

sibylline tones insinuating accusations as he goes along—all of which
makes Carmagnola soon recognize the trap into which he has fallen.
He responds righteously, but to no avail. He is sent off to prison,
where his final colloquy with Gonzaga and then with his wife and
daughter (who faint in anguish) reveals what the author really intended to bring out in his character: magnanimity, pride, nobility,
and tragedy.

> . . . Tell my comrades
> That I die innocent: you were the witness
> Of my deeds and of my thoughts, and this you know. . . .
> . . . I am
> The one betrayed. . . .
> Oh piteous God, in this moment so cruel
> You lead them off, and I do thank You. Friend,
> You succor them; from this ill-omened spot
> You remove them, and when light again they'll see
> Tell them naught remains for them to fear.

Critics have not disagreed in pointing to the tragedy's basic weakness: the psychological incompatibility between great strength of
character, displayed to the point of imprudent impetuosity, and
small, shrewd, cold, calculating political maneuvers on the part of a
suspicious oligarchy of potentates. It was on this irreconcilable
dichotomy, however, that Manzoni consciously wanted to build his
tragedy: of the noble Carmagnola he asks if "he is [not truly] a
dramatic character?"[6] The problem is not the concept but the execution, for the dichotomy remains dramatically unexploited, albeit
moving. There is little sense of tragic accumulation of events,
mainly because too many of them depend less on an individual flaw
than on human weakness generally, and less on tragic consistency
than on normal mutability under the dictates of suspicion or self-
interest. "The catastrophe," writes one critic about the protagonist,
"finds him too different from before; we have two characters: a not
too characteristic warrior, and a deeply melancholy man, with no
strong bridge between the two."[7] And even if we may counter this
argument by noting that there is nothing contradictory about
melancholy courage, and that, like Corneille's Polyeucte, there is
something abstract about this soldier accustomed to open combat
and not covert schemes, we might still refer to the comment of
another critic who says that Carmagnola is an adventurer who may

be more courageous than shrewd, but who really has no noble ambitions, leaps at the chance of revenge against Visconti, and so becomes "a wolf among wolves"; how is it that this peasant who has risen to power unscrupulously is now so ingenuously trusting and done in by a betrayal the likes of which he must have witnessed frequently?[8] But apart from Manzoni's insistence on historical accuracy—excessive to the point of dividing his characters formally between "Historical" and "Ideal" (fictional)—it is unfair to step outside the frame of the play. What Manzoni created was a Christian Romantic who ends like the Napoleon of "Il cinque maggio," purified of the need for earthly conquest and glory, and only at this point "naught remains . . . to fear." He may be "unverisimilar," but then again, and *artes poeticae* notwithstanding, what tragic hero finally is not?

In a deeper sense, however, it is Marco who strikes us as the more tragic figure. He is the victim of the capricious twists of worldly events and of his own conflicting perspectives on loyalty; his noble impulses cry for the heroism he does not possess, and his anguish in retrospect stems not from confusion or blindness but from a lucid recognition of his unheroic essence. Marco's long, self-inquisitional monologue in Act IV, in which he plunges as far down to scrutinize his self as any character can, gives us an insight into Manzoni's real dramatic abilities, but the passage is too fleeting and the Count claims (as he should) too much of our attention. Still, in a very necessary way, Marco deepens the tragic tonality of the play, so that it would be hard to conceive it without him.

This tonality is maintained uniformly by the regular, almost military, rhythm of the cadenced endecasyllables. Monti may have found the style, in his words, careless and prosaic, but another contemporary, Pellico, understood Manzoni's attempt to bring the language down from Olympus, and in good Romantic fashion make the work accessible to those untutored in lofty poetic diction (the play is written in blank verse). Therefore, having no linguistic tradition of this sort to back him up, Manzoni experimented with a balanced and simplified, yet musical, language, lest the drama not communicate directly with the public.[9] We must recognize that whatever appeal *Il Conte di Carmagnola* may still have is due in large measure to the sense of immediacy provided by the language.

According to the preface, Manzoni inserted the Chorus concluding Act II in order to have a "little corner" for himself, somewhere for him to enter the play, not in the Classical sense of interpreting the action and alluding to its denouement, but in the sense of a metahistorical comment—more intensely poetic, to be sure—on the ills of Italy and mankind. Apart from standing out because of its different pattern of versification,[10] the Chorus introduces new subject matter which many have deemed too inconsistent with that of the rest of the play. Manzoni's explanation is twofold:

The Chorus was certainly inserted with the intention of defiling . . . wars. . . . It seems to me that the spectator, or the reader, may bring to a drama two types of interest. The first comes from seeing men and things represented in conformity with that kind of perfection and desire which we all have within us. . . . The other interest comes from a representation closer to the truth, to that mixture of greatness and pettiness, reasonableness and foolishness, which we see in the big and small events of this world. This interest relates to an important and eternal part of man's mind: the desire to know what really is, to see as much as possible in ourselves and our destiny on this earth. Of these two types of interest, I believe that the deeper one, and the one more useful to stimulate, is the second. . . .[11]

Extraneous though it may be in a strict sense, then, the *Carmagnola* Chorus was to allow the useful and "modern" meaning not to go unnoticed, and it was to give the poet himself not so much a role in the play as an opportunity to give vent to his most urgent historical consciousness. Its function combined ethics with aesthetics: in reinterpreting the fundamental character of Greek choruses as he saw them, it was ". . . in no way *a caprice or an enigma* but what he really . . . wanted it to be: 'a personification of the moral thoughts inspired by the action, an organ for the sentiments of the poet who speaks in the name of all humanity.' "[12]

On balance, *Il Conte di Carmagnola* is an acceptable but not an exceptional tragedy. It can be read well, and can be appreciated if the reader interpolates the missing warmth and intensity, for there is more poetry than passion, more lyricism than drama, in it. We need not go as far as Foscolo who deplored it, or as the *Biblioteca Italiana* and London's *Quarterly Review*, which criticized it severely, but we can understand the reservations.[13] Structurally, particularly in the interrelationships between scenes, it is well conceived; otherwise, Manzoni himself recognized repeatedly the weaknesses of his "little romantic monster"[14] and did not need the critics' "open derision."[15] Pellico, however, liked it, though he thought that it dragged somewhat because the characters came too close to the truth. And Goethe praised it, taking up the cudgels in its defense in rebutting the journals. While he did not quite understand the need for Manzoni's distinction between historical and fictional characters, he was clear in his high regard: "I esteem *Carmagnola* very much, very much. . . . It is noteworthy for its depth; and the lyrical part is very beautiful. . . ."[16]

Goethe also extolled *Adelchi*, "something greater by reason of its argument."[17] He had advised Manzoni to choose in the future a subject with deeper pathos, and this the second tragedy has, not necessarily because the subject matter is more moving but because it is handled by the poet with more consistent mastery. It is artistically unified and presents a total poetic experience. But it did not become so painlessly. Manzoni was "not at all happy" with the original version, "and if . . . one ever were to sacrifice some tragedies, this one would not escape suppression. I imagined the character of the protagonist based on historical data . . . but I noted that for all of that there was nothing historical about what I did. . . . The result is something with a romanesque flavor which does not agree with the whole and which shocks even me as it would a badly disposed reader."[18] And when he went about revising it, he erased "perhaps a thousand verses."[19] Indeed, the second version, the one Goethe knew, was "purified": many of the harsh political allusions, such as to the Pope's greedy temporal ambitions or to the servile alliances with foreign predatory powers, are toned down and diffused throughout the tragedy by innuendo, implication, and overtone, thus permitting the protagonist to stand out in greater relief. This does not mean that the political suggestiveness of the play, with reference to the suffering of contemporary Italy under foreign domination, was erased: we need only read the two choruses to be reminded that Manzoni wanted the analogy with the Risorgimento. As the censor said: "Whom did Mr. Manzoni take us for? Does he perhaps believe that we do not know what he is aiming at?"[20] Manzoni's was not a call to arms, however; his Christian conscience could not permit incitement. Besides, for him the Risorgimento was a spiritual phenomenon, an appeal to men's civic and Christian consciences, and *Adelchi*, as its protagonist unquestionably suggests, stems from Manzoni's disappointment over the pitiful failure of liberal agitations (in Naples, Sicily, and Piedmont during that year, 1821) to make any headway toward independence. In fact, there are those who see Murat's failure in the inspiration of *Car-magnola* as an anticipation of *Adelchi*.[21] This play is so strongly pessimistic that it almost strikes a jarring note in Manzoni's generally unruffled philosophical manner.

Yet this was the ethical result rather than the historical purpose, about which he wrote to Fauriel: "I want [to depict] the fall of the Lombard kingdom . . . ; everybody regards the Lombards as Italians . . . , and you can see that by looking at things this way they judged falsely the facts, laws, people, everything . . . I should like you to send me some modern works (excluding the best known) by those who for better or for worse have tried to disentangle the chaos of practices (of medieval barbarians), and who above all have spoken about the conditions of the natives, subjugated and *owned*—which is the point on which history is the poorest."[22] As usual, his desire for historical accuracy outstripped necessity, and in his intense research he went to great lengths to verify details. A typical example is his letter to Luigi Paroletti, his cousin in Turin:

French and Italian historians who talk of Charlemagne's descent into Italy in 773, merely say that he took the mountain route and reached the rear of the armies of Desiderio, his enemy and king of the Lombards, who had made camp at the Alpine Chiuse, which he had fortified, and which without doubt is Susa. But the author of a chronicle in the Monastery of the Novalesa, who wrote during the following century and filled his book with stories, goes into greater detail, which, though mixed with fable, still might be worth looking into, since that place where Charlemagne sojourned for a while could contain a parcel of the truth. So then, he says that an unknown passage was indicated to Charlemagne, and that by following his guide he marched from the Novalesa *per crepidinem cuiusdam montis in quo usque in hodiernum diem Via Francorum dicitur* [along the base of a certain mountain which in our day continues to be called the Road of the Franks]. I find a Villafranca in the Aosta valley, which, given the similarity of the names, makes me suspect it to be this *Via Francorum*. Descending from this mountain, according to the chronicler, Charlemagne arrived in *planitiem Vici, cui nomen erat Gavensis* [on the level ground of Vico, the name of which was Giaveno]. The commentator interprets Giaveno, but I cannot find this Giaveno on my insufficiently detailed maps. Now, I should like to know if, by leaving the Novalesa, there is a road that leads through the mountains to Giaveno, and from there to Susa, and approximately how many days it takes to cover it.[23]

This time, Manzoni not only preceded his tragedy with "Notizie Storiche," as he had done with *Carmagnola*, but he also engaged in true historiography with his elaboration of the "Notizie" in the form of *Discorsi sopra alcuni punti della storia longobardica*. The historical situation of *Adelchi* (barbarian Longobards lording over the enslaved Latin people who look to the Pope to mitigate their suffering, and the Pope's beckoning the Franks into Italy, thus pitting barbarians against barbarians—not unlike pitting Austrians against French in the nineteenth-century context—but ultimately doing nothing to alleviate the agonies of the weak, oppressed Latins) blends intimately with its poetic inspiration through which the situation is relived. In this case, poetry more than ever becomes the spirit of history, "a vital and indissoluble wedding of history and fantasy, where fantasy is totally incorporated into history, and history dissolves totally into fantasy."[24] The "literary" society evoked—the courageous palladin, his faithful friend, the beautiful suffering lady, the prevaricating traitors, the rash defiance of one king and the obstinate power of the other—acts like an aura rising from the solid substratum of history.

The drama reveals a world presided over by force, by thirst for conquest, in which the conflict for Manzoni is "between the law of the Gospel and the historical necessity of violence."[25] At the beginning of the play, which opens in the royal palace in Pavia, a squire announces the arrival of Longobard King Desiderio's daughter Ermengarda, who has been repudiated by her husband Charlemagne, King of the Franks. Spurred by pride and vengeance, Desiderio's thoughts turn to Pope Adrian who, with the proper inducements, could put Charlemagne's nephews on the Frankish throne (they had been driven out by their uncle and were at Desiderio's court with their mother Gerberga[26]). Prince Adelchi disagrees, urging that his father first regain the Pope's support by restoring to him the lands he had promised years before to restore. Greatly saddened over his sister's treatment, he exclaims:

> . . . Oh bitter price
> Of kingdom! Oh state . . . more woeful
> Than that of subjects, if even their gaze
> We are obliged to fear, and hide our forehead
> For shame; and if we cannot even honor

> The ill-fortune of someone beloved
> In the open sun!
> . . . .
>   Remember
> Of whom we are the kings; for in our ranks
> Mingled with the faithful, and perhaps far more than they,
> Lurk our enemies, and that the sight
> Of a foreign banner changes every enemy
> Into a traitor. Oh father, to die the heart
> Alone suffices; but the victory and kingdom
> Are for him who rules over the peaceful.

These last words adumbrate the catastrophe, which seems fated even if by chance the Longobards should win. Nonetheless, his practical nature insists that, if any chance exists, it cannot take place without vacating the Vatican territory: "Let us clear out the Roman lands, and friends / Be of Adrian, for he so wishes." But Desiderio is too fired with the need for immediate military action:

> . . . To perish,
> Perish on the throne or in the dust I would
> Before I suffer such a shame. Let not
> That advice escape your lips again: your father
> So commands you.

Ermengarda's already painful situation is compounded by the king's brash attitude; her words sigh typically with a combination of lassitude and entreaty:

> My sorrow does not ask so much; I only wish
> To forget; this willingly the world accords
> The wretched. Oh, enough! In me
> Let ill-fortune end. I was to wear
> The candid badge of friendship and of peace:
> But heaven willed it not; ah, may it not be said
> I brought discordance everywhere I went
> And tears, for all to whom I was to be
> A pledge of joy.

She asks to retire to a convent, in whose solitude she might through prayer bring peace to her heart. When Charlemagne's ambassador arrives, there is no changing Desiderio's mind, particularly since the legate talks of Longobard restitutions to the Vatican, and the king urges his noblemen to war. A good part of them responds to his rousing words. The act ends, however, with another part of them bent on betraying their king; they meet at the home of Svarto, a common soldier bitter over his commonness and unscrupulous in the method he plans to adopt to overcome it.

> . . . At the bottom of Fate's urn,
> Covered over by a thousand names, my own
> Does lie; if this urn is not shaken, at the bottom
> It will lie forever, and I shall die
> In this obscurity of mine, without anyone ever
> Knowing that I dared to leave it well behind.
> I am naught. . . .
> Who thinks of Svarto? who cares to observe him?
> What foot turns to reach this lowest limit?
> Who hears me? or who fears me? Oh, if boldness
> But bestowed award! If only destiny had not
> Commanded in advance! and if the empire
> Were with swords contested, then you'd see,
> Proud dukes, just who among us would obtain it.
> If only it were up to the adroit! I read your hearts,
> All, but mine is shut to you. Oh! how much
> Astonishment would hit you, and how much disdain
> If you ever were to find out that a single wish,
> A single hope, now binds me to you. . . .
> Some day to be your equal! You might think
> I want my fill of gold. What's gold? to throw it
> At your subject's feet, now that is destiny; but humble
> And defenseless to extend my hand to grab it,
> Like a beggar. . . .

He volunteers to take the message of the duke's betrayal to Charlemagne; the trip is risky, but a nobleman would be detected more readily than he:

> If at roll call someone calls my name and asks:
> Where is he? let one of you say: Svarto? I saw him
> Running long the Ticino; his steed
> Got frisky, from his saddle shook him off
> Into the waves; he was with arms, and surfaced not again.
> Hapless one! they'll say; and none
> Will speak again of Svarto.

The second act moves to the Frankish camp in Val di Susa, where Charlemagne expresses concern over the feasibility of crossing the Alps. His predicament lasts until the arrival of Martino, Deacon of Ravenna sent by his Archbishop, who informs him of the Longobard position at the Chiuse (". . . there crowded / Are the horses and the arms; there gathered / A whole people stands . . .") and of the existence nearby of a hitherto unknown pass through the mountains—the one he took to slip unnoticed by the Longobards, and the one Charlemagne should take to descend upon the enemy from behind. Once Charlemagne's worries are erased, his true personality is revealed: the dominator, who in the face of conquest can easily discard moral responsibilities such as his repudiation of Ermengarda for purely political expediency:

> . . . I see again
> The star which sparkled at my leaving,
> Then lay hid some time. What seemed
> To push me away from Italy was but
> The ghost of error; lying
> Was the voice that said inside my heart:
> No, never, no, on the soil of Ermengarda's birth
> You cannot be king. Oh world! I am
> Of your blood. You are alive: why then
> Stood you before me stubbornly,
> Tacitly, afflicted, in act of rebuke,
> Pallidly, as if come from the tomb?
> God has damned her house; so was I then
> To stay united with her? . . .
> . . . A king cannot
> Travel his high road, without having
> Someone fall beneath his feet. . . .
> . . . .
> . . . Three more days,
> Then the battle and the victory; and after that
> Rest in lovely Italy, amid the fields
> Waving with the grain, and in the orchards
> Laden with fruit unknown to our fathers;
> Among the ancient temples and the palaces,
> In that land cheered by song, prized by the sun,
> Sheltering in its bosom the world's lords,
> And God's martyrs; where the shepherd supreme
> Raises both his palms, and blesses

> Our banners, where we have as enemies
> A puny people, still divided
> Among themselves at that, and half-way mine. . . .

The beauty of Italy attracts, and her divided citizenry makes the prey that much more enticing for someone for whom no law exists except success.

Adelchi dominates the third act; he is duty-bound to defend the honor of the kingdom, yet knows deep inside him that all is to no avail, and that an unhappy destiny hovers over the Longobard enterprise. For this reason, when his close and devoted friend Anfrido mentions the word "glory," his melancholy reply fits not only his profile but also the whole temper of the drama:

> . . . Glory? my
> Destiny is to crave it, and to die
> Never having tasted it.

He fights as he must, for a condemned cause. But he fights valiantly, even while all else crumbles about him, and in so doing offers a sharp contrast with the defecting dukes: Guntigi, Ildechi, Farvaldo, Indolfo, etc. The cowardly sight even revolts a noble, Frankish warrior, Rutlando (alias Orlando, or Roland), who cries his disgust to Charlemagne:

> . . . Oh king, I call you
> As witness, and you too, you Counts, for on this
> Vile day I unsheathed not my sword; let him today
> Wound whome'er he wishes. Frightened, scattered flock,
> I shan't pursue it. . . .
> . . . .
> . . . Friends?
> This we would have been much more, had we at the Chiuse
> Crossed arms. They asked me for the king; I turned
> My shoulders; you will see them now. No, if I knew
> What kind of enemy we marched against, for sure
> I would not have moved away from France.

Anfrido dies with honor, and Adelchi chastizes the "Day of infamy and ire," seeking for himself the same kind of honorable death. At this point, Manzoni introduces one of the two Choruses of the tragedy, a pessimistic comment on Italy's destiny:

From the mossy porches and the failing Forums,
From the woods and from the screeching smithies,
From the furrows laved with servile sweat,
A people frequently dispersed arises,
Perks its ears, uplifts its head
Rocking with new rumors rising.
. . . .
In their looks and faces, confused and uncertain,
Suffered contempt mixes contrastingly
With the wretched pride of times gone by.
. . . .
And on deserters, with sword flaming,
Like ransacking dogs loosed running,
Right and left he sees the warriors come;
He sees them, rapt in a joy unknown
Surveys the battle with lithe hope
And dreams the end of his harsh service.
. . . .
Would the wished prize, promised to the brave,
Be—deluded ones—a shift of fortune,
That a foreign people end your sorrows?
Return to your proud ruins,
To the faint-hearted jobs of your parched workshops,
To the furrows laved with servile sweat.

The stout will mingle with the foe surrendered,
The new lord will mix with the old;
On your neck will ride both nations.
They share the serfs, they share the herds;
They pause together on the blood-soaked fields
Of a dispersed race without a name.

Act IV finds Ermengarda in the monastery of St. Salvator in Brescia where she dies, the fragile victim of her enduring love for Charlemagne and of an irrational, insensitive world which substitutes blood for beauty and violence for peace. Among her dying words, she recalls to the abbess her sister, Ansberga, the happier times of yesteryear:

Smiling days! Do you remember? We crossed over
Mountains, rivers, forests, and with every dawn
The joy of waking grew. What days!
No, speak not of them, I beg you! Heaven knows

If I thought that ever in a mortal heart
So much joy could be contained, and so much sorrow!
You weep for me! Oh, wish you to console me?
Call me daughter: for at this name I feel
A martyr's fullness, and it floods
My heart, and casts it out into oblivion.

The scene concludes with the Chorus returning to sing the death of the afflicted heroine. It is one of the author's finest poetic efforts and, like the previous Chorus, is often included separately among his "lyrics" in the exclusive sense. It may be imagined as a chorus of nuns, to whom Manzoni has lent his most intimate feelings, and contains three parts: the heroine's final moments, the reevocation of her tragedy, and moral reflections on the theme of "provident ill-fortune," the Providential intervention of God in the turmoiled affairs of Ermengarda who through her suffering redeems her Nemesis-plagued race and attains salvation.

With her soft braids spreading
Over her troubled bosom,
Her limbs slow, and bedewed
With death her white visage, she
Pious lies, trembling
Her eyes seeking sky.
. . . .
As dew upon a tuft
Of grass that has turned arid
Makes life again freshly
Flow inside the withered blades,
Which rise once more green
In the tempered dawn;

So into her thoughts, by
Love's ungodly virtue wrought,
Descends the cooling balm
Of a friendly word; her heart
Delights in calm joys
Of another love.
. . . .
Descended from a line
With oppressors blameworthy,
Whose numbers spelled courage,

Whose offense became reason,
Blood their right, and fame
Was in no pity,

Provident ill-fortune
Placed you among the oppressed;
You die lamented, calm,
And descend to sleep with them:
No one will insult
The accused ashes.

You die; may your lifeless
Visage be reformed in peace,
As once it was careless
Of an erring destiny.
It colored only
Slight virginal thoughts.

Thus from the clouds rent through
The setting sun appears,
And behind the mountain
Crimsons now the trembling West,
Boding good farmers
A day more serene.[27]

The scene shifts quickly to the walls of Pavia, the town to which
Desiderio has retreated, and where Guntigi prepares the final betrayal in a speech ringing with Shakespearean overtones:

   . . . Loyalty? So let the saddened friend
Of a fallen lord, the one who, stubborn
In his hope, or, say, irresolute, stood
With him until the end, and with him fell,
Cry Loyalty! Hah, Loyalty! and with it
Let him be consoled—all right. For whate'er consoles
In it we wish to trust—no hesitation. But when
We might lose all, and yet we can
Save all; and when the lucky one, the sire
For whom God declares himself, the consecrated
Charles sends me a messenger, wants me his friend,
Invites me not to perish, wants to separate
Me from the cause of misadventure. . . .
What for, though always shunned, does this word
Loyalty return to assail me,

> Like a troubling bore? it always hurls itself
> In the midst of all my thoughts, consulting them,
> Upsetting them? This Loyalty! All destinies
> Are fine with her, and death is beautiful. Who says so?
> The one for whom you die. And so the universe
> Repeats it with a single voice, and shouts
> That, be he mendicant or derelict, the loyal man
> Is honor worthy, more than is the traitor
> Leisuring with friends. Ah, is that so? But if he's worthy,
> What's he doing being mendicant or derelict? . . .

The final act, in the Royal Palace at Verona, seals the end of the
Longobardic world. The petulant natures of the two rival monarchs
makes it impossible for them to behave toward each other with
civility, each only too quick to berate the other. Vanquished, Desiderio begs Charlemagne to spare his son's life and let all other
matters rest, not indulge his greed, for "Heaven abhors immoderate
desires," and when the Frankish king balks, he erupts:

> I begged you, so I did, though at the test
> I should have known you! You deny it; on your head
> The treasure of revenge grows thicker.
> Deceit has made you victor; let the victory
> Make you proud and merciless.
> Step on the prostrate, and climb; you offend God. . . .

to which the irritated victor responds:

> Silence, you who are defeated. What's this? Just yesterday
> You dreamed my death, and now you beg forgiveness,
> Which would be meet if, in the easy hour
> Of hospitable discourse, delighted I
> Would be rising from your table! . . .

Still, before the nobility of Adelchi, who is carried in mortally
wounded from the field of battle, even Charlemagne softens and
acquiesces to the Prince's words of friendship. To his father, at
whose side he has stood dutifully though in full knowledge of the
vanity of the situation, Adelchi utters dying:

> Life has its great secret, and the final hour
> Alone can understand it. . . .

Rejoice you are not king, rejoice that every course
Of action is now blocked: no place is there
For friendly, harmless deeds; all that remains
Is to do wrong, or suffer it. A force ferocious
Possesses this world, and it bears the name
Of Law. The bloodied hand of our ancestors
Seeded injustice; our own fathers
Cultivated it with blood; by now this earth
Will not yield another harvest. . . .

As the final curtain falls, Adelchi gives up his "tired soul" to Heaven.

The plot's underpinning reflects ideas Manzoni derived from French historians like Fauriel and other liberal thinkers of the Restoration, primarily Augustin Thierry.[28] The latter's dualistic vision of conquerors and conquered, oppressors and oppressed, with, in *Adelchi*'s case, Italy representing the Third Estate amid the clash of races bent on domination, gives the play an historical justification in the light of which the characters, fictional or real, engage a dimension of life greater than themselves. As one critic put it, Adelchi is "the soul of exile."[29] More than anyone else, he feels the guilt of his "race" and knows both the Papal diffidence and the reciprocal hatreds separating Longobards from Franks from Italic Latins. In the subtle ways of his restive conscience, he has compassion for the Italians, his serfs, for, as Croce stated, he is aware that the world is not based on the opposition between good and evil, rather on the shock of vital interests,[30] on whichever side these may lie. He has, then, a pragmatic sense of ruling, which with reference to personal behavior becomes transmuted into exemplary ethics. It is erroneous to try to see in him a typically Romantic hero. True, he is Romantic in his many inner contradictions: his desire for glory, yet his unwillingness to attain it by calculation, hypocrisy, or "politics"; his stern regal bearing, yet his inability to react with justified ferocity against traitors; his will to avenge the insult to Ermengarda, yet his too profound Christianity to throw pity to the winds; his confidence in his courage and in himself, yet his awareness that it will not avail his sister, his realm, or his father. He is Romantic in that he feels he was born for greatness, yet he kills its potential by his unquestioning faith in duty and by the attendant resignation. His stoic front hides a gentle heart. But his world-weariness is not Romantic lassitude in the poetic manner of Novalis' *Heinrich von Ofterdingen;* it is the realization of Christian renunciation, far more convincing than Chateaubriand's attempt to portray it in *René* through the mouth of Father Souël. To say, with De Sanctis,[31] that Adelchi realizes the ideal of the *Inni* (in preparation of Father Cristoforo and Cardinal Borromeo in *I promessi sposi*) strikes us as exaggerated, or needlessly facile. He does, however, represent the apogee of Christian fatalism in the theater; he does not permit himself to withdraw from the historical determinism which affects his duty, and if he obeys the dictates of necessity, he does so with his arm and not with his sword.[32] There may not be in him the agony of doubt, but there is the anguish of engagement. If only for this reason, he has been compared with Alfieri's Ildovaldo in *Rosmunda,* the Marquis de Posa in Schiller's *Don Carlos,* Sophocles' Antigone and Shakespeare's Cordelia, but above all with Hamlet—with the one exception, apart from the unparalleled depth of the Shakespearean hero, that Adelchi's is not a philosophical nature that stifles action but an active nature for which philosophy despairs. Hence he is to some extent a solitary hero in the Shakespearean tradition, but to a larger extent a representative hero, imbued with religiosity, illustrating a particularly symbolic situation.[33] In Western literature, he comes as close to the Christian tragic hero as we may witness; his only rival is Corneille's Polyeucte, but Adelchi's inner travail does not admit comparison with the former's abstract stoicism. We may admire Polyeucte; we feel for Adelchi.

Like her brother, Ermengarda is portrayed not as deluded by life but as a conscience of life. Both are victims, to be sure, but through their openness to justice, love, and charity something of them survives. Manzoni deifies his heroine, for in a sense she is Italy; he makes her ethereal, emerge like an elegy in an epic of armor, or, as Ulivi put it, like "the kind of blended and afflicted musicality we associate with Racine's Phèdre and Athalie."[34] But more than Italy, she is humanity, its drama. Though her emotions bear the stamp of regal refinement, she is more loving than queen,[35] and her passion churns only inwardly; outwardly it is tenderness and sacrifice, that is, an expression of spirituality. When Manzoni inscribed a copy of *I promessi sposi* for his daughter Enrichetta, he wrote in it, recalling his recently deceased wife, what her name meant to him— something which could justifiably apply to Ermengarda (or the

novel's Lucia): "faith, purity, wisdom, love of one's own, benevo-
lence toward all, sacrifice, humility, *all that is holy, all that is lova-
ble* (St. Paul)."[36]

Manzoni's genius for characterization is not limited to *I promessi
sposi* or to the protoganists of this play, for next to Adelchi and
Ermengarda, the other characters do not pale. He knew that he was
side-stepping tradition when he created the role of Charlemagne, as
he wrote to Cousin: "Charlemagne . . . will be neither Ariosto's
leader of the paladins, nor the saint of some ecclesiastical authors,
nor the legislator of some great men, nor the wise man of some
university faculty, nor the rascal of some philosophers, nor the hero
of those who received pensions from his younger brother, but
someone who after all that may still turn out to be a poorly conceived character."[37] He turned out well, however, the "most composite" character in the play, the "pure politician and all-time
Caesar,"[38] who has as many personalities as there are situations for
them in which to function. Indeed, Galletti alludes to "the Caesar-
ian profile of Napoleon,"[39] but a more apt reminiscence would con-
jure up the Machiavellian prince, for whom the political end is the
only rule, necessity must be faced with resoluteness, and power is
not to be measured by petty ambition. If his language swells with
the pomp of victory, it is because he can still remain human, or
rather return to his humanity, after the deed has been accomplished
and the power accrued.

Next to him, Desiderio appears less composite than complex,
because in his case we cannot speak of a pure Machiavellism but of a
confusion between fever of ambition, of dominion, rough pride and
petty egoism on the one hand, and on the other genuine paternal
compassion and sporadic bursts of magnanimity. Of all the characters who walk Manzoni's stage, he remains the most difficult to
grasp, beneath the obvious superstructure of a barbarian prince,
and therefore the one who arouses the most curiosity. The broad,
ethical dimensions of the crisis escape him; his vision is fragmented
by his impulses, good and bad. This is not the case with the leading
traitors, Guntigi and Svarto, who bring to mind "the tragic morality
of Shakespeare,"[40] without, however, overpowering us with the
fearsome evil of the Iagos. Their vision is not fragmented; they have
a clear view of "real" life, stripped of idealistic charismas, and use
cold logic to legitimize ugly calculation. Guntigi's "Loyalty"
monologue drips with sophistry and ably conceals the void of his

conscience, while Svarto climbs to become Count of Susa, acting like an elemental incarnation of that earthly "force ferocious" that Adelchi speaks of, before which decency has no chance, and in whose throes "ill-fortune" is merciful when it is "provident." Too bad that both Guntigi and Svarto, limited to their respective corners of the play, do not develop more forcefully throughout it, and that, as Carducci remarked, they are not endowed with a deeper, Michelangelesque or Shakespearean trait or two. Still, in their own corners, they remain impressive.

In the brief lapse of dramatic time from near the end of Act III to near the beginning of Act IV, Manzoni concentrated the lyrical essence of the tragedy in the form of two Choruses, regarded by many as the fruit of his historical and ethical meditation. Structurally, they "peak" the action by revealing its symbolism and by allowing the poet to intervene so as to draw the play out of itself, to summarize and to teach. Their importance in Manzoni's mind cannot be minimized: he talked about having had to "rhyme the two lyrical choruses . . . , in order to draw attention to what is most serious and poetic in the subject matter. . . ."[41] Thus their aesthetic placement serves a philosophical end, for by being juxtaposed they signal once again the tragic dualism in Manzoni's world view, the sense of collective and individual tragedy which underlies his pessimism regarding things of this earth. The first one is Italy's Chorus, or as Russo calls it, "a sorrowful epic of war," the peripeteia of a whole society aroused and dismembered by superior forces and adverse historical traditions. The same critic notes too that the national motif is colored with Manzoni's Christian consciousness, and that while we may speak of a certain "contemplative pessimism," we may also speak of another "active pessimism," that of teaching the people to work and be virtuous for their own inner redemption.[42] The second, Ermengarda's Chorus, points to the ensuing private tragedy, the solitary destiny of the individual, who in the nature of things will always be frail and haplessly suffering if he is going to be honest. Only endurance or forebearance marks the life of the good, at the end of which hope lies in the Providential reward of being removed from it. There is, shall we say, poetry in morality, and in the morality of death.

Before and after the two Choruses, the structure of the tragedy— the scene by scene progression and the feeling of spaciousness emerging from it—adumbrate the narrative artist of the novel. The interrelationship of the parts, rather than tightly confine the play according to Classical norms, yields through the subject matter to a broader, we might suggest cosmic, sense of the whole. Nowhere is this sense more pronounced than in Martino's recounting of his arduous journey across the beautiful Alps. Little knowing that the Franks will turn out to be invaders and not liberators,[43] he represents the Italian people's hope, a hope which becomes lyricized in the form of a sublime account of the country's natural beauty:

> . . . Here
> No trace of man appears, but only forests
> Of firs intact, rivers unknown, and trailless
> Valleys; all was quiet: I heard
> But my own steps, and from time to time
> The torrent's thunder, or the unexpected
> Falcon's screeching, or the eagle's darting
> In early morning from its raised nest, roaring
> Above my head, or in the afternoon
> The sylvan crackling of the pine cones
> Stung by the sun. I journeyed thus three days
> And I spent three nights under tall plants
> Or in the gorges. My guide was the sun;
> With it I arose, and then I followed
> Its course, facing last its setting. I walked
> Uncertain of the road, and crossing over
> From vale to vale; or if at times I saw
> Rising before me the summit of a cliff
> Accessible, and I did reach the top,
> More peaks more sublime, stood
> In front and all around, still others whitened
> From crest to base with snow, almost
> Like pointed, steep pavilions, pegged
> Into the earth; still others, iron-firm,
> Like walls erect and insurmountable. The third sun
> Was setting when I scaled a lofty mountain
> Which raised its forehead higher than the rest
> And was one long green slope, its summit
> Crowned with trees. . . .

Passages like this one highlight *Adelchi*. They make it Manzoni's lyrical masterpiece and, together with *Il Conte di Carmagnola*, augured well for the future of Romantic theater in a Europe seeking the theatrical ground for its new literature. Goethe alluded to Manzoni's "new dramatic school." But the Romantic "school" of historical drama went in other directions, in those—primarily in Germany and Austria—of Kleist, Hebbel, Grillparzer, and Ludwig (and the little recognized Grabbe and Büchner), while in France, Manzoni's intellectual center, it sank into the soap-opera platitudes of Hugo's *Hernani, Ruy Blas, Lucrèce Borgia, Les Burgraves,* etc. Disenchanted with such productions, Sainte-Beuve looked back to the promise held forth by Manzoni's dramatic works: "When I think of those two beautiful columns which seemed to shape for us in advance the portico of the edifice, providing we followed the example, I can hardly not blush at what, under our very eyes, has happened to this dream of a theatre."[44]

Goethe was correct: Manzoni's theater was "new." While the characters do stand out, they leave an impression on us more through what they do not say than through what they say, and therefore do not overpower us like Phèdre, or Lear, or Oedipus. Manzoni's propensity to write for readers rather than for spectators aided this attenuation which, combined with his ethico-historical concerns, produced what has been called a narrated representation. On this basis, one critic[45] has pointed to Manzoni's modernity, since his conception anticipates Brecht's epic theater, although the latter's objective depiction of events cannot blend with the former's subjective poetization of them. Still, there remains the same "ethical dissatisfaction with the conventions of the traditional stage," and conceived as an epic narrative, *Adelchi* presents possibilities involving stage and public, that is, a collective experience, which would be difficult in the conventional manner of stressing the imposing hero and the impressive heroine.[46]

The underlying pessimism is the same. More pagan and naturalistic, Shakespeare does not concern himself with Christian renunciation; Manzoni does, and Brecht does not know it. Greek Fate became Destiny in Shakespeare and Marxist struggle in Brecht, while Manzoni saw existence more Jansenistically as an infirmity, in which participation means fighting and in which good actions turn to, or are annulled by, worldly evil. Not the least cause for worry is history's ability to place fine men and women, princes or paupers alike, in the roles of oppressors; necessity makes no allowances for good will, and in short order all hands become soiled. Nonetheless, "fighting and active participation are the primary condition for salva-

tion. . . . Of course, to participate by fighting is not an optimistic
solution, and we might say that, along with admiration, a historical
pietas veils the eyes of the poet when he looks at man's tumultuous
incursions."[47] We may either obey reluctantly, like Adelchi, or absorb sacrificially, like Ermengarda. A troubling fatality hovers above
our heads; Thierry's racial determinants look, more philosophically,
like Jansenistic determinism if we consider, somewhat like Russo,
the unreconcilability between the Jansenistic world of Grace inhabited by Adelchi, Ermengarda, and Martino, and the Machiavellian
world of Realpolitik inhabited by Desiderio, Svarto, and Charlemagne.[48] Hence the veracious, tragic atmosphere of *Adelchi*. We
cannot feel that if the aberrations of the hero's historical age were
rectified, all would end well. If tragedy must encourage a metaphysical attitude through a poetic cosmology, then *Adelchi* fits the mode,
and the notion that Christian tragedy is not possible because of the
promise of salvation does not apply. For Manzoni, Providence operates in the infinite rather than in the finite, preparing salvation with
pain and ill-fortune, "but abandoning the earth and the living to the
whirlwind of evil and to the anguish of eternal shipwreck."[49]

To be sure, Hamlet, who looks upon his fellow man's hypocrisy
and injustice with equal aversion as Adelchi, cannot invite death as
confidently as his counterpart because he has no faith in the beyond.
But Adelchi is no less anguished and his tone no less pessimistic.
For this reason, the play should not be considered an exemplum to
which the human traits of its characters are subservient, or in which
inspiration drew exclusively from the Christian fountain; in fact, the
emphasis rests on the personality, albeit not overpowering, moving
as best he can in an evil world toward an attainment, in some cases,
of the Christian ideal. If the play's expressiveness stems from a
refined religiosity, its humanity stems from a sensitive psychological
assessment of human behavior. "The thought that moves the drama
is doubtlessly Christian, but the feeling that penetrates every scene
is one of horror for universal injustice and disdain for triumphant
perfidy."[50] Sansone insists that in its finest moments, *Adelchi* expresses not Manzoni's religious but his secular pessimism, his tragic
sense of life, [51] and to this we must add that he does so to the point
of near crisis. His "freest poetry" (the expression comes from
Croce[52]) may be free in a sense other than versification. For *Adelchi*
rings surprisingly with doubt, with the agonizing questions of Job:
why do the good suffer?; why do they die without realizing their

good?; how can Ermengarda be cast aside so shamelessly?; why are Svarto's ambitions fulfilled?; how can Charlemagne stoop to an acceptance of human fraud when his own knight Rutlando shudders? In other words, where is this divine, Providential justice which ultimately controls human history from above, which shapes the historical design? In the long run, Christianity shows itself in *Adelchi* only in the way its heroes accept death, in the "provident ill-fortune." The rest is cast with bleak thoughts.

CHAPTER 5

Upright Heart and
Perfectioned Mind

"RELIGION merely wishes to lead us to wisdom and moderation without unnecessary sorrow, and through calm reflection take us to that state of reasonableness which we would otherwise reach through weariness and some sort of despair." In their
tranquil, Manzonian way, these words underlie the *Osservazioni
sulla morale cattolica* (1819/1855), a fundamental, albeit informal,
essay for all those who seek an insight into the theoretical premises
of the author's major works. Analogies with Pascal,[1] who also left us
his "observations" in the form of the *Pensées*, inevitably come to
mind, though despite the defensive nature of the *Osservazioni*, the
polemical and anguished tone of the Jansenist is missing. Manzoni is
too modest for the aggressive discourse (especially in the *Lettres
provinciales*) of Pascal, too indulgent for dismay at the extent of
human ignorance, and too confident to despair at the fallibility of
reason and the enormity of human misery. Sansone speaks of "the
serene tranquility of him who feels he possesses an irrefutable
truth."[2] A letter written when he was forty-three makes the same
telling remark by way of confession: ". . . it is true that the evidence
of the Catholic religion fills and dominates my intellect; I see it at
the beginning and at the end of all moral questions—everywhere it
is invoked and everywhere it is excluded. Truths themselves, which
after all may be discovered without its guidance, do not seem whole
to me, or founded, or unshaken, unless they are redirected toward
it, and thereby appear as what they are: consequences of its doctrine. Such a conviction must come through naturally in all of my
writings. . . ."[3] We might argue with Pascal about the wager, man's
double nature, and the proofs of the Christian religion as we might
with Manzoni's theocentricity; but since the latter does not force his
constructs upon us, we feel less disposed to confrontation and move
along with the "serene tranquility."

At the urging of Tosi and Fr. Giudici, and with the encouragement of Dègola, Manzoni undertook to respond to Sismondi's accusations against Catholic morality, for which the Protestant thinker used Italy as an example. According to him, Italians practice religion ritually, neglecting its spirit, and as the Middle Ages show, when the Pope enjoyed almost absolute power in temporal matters, the adherence to external practices induces corruption. Manzoni sees the reason for institutional degeneracy not in the moral doctrines themselves, which correspond with the teachings of the Gospel, but in their arbitrary application by those in power. Is it not true that all Catholicism can do is to comfort man, improve him in a world in which human passions forever traduce and immorally deform good principles? Man may indeed be "the dregs of Adam," but his faith may contain many treasures. Sismondi's documentation about Italy is defective, among other things, through its generalities which give rise to out-of-context absurdities. As an example, by reading chapter 127 of the *Républiques italiennes* Manzoni says that one could easily envisage Italians as "living between hired killers and Carthusian monks." The argument of the essay runs along these religious and political lines. It does not pay close attention to Sismondi's assessment of the relation between the political Church and Italian history, but it has the advantage of voicing a personal credo, which is spared the grandiose designs of Chateaubriand and Lamennais and which yet professes a "genius" and speaks the "words of a believer." Too often it is criticized for having no "organic" presentation, or for argumenting without the rigors of logical speculation.[4] The fact is, as Angelini aptly put it, that the *Osservazioni* are not a treatise but a "praise,"[5] and, we might add, not a tightly structured dissertation but a free exposition of just what the title says, "observations." Similarly, the appended *Abozzo di un Capitolo sull'Utilitarismo* is nothing more than a "sketch." Perhaps for this reason, Manzoni insisted to Dègola before writing it that the work he had in mind "is not substantially religious, nor is it apologetic."[6]

Devoid of religious reasoning, secular philosophy, Manzoni believes, represents an imperfect attempt by man to use reason for his betterment. Compared with the constructiveness of revealed morality, "purely philosophical morality" is "naturally defective," and only the blend of reason and faith can offer him the possibility of integrating his values with the wholeness in whose terms alone life can be conceived. Instinctively, the effects of reason aspire toward happiness; they ascend and hope to transcend, but left to its own resources, reason tends to descend to covetous attachment to particular—as opposed to universal—goods. As the important *Abozzo* clarifies, utility, a pragmatic characteristic of one's attachment to particular goods, needs something greater than itself to rise to the stature of an absolute; in no way, as utilitarians claim, can it shape itself into a principle of morality. How can man really ascertain in advance what will be useful to him? How can justice be seen in entirely pragmatic terms and be identified with utility? Justice is useful, to be sure, and justice and utility are mutually servicing; but without the transcendent view provided by Revelation, without the paralegal criteria by which alone we understand the meaning of the concept of justice itself, how can we acquire that sense of what is "whole," "founded," and "unshaken" that is so necessary if we are not to be traduced by a mere succession of responses to contingent considerations? What is just is not *ipso facto* useful. The danger lies in confusing "universal utility" with "utility for the largest number," which removes man from the transcendent context and, as one critic remarked, brings us back to the thesis of the worldly Callicles in Plato's *Gorgias* for whom the weak and the many make laws for their own protective utility.[7]

For Manzoni, "the Church . . . possesses moral truth in its entirety, which includes the particular truths of morality: those which man may come to know through the sole use of reason, and those which form part of Revelation, or which may be deduced from it." One admission here, as in the letter of 1828, is that man can come to know moral truth outside of the Church, so that despite the lack of wholeness reason does have *some* operative autonomy. What is always intriguing in Manzoni's liberal Catholicism is the perpetual moderation between conservative and libertarian principles. The Jansenist and the "ideologue" mingle. But above all, it is the man of "intimate sense" (what becomes the "common sense" of *I promessi sposi*) who impresses us with his gentle logic. He opposes the fundamentalist or fanatic who blindly defends the "corruption" and "bad administration" of the Church simply because, being the Church, the institution supersedes its own practices, its own abuses of authority, its abstinence from self-criticism and revision, and its misuses of position: "One of the gravest symptoms of degeneration in man as in society is that of being content with one's mortal state, of not finding anything to remove or perfect. I do not intend in any way to defend abuses which are justified under religious pretext, but which in fact reflect temporal goals; indeed I declare that I hope ardently that they be made known time and again, and be condemned by the very people to whom they might appear useful. . . . That these abuses exist is all too undeniable." If, then, the Church conscientiously directs its enterprise with spiritual purpose, it possesses the most meaningful set of moral truths with which to lift "the dregs of Adam" to a better life.

Momigliano and Galletti are among the more perspicacious interpreters of the *Osservazioni*. While the work is of small merit, for Momigliano, compared with the gigantic spiritual structure of the novel, he discovers a number of valuable insights in it, such as the indivisibility of faith and morality from logic, a central tenet in Manzoni's philosophy. Another is the constant accord between the true and the good, an inseparable partnership of values as much Romantic as Classical, and therefore eternal, or absolute. Catholic morality is endowed with absoluteness or unity, and the *Osservazioni* suggest how genuinely Manzoni possesses it and how consistently it is capable of resolving his most complicated doubts. Correctly, Momigliano finds chapter 3, "On the Distinction between Moral Philosophy and Theology" along with its appendix "On the System Which Bases Morality on Utility," the intellectual core of the work. We should add also that small section in chapter 5, "On the Correspondence of Catholic Morality with Natural Upright Feelings," which asserts that in building a code of ethics (on the Word of God), the Church could not "have destroyed the natural bases of morality, that is, upright feelings, toward which all men are inclined." Hence it makes no sense to separate ethics from religion because being God-inspired both are mutually inclusive. In chapter 3 Manzoni writes: "In whatever system of morality *absolutely distinct from theology* . . . , there are two innate and irreparable defects: a lack of beauty, in other words, of perfection, and a lack of motives. For morality to be accomplished, it must unite these two conditions in the highest degree; that is, it must not exclude, indeed it must propose, the most beautiful feelings and actions, and offer motives for preferring them." In uniting these two basic human tendencies, Catholic morality allows man to find "his unity in the recognition of the eternal and supreme unity of the true and the good." Armed with such cognitions, Manzoni claims that faith is not an irrational force but a rational act of the will, an act anchored on one's willingness "to examine and admit or reject proofs." The "disposition of the heart" must not be discarded, but the "will to examine" is central.[8]

The appendix, appropriately from the point of view of Manzoni's argument, considers the fallacies of utilitarianism and focuses in large part on Jeremy Bentham's assumption of the connection linking interest with duty. Bentham emphasizes the former, arguing on pragmatic grounds that since it is more concrete and precise as a concept it provides a clearer basis for behavior than the latter which is more abstract and less immediate. But duty is a moral concept, and Manzoni cannot admit the primacy of utility. His postulations here are weak, and in the long run he gives the impression that "his originality lies only in demolishing: the positive part of his thought is but an application of the Gospel."[9]

Yet, even this critic must admit that on balance the *Osservazioni* distinguishes itself through its logical rigor (which seizes upon the slightest contradictions and eschews generalities), its consistent discernment of truth from falsehood (which gives prominence to the "intimate sense" over the *arguendo* assumption), and its absolute unity of thought (which springs from the author's omnipresent conscience of faith). Furthermore, as the notion of "intimate sense" suggests, the work's acumen gains through the "psychological penetration" of his observations on modesty, pride, hypocrisy, malfeasance, slander, etc. Hence "he never bores you, because his morality is rooted in a concrete psychology and is enlivened by a moving humanity."[10]

Galletti turns our attention to another aspect of the *Osservazioni*.[11] To the extent of his fideism, Manzoni shares with Pascal a certain anti-intellectual approach, but in political and social matters he does not fear reform and novelty; "in fact he loves them and seeks them, convinced that if they are really good they cannot go against the spirit of the Gospel. . . . [Hence he remains democratic] like a follower of the first Apostles, persuaded that men will be able to build a society and an order of things less unfair than the present only on the idea of equality and fraternity."[12] In his mind, religion and freedom can go hand in hand, and as Sapegno remarked, the *Osservazioni* offer a Catholic morality which coincides frequently with the moderate liberalism of the earlier nineteenth century.[13] Politically and otherwise, "man will be reasonable and enlightened in proportion to his faith"; like Dante, Manzoni's goal is "to bring himself to the point of uniting reason with religion," to be a rationalist with faith—given his overall pessimistic idea of man—in whom the "perfectioned mind" accompanies the "upright heart." The demands of modern life, so wrought with the turmoil of change, seem to belie the merits of historical traditions, but in fact the "intimate sense" of his evangelical morality encourages a different perspective, a cosmic view whereby the divine design may be periodically examined to reveal how all new ideas—though by addition we keep expanding the truth—already existed in some form in the Gospels. If man reads them properly, he comes to know how the finite is continuously absorbed by the infinite. To read them properly means to study them not as catechism but as a text in which the troubled drama of moral values unfolds. And this is revelation.

The central issue is always morality, conceived with all of its human and psychological facets, under the aegis of divinity. The focus rests more on the actions of men, or human dimension, than on historical cause and effect, or neutral dimension. Manzoni's analyses of historical and political questions resolve themselves in moral terms. Accordingly, his last and unfinished historical essay, published posthumously in 1889, gives moral precedence to the Italian struggle over the French. The *Saggio comparativo su la rivoluzione francese del 1789 e la rivoluzione italiana del 1859* was to be a comparison between the effects of the two revolutions, a discussion of the oppression and the governmental difficulties which resulted from the French regicide, and an examination of Italian conditions which made it mandatory to remove the preceding government (Manzoni never got to this last section). Much controversy surrounded European opinion about the event of 1789. Carlyle, Ballanche, De Maistre, and De Bonald pointed to divine punishment for the hypocritical humanitarian rationalism of the previous century which concealed satanic power and needed purification by blood; German thinkers looked down upon it; Hugo, Quinet, and Leroux saw it as divinely ordained and nobly progressive toward freedom; Alfieri hailed it for its liberal spirit and then condemned it for its excesses, not finding in these the fascination Taine did years later. Manzoni typically viewed it as an all too human drama enacted by sincere, generous, dedicated, selfish, and cruel men. Though originally useful and legitimate in its principles, the French Revolution was unnecessary and inconclusive, because it degenerated into civic strife which culminated in the overthrow of a legitimate government which was about to find ways to better the plight of the poor, and the great difficulty in replacing the fallen government with a new one which turned out despotic, helped not at all and erased the original benefits. On the other hand, the Italian revolution was necessary, legitimate, and just, because it united a country divided by foreigners and represented a holy (moral) aspiration. It did not, like the French, have to "seek out a goal in the fury of the chase." With more wishful thinking than accuracy, Manzoni believes the Italian revolution brought "true liberty, which, through just laws and stable institutions, insures the citizen against private violences and the tyrannical orders of power, since power itself is immune to the domination of oligarchic societies and does not buckle under the pressure of the masses. . . ."[14] It is not surprising that Croce took Manzoni to task for "a sophistic trial of the French Revolution" and that he lamented in general his ahistorical mentality, his lack of dispassionate, scientific interest in the study of history. De Lollis, too, has argued that Manzoni "lacked historical sense" and that this antihistoricism provoked a misunderstanding of the French Revolution, particularly because historical bases keep yielding to moral grounds.[15] But Croce had to admit that Manzoni erred through nobility; by "leaving the field of history and entering that of moralism" he insisted on "guaranteeing human responsibility."[16] It could be argued, too, that by focusing on the human Manzoni's purpose was not historiographical but judgmental. His Christian conscience suffered in the written—let alone the physical—presence of acts of cruelty, and this was especially true in his old age. They might be rationalized on divine grounds, as Quinet did, but on human grounds the necessary violence and the suspension of justice in chaos loomed as immoral. The Italian revolution was different: it seemed waged by "upright hearts," and did not sully itself with abhorrent abuses. Along these lines, it would have been rewarding to know his thoughts on the American Revolution, for the evidence shows that he became very interested in it in 1866. In speaking about Carlo Botta's study, he had referred to a "felicitous" subject consisting of "great actions . . . , generous passions for the welfare and foundation of a people, and I am tempted to say the almost ancient and classical nature of some of the heroes . . . of the American nation."[17] It was in this spirit that he viewed the Italian revolution.

The key word, not without Christian implications, is mentioned in *Dell'indipendenza dell'Italia* (probably 1872), a factual enumeration of those events which brought about the "admirable foundation" of the country. It is: "concordance," a notion Manzoni clung to zealously, to the point of objecting to Lamartine's use of the word "diversity" to describe Italy (*Lettera ad Alphonse de Lamartine sulla causa della indipendenza e dell'unità italiana*, Milan, April 6, 1848). Concordance is what even a superficial glance at 1789 convinced him the French movement lacked; but 1859, which fulfilled a moral function, envisaged a concordant goal. "A horrendous faction" did not corrode it. In these simple terms, Manzoni separated the good from the bad, always drawn to the event which embodied a moral purpose whose unfolding was defensible on Christian grounds, or through which he could investigate the moral consciousness of man. Had his sense of Providence not been so pronounced, he might have developed a dialectical perspective of history. But he did not.[18] The good and the bad, depending on the moment, divide the world: ". . . great political events . . . differ among themselves only in being morally good or perverse, depending on whether, at one time or another, there prevails either an honest and wise force which, powerless through legal justice, is moved by a feeling of natural justice and seeks to obtain some good, to hinder some evil, to modify that very sad state for the better, or a force moved by sad passions and criminal ends, which is used to maintain and worsen them."

In other writings, however, Manzoni belies those who charge him with antihistoricism. He is factually meticulous and understands fully the value of the background evolutionary process of a given event in his *Discorso sopra alcuni punti della storia longobardica in Italia* and to some extent in the *Storia della colonna infame*. Of the former, one critic says that it is "an important work, which has the right to be remembered with honor in the development of Italian historiography."[19] In it, Manzoni demonstrates consistency with his criticism of contemporary historians: "As for modern historians, I confess to you that I have difficulty understanding how they have skirted some of the most important problems without noticing them, or believe they have solved them with vague, loose, everyday formulas which are not applicable to the totality of the facts, and where with the slightest clarity you discover a big mistake." With his usual modesty, he stated that he did not intend "to clarify the history of the Middle Ages" but simply "to make obscurity visible,"[20] and, for that matter, he did not claim that this "cursed discourse"[21] (it caused him much labor in research and revision) dealt with important problems. But it dealt with an important principle: to revise the criteria for looking at medieval history. Furthermore, it was important to Manzoni who was writing *Adelchi*, just as the *Colonna infame* was important to him with reference to *I promessi sposi* (it was to be a chapter in the first draft, *Fermo e Lucia*). Both are good examples of how to avoid "vague, loose, everyday formulas." And both exhibit the best of the "historian" Manzoni: a live feeling for what is human, and an equally live sensitivity for the problems afflicting society at various times, not to speak of his rigorously documented and applied methodology and his broad sense of history.

Hoping to blend Muratori and Vico, and with Machiavelli, Cuoco, Thierry, and Giannone present in his mind, Manzoni breaks new paths in interpreting the Middle Ages by examining the specific question of the relationship between Longobards and Italians in the *Storia longobardica*. To do this humanely and sensibly, and not in the glib fashion it had been done repeatedly before, he asks himself about the conditions of all defeated peoples in Europe at that time—something previous historians had not asked themselves. What these historians had loosely said was not only that the Longobards and Italians had amalgamated before Charlemagne's descent but also that the barbarians had been good to the natives. In addition, it was believed that Italians had continued to live by Roman laws, and that the popes had disserved them through foreign alliances, such as the one with the Franks. Given the ease with which errors of historical interpretation are transmitted once a particular point of view becomes established, Manzoni insisted on the constant need for revision of the data and reassessment of the evaluations. Thus he came to the conclusion that Longobards and Italians had not become "one people," that the notion that the natives kept their own laws was "kind words, as Mephistopheles said, which are used when the concept is missing," that there are plentiful reasons to doubt the goodness of the Longobards to the Italians given the fact that "the temptation to be unjust must have been great in proportion to facility, impunity, and profit, and, as man's common nature shows us, moral actions, ideas, and theories could adapt easily to these circumstances," and finally that the pontiffs were in many ways the only defenders of the natives—hence the call for Frankish help against the barbarian occupiers. With the frequent appendage of observations, appendices, and notes to each chapter, Manzoni validates the best in Romantic historiography: a wide documentation established for the analysis of the individual and of human events. Sansone's comment is accurate: "Important to Manzoni was not the mere historical reason, not, that is, the explanation of events, which grows out of an anonymous and impersonal valorization of forces, but the concrete actions of men; history is the theater and the test of human responsibility and human freedom, and his value lies precisely in this secret examination and revelation of consciences."[22]

The moralistic historian found the richest test of human responsibility and freedom in a heavily documented examination of the juridical mentality of the seventeenth century in the context of events surrounding the *untori*, or "greasers" (people suspected at that time in Milan of spreading the plague by smearing a poisonous substance on walls). The examination gains for being narrative rather than analytical. The *Storia della colonna infame* recounts the trial of Health Commissioner Guglielmo Piazza and barber Giacomo Mora in 1630 (both are sentenced to death, though innocent), and recalls the column which was erected near the Porta Ticinese on the site of the former's house, which was destroyed, to commemorate this trial (it was knocked down in 1778). Without historical pretentions but with typical Enlightenment polemics, Pietro Verri had inveighed against the criminal weaknesses of seventeenth-century jurisprudence which sanctioned torture and destroyed the integrity of the individual. Manzoni's thrust was at once more psychological and juridical. "While Verri had justified the judges' procedure and condemned juridical science, that is, the work of legal authors of the time who theorized on principles which were then applied by the executors, Manzoni reversed the judgment, showing with ample documentation that the juridical science of the time sought to limit the use of torture, while the judges used it profusely, indeed applied it in detail with a kind of sadistic satisfaction."[23] First Manzoni measured the judges in accordance with the laws of the time, then as a Christian thinker and by concentrating on the juridical behavior itself he lamented the barbaric mores. The "real" background of the events included above all the psychological reality involving the *untori*, a syndrome in which even the famous Cardinal Federico Borromeo participated. The panic following in the wake of the plague's numberless casualties and horrors disrupted the public's mind despite the century's nascent scientism, and the need for scapegoats was felt compellingly enough to wrench legal judgment out of shape. It is useless to charge Manzoni with antihistoricism simply because the piece does not conform with dispassionate historical methodology; as he judged the law according to its intention, so we judge him. The *Colonna infame* intentionally partakes of novelistic characteristics, and among other things brings forth the plight of the humble: not those who will be comforted ultimately, as in the *Inni sacri*, but those who are buffeted now by the powerful, who awaken our pity, and who play out their roles in what someone has called "the novel of man's bewilderment."[24] Russo calls it an "essay of subtle analysis about the complications and weaknesses of man's spirit,"[25] but it is more acceptably a novel (or quasi-novel) of law and its practice, human superstition and innocent suffering, written by a moralist with a fine historiographical sense. A feeling of absurdity emerges after permeating the story, more through what remains unsaid than through what gets said. The contrast between Cavalry Captain Giovanni Gaetano de Padilla, the son of the Commandant of the Castle of Milan and therefore a member of the privileged class (to be sure, falsely indicted by the accused in the despair of torture), and the unprivileged, hence unprotected and torturable Commissioner and barber, speaks tacitly to issues of inequality before the law which will fill the pages of later reform movements. Yet for being eternal, it seems, this human ill, abetted in this case by the "perverse passions" of the judges, strikes an absurd note worthy of Beckett. "How blind is fury." In the *Colonna infame*, the poetry often lies between the lines.

If Manzoni employs various methodologies, depending on subject matter, his goal is uniformly moral and his conscience consistently ethical; by investing the historical event with moral consideration, like Rosmini he does not hesitate to make history a means to a greater end—something Rankean historians did not take to with enthusiasm. But where, except in personal preference, is the difference between conceiving history within an objectively formalistic or a religiously committed framework? Rationally presented, the latter is no less valid a point of view than the former, just as a deductive philosophy is no less valid, as a possible philosophical point of view, than an inductive one. Who is to say that *Die römischen Päpste* commands more authority than Burckardt's *Kultur der Renaissance in Italien?* Galletti pinpointed the question when he observed that nineteenth-century historiography, which led the assault on Manzoni's method, is merely a secularization of the usual theological concept of history that dominated Christian thinking from St. Augustine to Herder.[26] This is the concept Manzoni embraced, as poet, dramatist, novelist, and philosopher, which made him see society in the broadest of human perspectives: "that state so natural to man and so violent, so willed and so full of sorrows, which creates so many goals whose fulfillment is impossible, which bears all ills and all remedies rather than cease for a single moment . . . , that state which is a mystery of contradictions in which the mind loses itself, unless it considers it a state of trial and preparation for another existence."[27]

If, as Manzoni would have it, historical phenomena stimulate artistic creation, then the whole question of aesthetics cannot be separated from history any more than the usefulness of art can be divorced from its moral inpact. This means that the logic of history and the promptings of morality must underpin artistic expression, and literary criticism adjusts itself according to this optics. Even to his friends, Manzoni the artist presented himself as a literary critic; we might even say that his art derives from, or is a function of , his logical, critical mind which harbored an ineradicable concern for the truth. As one of his friends wrote about him, ". . . in him the artist was inseparable from the critic, so much so that the former could never do anything, or get anything under way, without the latter."[28] Certainly, he possessed one of the most reflective, critical minds among European Romantics, and one of the most profound, if only because he judged not as a partisan of a school of thought or as one steeped in a particular cultural atmosphere, but as a conscience. What is interesting in his case is the evolution of the meaning of truth in his poetics.

His first critical text was the Preface to *Il Conte di Carmagnola*, in which he stresses the need for faithful adherence to given historical events in order to extract from history its poetry—something that the introduction of choruses can do much to enhance. Furthermore, truthfulness does not mesh with observance of the unities of time and place. This last argument became ostensibly the subject for his more elaborate *Lettre à M. C*** sur l'unité de temps et de lieu dans la tragédie*, but as the thesis unfolds, he delves into matters of greater significance. Unity of action is defined for Chauvet, who had maintained that the first act of a drama must communicate to the spectator the situation and designs of each character, including their attendant results, and that all subsequent material must bear narrowly on these premises without temporal interruptions or spacial dislocations. Manzoni, with more historical consciousness, insists simply on "a succession of interconnected events." But more significantly he broaches the whole question of the relationship between historico-moral truth and poetic truth. We may not wish to accept Sansone's declaration that the *Lettre* is the author's "most important theoretical work,"[29] but we must recognize its purport and implications.

De Sanctis was among the first to detect the potential error on Manzoni's part in confusing poetical with historical truth, or artistic with natural reality, when it comes to the problem of combining the two in logical terms. Given the author's pronounced historical bent, it has also been pointed out that in this document he relegated poetry to an ancillary, not to say subservient, position with respect to the primacy of history and historical truth. But while it is true that for him an historical error consititues an aesthetic error, it is also true that he freed Italian poetry from many eighteenth-century shackles. Real poetry, he once wrote, "is quite rare among poets, particularly in Italy, where habit and rules—all ideas—have tended for a long time to remove poetry from naturalness, and to make a mere conventional language out of it."[30] He reacted against his compatriots' adherence to antiquity as the only path to beauty, but he criticized even more the intransigence of so many Frenchmen (like Chauvet) on this subject, asserting his belief that "certain works containing veritable beauty have been neglected [there] simply because they do not follow the common rules."[31] While he did not consider the mixture of the sublime and the grotesque in drama, or "the pleasant and the serious," to have been productive, even in Shakespeare, he nonetheless recognized the possible "felicitous" application of the theory in the future, and refused to abide by "arbitrary limitations."[32]

Among the most flagrant arbitrary limitations are the unities of time and space which offend historical reality and which Chauvet defended. The Preface and the *Lettre* both attack the resulting un-verisimilitude, and in justifying his view Manzoni turned to a comparison between Voltaire's *Zaïre* and Shakespeare's *Othello*. The moral undertones of the English bard make his drama infinitely superior to the Frenchman's, which is seasoned with superficialities. Classical rules condemn the playwright to the artifice of long speeches to disclose the background of actions, to an abusive selection of facts of violence, many inviting suicide or madness, and to a congestion of events inside a brief span of time, not to speak of an excessive reliance on the subject of love, that is, passion—the case with French tragedy (he had read Lessing)—in order to give these time/space-limited events a certain dramatic coherence. Not being so constrained, Shakespeare emerges as more moral. No wonder that Nicole, Bossuet, and Rousseau censured the theater with immorality, since they did not look beyond the "French system." Manzoni urges

a system leading to a moral goal, . . . leaving aside in many instances one's interest in curiosity and uncertainty [through suspense] . . . , but containing something interesting, rather, interesting in a lively way through a portrayal of man's emotions, his intimate feelings, developed by a progressive series of circumstances and events; through a depiction of human nature, and the creation of that interest which comes from seeing errors, emotions, virtues, enthusiasm and dejection portrayed, to which men are drawn during the most serious periods in their lives, and from considering in the case of others the mystery of one's selves.

Manzoni's reverence for history did not compel total obedience to it, however; though "invention" may not be loosed arbitrarily to indulge subjective whims, the artist relies on fantasy to penetrate all the undocumented niches of history. The *Lettre* makes reference to the "fecund liberty of fable," and contains many clues to suggest that historical truth is one thing, and poetic truth quite another, even if they enjoy each other's reciprocal merits.[33] Indeed, through historical research, poetry becomes more "true," which means more beautiful and useful. This notion may be said to underlie *I promessi sposi* from beginning to end. But as Manzoni's argument develops, we come to realize, too, that the emphasis shifts from historical truth, the *sine qua non*, to poetic truth, the *raison d'être*, and that, as Barbi said, from the *Lettre* begins a natural evolution in this direction, "a continuous progress toward free poetic creation."[34] Poetry cannot be sacrificed. By "poetry," Manzoni means a considered, penetrating look of empathy (German *Einfühlung*) into human emotion; it is not what is commonly meant by creation or invention but reflection, or, more aptly put, "felt reflection": "The portrayal of passions which excite no sympathy, but felt reflection, is more poetic than all others." Years before, he had expressed the binomial in terms of "to feel and to meditate" (*Carme*), then in the paraphrase of an "upright heart and perfectioned mind" (*Osservazioni*). This, in a non-Parnassian or non-*ars gratia artis* way, is "pure" art, for Manzoni; the adjective implies purification. "It is above that narrow, troubled sphere," he writes to Chauvet, "it is in the pure region of disinterested contemplation, that before the useless suffering and the vain pleasures of men we are struck vividly with terror or pity for ourselves."[35] No finer example of a moral aesthetic exists than Manzoni's, for the morality operates dialectically inside the work of art itself. From this point of view, it is possible and logical to develop the modern notion of art's autonomy and still be satisfied as to its moral obligation.

Manzoni's distinctions between history and poetry, poetry and morality, morality and art, art and history are as finely conceived and delicately balanced as the more essential interdependence of these elements. "Felt reflection" allows the incorporation of the consoling and redeeming truth of Christian history into art; it is not produced by the invention of facts (reality, for him, is rich enough poetically); it shuns Romantic vagueness, or the current attitude derided by Manzoni as "the lovely principle that all that is vague, uncertain, fabled, confused, is poetic by nature, and that when one knows nothing about a given subject one must commit it to verse."[36] Poetry stands "real" by being a moral commitment, a "life" force. Manzoni cannot be said to adopt a posture of facile moralism; he places his emphasis on art's seriousness of purpose, converting it simultaneously into aesthetic truth.[37] Like life, art, to be worthy of its name, depends on the coincidence of truth and morality within it, and it is attained through the contemplation of reality, not through the fancy of invention. As a result of this contemplation, it can put aside that quality of abstraction which it had acquired in the hands of Enlightenment rationalists, and invest itself with the tangible verities of Christianity. There is no need to fear slipping into intellectual pedantry or factual dullness. In a telling passage which betrays an enlarged meaning of truth in his poetics, he tells Chauvet:

But, you will say perhaps, if you remove from the poet that very thing which distinguishes him from the historian—the right to invent facts—what is left? What is left is poetry; yes, poetry. For in the long run, what does history give us? Events which are only known from the outside, as it were: what men did; but what they thought, the feelings which accompanied their deliberations and plans, their successes and failures, the words they used to make or try to make their passions and wills prevail over other passions and other wills, to express their wrath, pour out their sorrow—in a word, reveal their individualities: all this, more or less, is passed over in silence by history; and all this is the domain of poetry.

In other words, poetry not only completes history but illumines it as well.[38] It intuits. In the final analysis, the only *real* history is poetic metahistory.

Many thoughts of the *Lettre* of 1820 find logical development in the *Lettera al marchese Cesare d'Azeglio* of 1823, known as the *Lettera sul romanticismo*. Though great attention has been paid to its "Romantic tenets," its main interest lies in the near autonomy that art acquires in Manzoni's thought. Italian Romanticism, we know, differs from the individualistic and antirationalistic Northern Romanticisms by being more sociopolitical and above all more moderate in inspiration (what else does the title *Il Conciliatore* mean?), and in this context Manzoni's precept that art must have "truth as its subject, the useful as its goal, and the interesting as its means"[39] bespeaks a reasonable, one would say Classical, conscience at work. To be sure, the "negative part" of his letter dismisses mythology as idolatrous, criticizes the emulation (not the study) of Classical texts, and denies the authority of rules (like the unities). And the "positive part," generally regarded as the weaker of the two because it does not construct guidelines to replace the demolished principles, does little except to reaffirm the primacy of truth, direct attention to the need to create a more popular literature, and stress the value of Christian faith as inspiration for poetry. This third point is typically Manzonian: Romanticism derives its essence from faith, and Romantic aesthetics provide the best way to dignify or glorify that faith. The first point is Classically based on the ideal of ancient aesthetic pedagogy, blending historical with moral truth. The second remains the most significant, since it relates to his Christian, democratic ideology which establishes a continuum from the *Inni* and the *Colonna infame* to the novel, as well as to the heart of his linguistic theory.

In the aggregate, then, one must agree that, while Manzoni defended Italian Romanticism (along with its own vigor, it culled the best—the vital, organic values—and discarded the worst—the polemical tenets—from other countries) and personally saw himself as an Italian Romantic (as distinguished from other European Romantics), his very concept of Romanticism is so Classically grounded as to be considered a form of purified Classicism. How else are we to interpret his references to what amounts to a socialization of art? As for the apparent subordination of fantasy to historical truth,[40] we should exercise caution in accepting without circumspection this commonplace in Manzonian scholarship. For the suggestion in the *Lettre* that truth exists "even in fable" may not be discarded in the light of certain clues in the *Lettera* which adumbrate the *Discorso sul romanzo storico*. Historical and poetic truth do emerge as different: one reads Vico between Manzoni's lines, and the fantastic ends by being as "true" as any reality. By extension, and even if Manzoni did not go quite so far in this writing, the work of art may be considered as autonomous—albeit with all the moralistic and realistic obligations the author would impose.

By the time Manzoni completed the *Discorso sul romanzo storico* (with the subtitle *e, in genere, de' componimenti misti di storia e d'invenzione*) in 1831, his thought had evolved—some say to the point of aesthetic crisis—to the level of pure aesthetics. Though begun in 1828 as a letter to Goethe, it was published in 1845, after *I promessi sposi*, and in it "he destroyed with his reason what he had created with his fantasy. . . . Manzoni's aesthetic morality was becoming artificial, through an excess of logic."[41] It may be that Manzoni became too sensitive to various criticisms leveled against the historical novel by those who considered it an insult to the truth, and by those who looked at it more aesthetically and regretted the lack of artistic homogeneity with which historical data inevitably interfered. And Manzoni was always especially attentive to discussions involving the words "truth" and "history." Let us recall his comment of 1821: "I conceive historical novels as portrayal of a given state of society by means of facts and characters so similar to reality that one may believe one has just discovered a veritable history. When historical events and characters are included, I believe one must portray them in the most strictly historical of ways; thus, for example, Richard the Lion Hearted seems defective to me in *Ivanhoe*."[42] We know, however, that as a creative artist he had

also been sensitive to the need for fantasy, even while he talked of
Scott's King Richard: "how many works of the greatest importance
would never have seen the light of day if their authors had not
resigned themselves to mixing a lot of maybes into it, and many
more-or-lesses."[43] By now he realized that while truth is one, there
are different legitimate manners of truth.

As usual, the matter was one of verisimilitude, and verisimilitude
for the sake of broad communication. In his letter to Marco Coen,
he had made it clear that poets who write for their own kind and not
for humanity are not worth considering, and if they do write for
broad reception, what they say must be tested for truth. Therefore
Manzoni's thrust was to confer an objective value even to verisimilitude, which the poet might manage in such a way as to integrate the facts of history.[44] "Verisimilitude . . . is a form of truth,
different of course, in fact very different, from reality, but a truth
seen by the mind forever, or, to be more precise, irrevocably."
Manzoni approaches a modern distinction between historical and
poetic truth, noting that a reader's "agreement" is qualitatively different in both cases, indeed opposite. The historical novel,
therefore—and here Manzoni's conclusion suddenly startles us—if
not a misnomer in theory becomes one in fact when it confuses the
two types of agreement. Worse than a misnomer, it becomes a
mistake. Given this rigid perspective, a paralyzing respect for truth
in the study of reality, provoked, we feel, by "an excess of logic"
rather than by a genuine aesthetic conviction, we may be thankful
that he engaged in this ratiocination only after having written his
novel, and that his revision of it was not impaired by his theory.

But the interesting aspect of this document, which Sansone called
"the death of Manzonian poetry,"[45] lies in the fact that it provides
unwittingly the high moment of Manzoni's aesthetic meditation: an
implicit discovery "of the autonomy and essentially arational nature
of art—a discovery that constitutes a step forward, on the theoretical
plain, a promise for the future, for possible later developments, but
that, as far as Manzoni's own art is concerned, which was fairly
exhausted by now, finds no use, no possibility for concrete application."[46] A tacit suggestion of the freedom of art by a leading literary
personality opens new horizons to Italian Romanticism, and beyond
it, to Naturalism generally. If the novelist is restricted by verisimilitude but not bound by history (Manzoni's own conclusion notwithstanding), he may invent real facts, whose moral resonances will

grant them visibility, will transcend the real with a higher reality of their own. In the horizon stood Balzac and Dickens, Verga and Zola, Tolstoy, Keller and Galdós, who wrote, it has been suggested, the novels Manzoni did not get to.

Language being the most important tool of the author, Manzoni looked to it with increasing concern as he advanced in years, not only because the spiritual autonomy of a work of art depends to a large extent on the formal aspect fashioned by the words themselves, but also because in his Italy the linguistic question emerged as fundamental to the movement for national unity. Style may be "nothing more than the manner of putting together the materials of a language,"[47] but this language itself is deeply rooted in the primitive conscience of man and becomes ideologically significant. Not that Manzoni stressed this latter point; he focused on questions of general linguistics and linguistic psychology, as well as on questions of grammar and vocabulary, usage and dissemination. Still, the importance of *la questione della lingua* to the Risorgimento remained implicit. Linguistic concerns occupied him from as far back as 1806, to which a letter to Fauriel testifies. There followed an uninterrupted series of statements or works, fragments or projects: another letter to Fauriel in 1821, one to Rossari in 1825, two more to Borghi in 1829, a manuscript brought to light by Barbara Reynolds[48] of 1831–1834, *Sentir Messa* of 1835–1836 (the important treatise he worked on assiduously from 1830 to 1840), the letter to Giacinto Carena known as *Sulla lingua italiana* of 1850, the letter to Ruggiero Bonghi of 1868 entitled *Intorno al vocabolario*, another about Dante's *De vulgari eloquio*, the 1868–1869 letter to the Minister of Education, Broglio, called *Dell'unità della lingua e dei mezzi di diffonderla*, followed by an *Appendice* in answer to Lambruschini, and the letter to the Marchese Alfonso della Valle di Casanova of 1871.

The same fascination the Romantics exhibited for folk songs they exhibited for dialects, folk songs being to music what dialects are to language. As Herder said, they represent the "collective soul" of the people. In responding to Pietro Giordani's criticism of dialects, Pietro Borsieri had defended their revelatory virtues and their ability to teach us more about ourselves.[49] Manzoni's linguistic thought stemmed from philosophical questions and was too concerned with universals and a total Italian idiom to grant dialects their due. At the beginning, he envisaged a composite literary language which would transcend all dialects; then, thanks in part to his trip to Florence in 1827, he noted that there existed perhaps more similarities than differences among Italy's dialects, enough for him to see Tuscan (later Florentine) as central. Simultaneously he developed the notion that usage alone could serve as the determinant: "where Usage. enters the picture, Vocabulary [all other language matters] does not count at all for me."[50] This attitude underlay his refusal to separate the written from the spoken language. His 1821 letter to Fauriel expands on premises stated briefly in the 1806 letter, and deserves special attention, since it contains some of his seminal ideas. After lamenting "the poverty of the Italian language," he writes:

When a Frenchman tries to express his ideas as best he can, look at the abundance and variety of *modi* (possibilities) he finds in the language he has always spoken, in that language which has been developing for so long, and daily, in so many books, conversations, and debates of all kinds. On top of that, it has a rule for the choice of expressions, a rule he finds in his memories and daily habits which give him an almost sure feeling about his style's conformity with the general spirit of his language. He needs no dictionary to consult to see if a word will shock or be acceptable; he asks himself if it is French or not, and he is almost certain of the answer. However, this wealth of expressions and this habit he has of using them, give him the means to invent more for himself with some sense of assurance, for analogy is a wide and fertile field with respect to the positive quality of language. Thus he can render what is original and new in his ideas with formulas which are still reasonably close to common usage, and he can mark with fair precision the boundary between boldness and extravagance. Imagine on the other hand an Italian writing—if he is not Tuscan—in a language he has hardly ever spoken, and who (even if born in the privileged province) writes in a language which is spoken by a small number of inhabitants in Italy—a language in which large questions are not discussed verbally, in which works relating to the moral sciences are quite few and far between, and which (if you believe those who talk more about it) has been corrupted and disfigured by the writers themselves, the very ones who recently have treated the most important subjects, so that if you look at what one has done in Italy up to today you will not find a common way of expressing good modern ideas. This poor writer lacks completely a feeling, so to speak, of communion with his reader, that is, that certainty of handling an instrument known equally to both parties. Let him ask himself if the sentence he has just written is Italian. How can he give a sure answer to a question which is imprecise? For what does *Italian* mean in this sense? According to some, what has been registered by the Crusca; according to others, what is understood in all of Italy, or by the educated class; but the

majority does not give this word any definite meaning. . . . I believe,
however, that even for us there exists an approximate perspective on
style. . . .[51]

The theory implied in the letter is premised on the desirability of
a single language, understood by Italians; rather than a combination
of spoken dialects, which would of necessity be accessible to different people in different degrees, Manzoni argued, in the best
Romantic tradition, for one linguistic organism claiming both historical definition and development, and that organism, even more than
Tuscan, was Florentine. There exists an "approximative perspective" on what the "Italian" language means, let alone style. For just
as society for the Romantics meant less a social contract than a
spontaneous development of a national spirit, so language was
formed less by logical, studied evolution, as outside of Vico the
Enlightenment maintained, than by spontaneous creation bound to
the development of the national organism. Now, in order to enter-
tain the practical possibility of an Italian language, Manzoni had to
consider the question of the origin of language—something he undertook in the first part of his unfinished treatise.[52]

Whether or not influenced by the Ideologues (who in any event
prepared him for the problems he was to consider), Manzoni went
beyond their concerns by entering the psychophilosophical question
of language. Taking a hint from Victor Cousin and Maine de Biran,
and in opposition to Locke's and Condillac's theories on the origin of
language, Manzoni observes that language is innate (the subject
begins by saying "I"), which extends to mean that general ideas are
also. As Momigliano points out,[53] implicit in this observation is that
the fundamental problems of life may not find rational explanation,
just as, we might add, implicit in the rational structure Descartes
built upon *cogito ergo sum* is its grounding in intuition (in fact,
Manzoni criticized Descartes' system in his *Lettre à Victor Cousin*
which "consists in supposing that one can begin by recognizing any
special thing as true before having admitted its truth"). For Manzoni, the logical deduction points to Revelation as the innate source
of man's linguistic knowledge. French, German, and Italian thinkers were debating the validity of such a concept; Manzoni opted for
the theory of the God-given Word, as we might expect, but once he
put aside the question of origin with simple religious logic, he had
many important and modern things to say about the nature of lan-

guage and the Italian language particularly, the "beautiful tongue."
His philosophical preparation made him aware of all phases of the
European debate: the grammars of Port-Royal, reasoned grammars,
Vico's contributions, those of the Ideologues, Herder, Cesarotti, Fr.
Soave, the *philosophes*. Manzoni discarded the French notion of "a
science of laws of language common to all languages," of "necessary
relationships between language and the laws of thought."[54] Some of
his basic premises include the view expressed in a letter to Emilia
Luti: "What is a language . . . except the aggregate of vocabulary
used by a society to say all it says?,"[55] repeated in the treatise as the
"aggregate of vocabulary subject to rules." It is vocabulary which
constitutes language in its pristine sense, not grammatical rules or
verbal inflexions—which come later, and through stylistic variations
create the *modi*. Usage alone governs vocabulary; usage alone
creates new words, invents through analogy, but what interests
more the student of culture is its transformation of the meaning of
existing words, its evolution into metaphor, however irrational or
strange for him who is accustomed to literal usage. "Manzoni demonstrates a singular tendency to transfer his psychological tendencies into the study of language, to consider language as live matter,
as the mirror of the soul."[56] In fact, Manzoni asserts with keen
observation, "the intent and effect of such transformations is to
produce new meanings without new vocabulary." The pleasure they
produce leads to linguistic aesthetics, a sense of style, the recognition of the distinction between boldness and extravagance, and the
variations of lexical analogy. Part of what we mean when we speak of
expressiveness is the creative intercourse between euphony and
analogy, or analogy and etymology (he discusses this also in *Sentir
Messa*), and even here usage ultimately becomes the arbiter, mark-
ing over a span of time what communicates and what does not.
Being as innate as language itself, usage is varied and follows no
rational laws. Similarly, any positive grammatical rule can be forgotten, or revised, by the imperative of usage. Authors of reasoned
grammars err if they believe they can *fix* or classify grammatical
laws, for all they are doing is codifying a certain repeated number of
instances, relegating the many differences to the category of excep-
tions.

But if grammar is false, then usage is always right, and usage does
suggest daily to the speaker a sense of rule whereby, like the
Frenchman, he does not depart from "the general spirit of his lan-

guage." In Italy, such a spirit, if it exists anywhere, exists in that dialect which for linguistic, historical, and artistic reasons, has had the most sustained possibility for organic development. "And where to find this in Italy, if we do not accept as the common language one of the real languages we have . . . ? [I mean] Tuscan, accepted now for five centuries, . . . the only one accepted in some way or another."[57] Again, "There is no other Italian language than the Tuscan language."[58] All dialects are veritable languages, for Manzoni; no distinction exists (*Sentir Messa*). But the small Italian peninsula harbored many, many dialects, each—outside of Tuscan—with a limited range of vocabulary and therefore ill-suited to the practical and spiritual exigencies of the coming nation (*Sulla lingua italiana*). Indisputably, important issues and modern ideas may best be discussed in Tuscan. Manzoni adduces as proof of his contention of the wider understandability of Tuscan the fact that while any number of dialectical dictionaries existed, no one had thought of compiling one for Tuscan (*Intorno al vocabolario*). Furthermore, where Florentine, which stands at the heart of Tuscan idioms, will be lacking, one will be able to turn to other Tuscan dialects, even to foreign languages; one will be able to forge new words, indeed create usage itself, for usage is flexible and can absorb new locutions into the corpus of language.

As we may note, Manzoni is motivated by a mixture of practical and transcendent considerations, where the former get fully discussed and the latter hover in the background. Italy must have "a language like other languages":[59] this is a practical consideration, though it serves an idealistic end. The main idea, for him, is that language exists only if it is one, homogeneous, and organically living, based practically on usage (*Dell'unità della lingua . . .*), and —again the democratic Christian comes forward, convinced of the essential equality of all men—the focal importance of usage implies that there is no difference between the literary and the common idiom.[60] In turn, this means that there is no difference between the written and the spoken language—one of Manzoni's most dominant thoughts. One may take issue with him on this score, as has happened, since a further implication suggests that art must always be accessible to everyone, thus denying what merit may lie in either cultural elitism or accentuated artistic individualism. But there is nothing dogmatic about his posture; he would of course allow each artist to select his own manner of expression, while he himself would prefer to focus on universals than on peculiarities or bizarre individualities. Hence, behind the practical question of *fiorentinità* stirred the broader question of *italianità*.

Manzoni's theories of language derived from a gnoseological background, in which we find his historical bent on the empirical level, and his blending of beauty and utility and the aesthetic and ethical. They reveal a philosophical dimension to us, though, despite Rosmini's acclaim, a systematic philosopher he was not. In the *Lettre à Victor Cousin*, he modestly admitted to being only "an eavesdropper" on philosophy. Yet he was a philosopher by nature: the "perfectioned mind" is distinguishable but not separable from the "upright heart," for in the final analysis the two coincide, and in their coincidence lies Manzoni's whole philosophic posture. On a functioning level, he defined philosophy as "the study of . . . implications—so little studied and so continuously, so inevitably, employed." On the ideal level, it is "the science of ultimate reasoning" which proceeds beyond intellect into faith. Philosophy looks to a Platonic and transcendent affirmation of universals.

Manzoni was right to hesitate repeatedly (as in his letters to Fauriel his many allusions demonstrate) about considering the *Lettre à Victor Cousin* a finished piece; it not only remains incompleted, but it suffers from pedantry and disorganization. It has throughout a scholastic quality really aiming at a constant argumentation, and, more seriously perhaps, the negative argument dominates, leaving nothing for a constructive argument to contribute. Its importance lies in its proof of his philosophical interest which reiterated in many ways his postulate that a moral error comprises somewhere a logical error, and that a moral achievement constitutes a victory of truth. Cousin had asked Manzoni for his opinion of his *Cours*, and Manzoni obliged. Some of its ideas he could accept: Cousin's theory of the advance of the human spirit, and the notion of an active eclecticism, were not disagreeable to him; but most of the ideas he could not accept. Cousin's usual combination of sensationalists like Reid and Stewart with idealists and intuitionists like Schelling and Hegel, while it did not inform his response to the *Cours* directly, probably struck him generally as awkward. Specifically, Manzoni criticizes in the *Lettre* Cousin's inability to perceive accurately the relationship between the conditions of being and knowledge on the one hand, and their universal bases on the other, along with his distinction between thought and reason's spontaneous intuition. Again, and predictably for anyone who had read the *Osservazioni*, Manzoni opposes all attempts to reduce morality to interest even while recognizing some of the benefits of utilitarianism. And finally, in a rather weighty expose, he attacks his friend's notion of authority, viewed by Cousin as identifiable in the nature of the act being performed rather than in the performer of that act. Manzoni believes this view to interfere with all possibility of verifying authority, which consequently becomes a blurred concept for both those who undergo it and those who execute it.

Manzoni's disagreement with Locke and the sensationalism of the Ideologues was well known to Cousin. Indeed, Manzoni looked askance at the sensationalist background of the French Revolution. The senses are not, for him, the only suppliers of passions and cogitations, as the Englishman's disciple, Condillac, proposed, nor, for that matter, is reason. Both Locke and Descartes neglect an important source—spirit, religion; Condillac pays lip service to it, and Cartesians (like Galluppi) are content to use it as a point of departure and then forget it. They get confused with their own methodology, even while opposing the sensationalists: "if [Descartes] knows that the senses deceive him—that is, make the false appear true—he must then know what the truth is, since he denies that it is found in what appears to the senses. One cannot doubt without reason; and the reason for doubting is *believed*." Manzoni's philosophy submits primarily to faith, not so much to experience.

There are truths which transcend reason and the senses, and can only be secured in a superior light, though it is reason which must make the disclosure of the need for the superior optics. Almost by definition, an artist is one of those who possesses such optics. Universal being unites all knowledge, Rosmini had stated, and Manzoni followed in the footprints of his revered friend. The dialogue, Platonic in more ways than one and decidedly Rosminian and anti-sensationalist, *Dell'invenzione*, centers around a discussion by two "intimate friends" of what the artist does when he "invents." What he does, as the etymology of the word tells us, is not to create but to *find*, find those ideas (art relies for excellence on ideas) which his mind already conceives ideally, "intuits"—which means that they preexist in the mind of God, as do justice and morality. Manzoni is not dealing solely with antecedent existence here ("for how could we arrive at truths, if these truths did not exist?"), but also with an anti-idealistic autonomy of existence, for what the artist "finds" enjoys its own and separate reality.

Common sense, too, becomes a focal point, as a result of what he saw in Rosmini, "a firm purpose to observe things in themselves." Momigliano[61] has selected three passages from *Dell'invenzione* which he deems the most important utterances in all Manzoni's philosophical writings. They are worth restating:

[Here in Rosmini] you will find in the end, in formulas quite abstruse at first glance, the summary of what each person either believes habitually or habitually implies. For one of the great results of this philosophy is precisely that it maintains and claims for humanity the possession of those truths that are like its natural patrimony, against systems which, if they do not succeed in erasing them from the minds of their followers, still remain there like contradictions.

Here you will rejoice in seeing a true respect for human intelligence, a faith founded in human reason, . . . a true and deep respect, I say, for intelligence and common sense, imprinted in all men by an omnipotent goodness, compared with which the superiority of the loftiest minds is like the height of mountains compared with the depths of the earth.

With the claiming of possession of universally known truths comes naturally another excellent result: the revelation of concealed truths. One cannot defend (I mean defend well) the domain of common sense without proportionally extending that of philosophy.

Like art, Manzoni argues, truth is accessible to all; common sense is universal. His democratic philosophy flows into a democratic aesthetics. After all, he would say, God created spiritual goods for *all*. The goal of his thinking is to stand before the ultimate questions, and he criticizes those who stop short of it, who, therefore, do not love the real truth. (So Rollin and Crevier treated Roman history, he complains.) "One cannot examine something unless one first believes in something else." And that something else is God, the center of truth, creator of ideas, language, and the real good. *All* can participate in these virtues and partake of His bounty. While there are spiritual truths and logical truths, only he who, for reasons best known to him, does not want to get to the bottom of the truth will deny that logical and spiritual truths are one. The Cartesian rationalist or the Ideologue sensationalist will proffer such denials.

We see, then, that Manzoni's conception of reality stems from such a highly personal intepretation of it that the ultimate vehicle by which it can best be expressed by a human being is art—art, therefore, which must be conscious of human history and ideas, moral values, and religious truth, and must communicate with everyone. This is Manzoni's unitarian faith, one that in this case comes closer to German than to Latin Romanticism in its coherence between a philosophico-moral and an aesthetic concept of life, a coherence consummately illustrated by *I promessi sposi*.

CHAPTER 6

That Branch of Lake Como

SOMETIME around the turn of this century, it is said,[1] a congress of European critics voted *I promessi sposi* the best novel of the nineteenth century. Whether the story is apocryphal, and whether a group of learned men could actually assume the existence of common criteria by which to measure, say, *War and Peace, Crime and Punishment, Moby Dick, Madame Bovary, Old Goriot, Great Expectations, Pride and Prejudice, Germinal, I Malavoglia,* and *I promessi sposi* against one another does not matter here. What matters is the possible reason for assuming such an outcome to the ballot: and that is the remarkable comprehensiveness of Manzoni's novel. For it embraces the major novelistic modes of the whole century and more, as the countless adjectives applied to it by readers of various persuasions suggest: historical, philosophical, sociological, metaphysical, psychological, realistic, naturalistic, idealistic, lyrical, epical, dramatic, religious, optimistic, pessimistic, moralistic, ironical, oratorical, and universal. The list could be extended. All of this suggests that it is a work of *art*, the aggregate likes of which the Western world had not come across since *Don Quijote.* "The work far surpasses . . . any generic classification."[2] As a classico-romantic tapestry of existence, it is woven broadly with many threads, presenting an organic, polysemantic spectacle in which individual and society interact in an intricate system of interrelationships, yet in which the single conscience can still find its own tie with the universal. The tapestry is formed as the individual, humble scenes, at first sight little more than isolated episodes, are made to ramify and expand, by the nature of things, into a panoptic view of life. "That branch of Lake Como . . .": the story's opening words amplify stylistically into a complex period, just as they expand the simple situation they introduce into an encompassing experience.

The three versions of the novel represent over twenty years of arduous, patient meditation and labor. A first draft, called *Fermo e Lucia*, occupied him from April, 1821, to September, 1823. Its heavy Romanticism, not to speak of many digressions of a theoretical, historico-documentary nature, prompted him (with the urging of friends like Visconti, Fauriel, and Grossi) to revamp it for the first edition, in (1825–)1827, and for which he thought briefly of the title *Gli sposi promessi* before deciding on the definitive *I promessi sposi*. He gave the novel a subtitle: *storia milanese del secolo XVII scoperta e rifatta da Alessandro Manzoni*. But the linguistic and technical modifications were still not enough to give the novel the measure and balance Manzoni sought, so that he kept working on it long after 1827, focusing especially on the Tuscan idiom his trip to Florence had made him recognize as focal for Italian expression. The final version is of (1840–)1842.[3]

It is well known that Manzoni immersed himself in prolonged historical studies of all kinds to research the novel (a document of the Spanish Governor of Lombardy, dated October 15, 1627, began the whole process), deriving many indications from the *Storie milanesi* of Giuseppe Ripamonti and the liberal economico-political ideas of Melchiorre Gioia (*Economia e statistica* and *Sul commercio de' commestibili e caro prezzo del vitto*). He had taken copies of these works to Brusuglio with him in March, 1821. From there, his investigations broadened enormously. "I must constantly consult a pile of books, pamphlets, even papers, some of which are rare, even unique. . . ."[4] In libraries, archives, and at home, he checked and double checked each event or fact (though it is said he missed on the Capuchins' beards) before committing it to his story. Much—more than necessary—has been made of the influence of Walter Scott and Manzoni's genuine respect for the father of the historical novel, whose method of "depicting a period by means of a tale of his invention" he found appealing. Manzoni, however, insisted on "poetry" more strictly than Scott, by not trying to do what history does better and by "profiting from history without competing with it."[5] This approach permitted a deeper and more intimate treatment.[6] Indeed, *The Fair Maid of Perth*, which Scott wrote after Manzoni's novel, resembles *I promessi sposi* more closely in plot than the latter resembles *Ivanhoe*, so that the influence is at best reciprocal. But Manzoni's "poetry" remains more real than Scott's *merveilleux romantique*. In fact, there is evidence that he studied the works of people like Scott not to imitate them but to avoid their errors: "I dare flatter myself . . . that I avoid the criticism of imitation. To this end, I do what I can to become imbued with the spirit of the time I am to describe, in order to live in it."[7]

To summarize the events of an epic not only borders on futility but also risks counterproductiveness. Suffice it to say that Manzoni, pretending to discover a very interesting and worthwhile but badly written, anonymous manuscript of the seventeenth century, decides to tell the story in his own way. At the beginning, somewhere in the Milanese near Lecco, two good young peasants, Renzo and Lucia, attempt to get the village priest, Don Abbondio, to marry them, but he refuses because, as they soon discover, the local tyrant, Don Rodrigo, has taken a fancy to Lucia and threatened the priest if he agrees to the ceremony. Almost eight hundred pages later, the two finally get married; but there is a saga in between.

Fra Cristoforo, a sternly moral monk, gets involved, opposing Don Rodrigo and arranging for Lucia to leave her home town and remain secluded in a convent directed by an awesome nun with a dark past, Sister Gertrude. Meanwhile, Renzo seeks help from a crooked lawyer, Azzeccagarbugli, and, failing this, proceeds to Milan. Here he runs into bread riots and other difficulties, some of his own making (like getting drunk and talking too much), but manages to escape his pursuers by reaching the Adda river. In his corner, Don Rodrigo is not to be foiled; he seeks the assistance of a formidable, evil figure, whose name is never revealed to us and who is referred to by everyone, including by his band of henchmen and cutthroats, as the Unnamed (the Innominato). The evil man has Lucia kidnapped and brought to his castle, where, before her spiritual radiance, and in a scene of gripping power, he begins to doubt the worth of his previous existence and eventually, in another outstanding scene, converts to the good life as he seeks out the comfort of the saintly Cardinal Borromeo. The ills are not over, however, for the injuries of drought, famine, and war, and the infections introduced by foreign troops in Northern Italy, then under the Spaniards, bring about a devastating plague with which thousands are struck and carried off by hooded *monatti* (those who bury the dead of the plague) to the *lazzeretto* (Milan's hospital camp), where vast numbers of the victims lose their lives. Among them are Don Rodrigo, his henchman Il Griso, Fra Cristoforo, the village priest's gossipy housekeeper Perpetua, and the intellectual pedant Ferrante and his wife Prassede. Lucia miraculously recovers. Fires burn diseased objects, and finally rain purifies the land. And Renzo and Lucia, somewhat wiser now than before, are united in marriage.

There should be no *vexata quaestio* concerning the unity of this novel, that is, concerning the success of the relationship between its aesthetico-poetic and its ethico-religious elements, or between its moral and artistic inspirations. Yet scholars have chosen to raise it, as they have with *War and Peace* or the *Aeneid*. The question of the "truth" (reality) of an historical novel, which *I promessi sposi* assumes from the outset, should not lead us to the antiquarian expectations of Scott (*Ivanhoe*, *Quentin Durward*, etc.), the reliance on rumors of Vigny (*Cinq Mars*), or the imagined vantage-point perspectives of Hugo (*Notre Dame de Paris*). Some have attacked the truth/falsehood defect of *I promessi sposi* as an insult to both historical veracity and aesthetic propriety, while others, maintaining the opposite, have stressed that the novel's merit lies in its historicity rather than in its invention.[8]

Yet it should be obvious that Manzoni's aim was not to use history simply as a convenient mold into which to pour the adventures of Renzo and Lucia; moreover, his execution reveals a concern to conceal the separation between invention and document. Rather than a display of erudition, *I promessi sposi* represents a creative synthesis of his research and his "influences," which he absorbed and reshaped inwardly in conjunction with his artistic desires and moral promptings. For him, the historical novel was not a fad, but the most aesthetic vehicle for the presentation of truth and the educational value of history.[9] What Helen Cam said theoretically about a desideratum of the historical novel may be said about Manzoni's, that it enlarges the sympathies by compelling the reader to see abstract generalizations, whether political, social or economic, in terms of the human individual.[10] But the individual is not projected into 1627 simply because the period happened to interest Manzoni. His novel fulfills Lukács' requisite, that the characters and their actions develop out of the epoch in which they play, while they simultaneously "rouse the present, which contemporaries would experience as their own prehistory."[11] Truth so conceived is a form of poetry, for Manzoni, not because it derives from history but because it transcends it. The advantage is that while history lies by its nature and through its particulars anchored in time and space, the poetry which is rooted in it rises above the categories and attains the universal. Manzoni's feat was not in being able to theorize this, but in having been able to forge the theory into a convincing work of art which is as much documented as it is invented. This is, in Lukács' words, his "superb and historically profound conception."[12]

The historical dimension of the novel, including the unified linguistic theory underlying it, lends itself to metaphor and has given rise to patriotic ("historical school") interpretations of it, interpretations which suffer, again, for being too one-sided. "The very contrast between the suffering population and the violent oppressors lends the book a pugnacious cast."[13] While national-democratic implications abound along with implicit laments over the country's fragmentation, and while the Machiavellian, historically Italian motif of opposition to foreign troops on native soil is unmistakable, Manzoni's Christian and humanitarian impulses outweigh the narrowly political and patriotic. If Metternich's observation that the novel's surface message was directed at Spain and the underlying one at Austria was valid from the point of view of his own historical role, Settembrini's (and Carducci's) contention, amplified by Crispoli, that the overriding pietistic considerations displace the political significance[14]—not to speak of the frequent injections of humor and irony which tend to turn the mind aside—makes greater sense. Without abandoning the framework of period, place, and the age- and class-conditioned psychology of the characters, the story of the lovers grows not only into *the* tragedy of the Italian people as a whole, as Lukács said,[15] but also into a synoptic view of the human condition. For Manzoni's patriotism was generic: it is in the nature of morality to extol civic and moral virtue, to denounce oppression, and to condemn violence and harsh revolt. But it does not bring the torch to the buildings. Manzoni was always too reserved to present himself as a teacher of activist patriotism or as an instigator of propaganda.

The many who, after De Sanctis, have insisted on the oratorical quality of the work ("a too oratorical emphasis, almost worthy of the pulpit"[16]), written under the dictates of an intransigent, religious morality, confuse oratory with poetic reality, which in this case happens to be a Christian reality. If oratory exists, as D'Ovidio pointed out,[17] Manzoni was careful to place it in the mouth of friars and bishops. Whatever moral norms appear to prevail do not stem from an abstract, religious view of what ought to be, but from the inner workings of the poetic concept. Providence operates not from without but from within, thus reconciling the individual with the universal and not forcing the individual to submit to the universal. The unity of the novel, therefore, consists "in its universality, which on the level of moral vision absorbs the historical and realistic particular; it consists in the profound accord between man's autonomy and the existence of an Absolute which transcends us; it consists in the dialectic of historical truth, which becomes myth and with which corresponds that other dialectic of feeling and linguistic objectivity."[18] Oratory is by nature emphatic, and its goal is persuasion. Manzoni's aesthetic, instead, favors impartial truth, garnered through a close study of history and presented with such indulgence that it converts reality into poetry. His objectivity speaks for itself; it creates its own faith, its own ethical norms. It says: "This is how it happened because this is how I see human life," and not "This is how I am making it happen because this is the creed which shapes my view of life." Only a Moravia can see the poetry as propagandistic: "Catholic realism," as he calls it,[19] when what it is is simply a "poetic realism."

From this point of view, Manzoni's so-called Jansenism—that supposed heterodox streak inside his orthodox faith[20]—especially when applied to the novel, betrays an attempt on the part of some critics to convert artistic invention into theological argument by giving his Parisian experience more prominence than is called for. Rather than view the Manzonian world as Pascalian, "always . . . a contemplation of the greatness and the misery of man,"[21] it is less dramatically a contemplation of the world as it is, and of man as he is. It is surely a world we recognize. While fallen man is swept along epically by forces greater than himself, the notion of determinism fits only tangentially in a diversified world where passive acquiescence and heroic will stand side by side. As the *Osservazioni* tell us, Manzoni could not brook the idea that Grace arbitrarily elects some while turning down others. While pessimism, the kind that exists more pronouncedly in the tragedies, conditions mortal life, Providence provides the immortal counterbalance. To be sure, the individual conscience someone like Fra Cristoforo persistently appeals to amounts to an antiauthoritarian insistence on Christian subjectivity, as does the inner working of Providence itself (magnificently illustrated by the inwardly wrought conversion of the Innominato), but the fact that we cannot enunciate a clearly discernible Jansenistic posture by Manzoni lends authority to Russo's belief that the only way to understand his Jansenism is not as a doctrinaire position but as a sentimental attitude.[22] The poet is not theologian. Indeed, as Montano correctly stresses in reminding us that Manzoni never claimed there was no moral truth available outside the Church, what we come across in him, and quite apart from the fact that such considerations do not help our understanding of the novel, is a pronounced anti-Jansenism.[23]

Seen in these terms, *I promessi sposi* strikes us as a modern novel, written by a self-conscious artist, a novel modern in intent, committed and intellectualistic, an aesthetically conceived essay-novel. Its world view captures the perfect synthesis of the real and the ideal which *Il Conte di Carmagnola* and *Adelchi* had striven to capture. The novel, given the genre's at once expansive and synthetic virtues, avoided the problem of the encroachment of invention on reality, Mazzamuto indicates,[24] and encouraged the enriching introduction of the comic inside the tragic. The result was an integrated realism which mirrors human reality, the individual's perplexity before plain good and evil, churned in a world of necessity and utilitarian reason. Onto this world, Manzoni superposed the moral concepts of sin and expiation, where cynicism breeds self-indulgence and acceptance fosters divine aspiration. In a world of nature against man and man against man, what is hopefully to be shunned is a situation of man against God, or an ethical perversity. The *Inni sacri* had made man aware of how passion and hate preclude spiritual serenity, but their scope, like their form, appeared more limited than the novel's. The struggle and dangers of life, adumbrated in "Pentecoste" and "Cinque maggio," could be presented more fully in the format of epical narration, in a broad tapestry humanized by personal lyricism and objectified by history, where the ideal and the real interpenetrate, even explain man's presence in the evolution of time. "The abyss, in which man struggles deluded by his own greatness, would be a chaos of solitude and despair, unless some kind of providential assistance did not reveal to him a luminous world beyond caducous and transient glory."[25] And this providential assistance every man can find within himself.

CHAPTER 7

Right and Wrong Never Neatly Divided

S COTT had nothing to do with Manzoni's creation of characters, whose paradigm, if anyone, was Shakespeare. He extolled "that master of the human heart," and added: "Anyone who wants to write poetry must read Shakespeare; how he knows all the feelings!"[1] And it was feelings that elicited Manzoni's interest—feelings and their corollary, the motivations for human actions. Hence his propensity for psychological examination. Types, therefore, in the manner of Theophrastus or La Bruyère, or of Jonson or Molière, struck him almost as allegorical abstractions corresponding little with human nature, that is, human individuality. The *Lettre à Chauvet* speaks of the many anomalies and the infinite variety of passions, and of their particular combinations which make for individual characteristics. Shakespeare was great because he did not slip into the easy predictabilities of typification. The *Lettre* criticizes those who create "abstract types of certain passions instead of beings endowed with passion: . . . allegories of love and ambition, for example, instead of creatures who really love or who are really dominated by ambition." For better or for worse, there is an inner wealth in each individual which precludes the formulization of types. Indeed, Manzoni's gallery of portraits, as the expression goes, far subtler than Balzac's and on balance far less tormented than Dostoievsky's, has been described as second only to Shakespeare's. The difference is that Shakespeare isolated the feelings of a human being, making his protagonist a solitary hero. Manzoni makes him a representative "hero."

Since there is no protagonist in the novel in the sense of an Emma Bovary or a Captain Ahab, the usual number of attempts has been made to fashion one from less immediate criteria. These are epitomized by Russo, who at different times finds different "hidden"

118

centers. Thus the control which, according to some, Manzoni's ethico-religious inspiration exercises over the molding of all characters and events leads to the view that the true protagonist is Manzoni's own feeling, or his intellectual inclination. On the other hand, his historical inspiration leads to the view that the subtitled seventeenth century, "lavish and baroque, religious and hypocritical, warlike and wretched,"[2] deserves the spotlight.

Perhaps the most convincing argument can be made for the humble folk; the "betrothed" are, after all, two poor peasants.[3] They belong to the anonymous crowd that "walks the earth, unobserved, leaving no trace," except that, by receiving life, as it were, through the conflict of great natural and historical events, they give history a sense—a "common sense" (in at once the strictest and the general sense of the term), because of the way these events ultimately reveal their suffering, to which we should all be sensitive. When caught in the maelstrom of wars and droughts, famines and plagues, their misery appears with stark, brutal nakedness, from which they cannot emerge as heroes, but surely as creatures of worth. "Misfortune reveals the value of the humble."[4] Hence Manzoni's "deheroization" of history, and, in fact, his removal from the novel of any example of exalted individualism.

The humble inject automatically into reality qualities of simplicity, warmth, and sympathy which tacitly bear their own message. They represent a counterpoising world away from intellectual and political fermentation, the kind that suited Manzoni's temperament. We think of the agrarian author in Brusuglio, and Colombo correctly reminds us of his letter to Marco Coen.[5] With even the most cursory acquaintance with Manzoni's intellectual biography, one realizes how natural it was for him to want to weave minor events inside major ones, and how likely it was that he should be the first on the literary scene to suggest the unheroic novel in modern terms by spinning an entire epic around two simple peasants. The progressive involution of ethical and social criteria along political, democratic lines, shaped by moral concerns, made the humble conveniently bridge his early Jacobinism with his later evangelical morality. He chose them because, being religiously oriented, they would give his novel a Christian coloration, and because, as an appreciator of the liberal historian Thierry, he saw merit in the notion of the dichotomization of races between the oppressors and the oppressed, or the victors and the vanquished. In *I promessi sposi*, the notion expanded and matured, under the guidance of more spiritual precepts, into a dichotomy between the powerful and the humble.

Had Manzoni stuck to the narrower class separation between the social oppressors and the socially oppressed, Marxist critics, who tend to regard Manzoni with suspicion—for they see his liberal, democratic Catholicism as belonging to the aristocratic variety— would perhaps not complain of his not having gone far enough. There are those like Lukács, of course, who see a prefiguration of class-struggle. But others, like Ferruccio Boffi, see Manzoni as the Italian bourgeois who views the humble sympathetically but with detachment (forgetting that Manzoni was generally a detached person), or like Antonio Gramsci, who interprets him as "wavering between an aristocratic Jansenism and a Jesuitic, popular paternalism."[6] And there is, too, the opinion of Moravia, who is bothered by the conservatism of Manzoni's "Catholic realism" which permits the illustration of individual and social corruption, but which also permits the concept of humility in the end to allow the master to remain master.[7]

Manzoni surely would not have understood this verbiage, whose motivation seems based more on a desire to rewrite the novel under the shibboleth of class-struggle than on a criticism founded on Manzoni's own intention. We should like to suggest that this intention was simply that of the artist's Christian compassion for the have-nots, those who finally make history *signify*, and that he gave form to his compassion by making the humble the protagonists of his novel—something all three of its successive titles leave us little room to doubt.

Though they remain unaware of the realities buffeting their lives, and in the end have learned a few things while still remaining ignorant of the historical forces which overwhelmed a whole society, Renzo and Lucia stand at the center of the epic. Moravia correctly sees them as the catalysts.[8] Through them, "the true, complete image of the life of man"[9] reveals itself, a life of weakness and error, of tragic confusion and bitter struggle, on all levels. The humble meddle through, with a reservoir of instinct and common sense, less conspicuously perhaps than the more advantaged, but more tenaciously for being more elemental.

Renzo provides the best example, in that he symbolizes this instinctive endurance, or perdurance, of what is ultimately the human race.[10] He is candid, faithful, youthful and easily excited, generous, ingenuous, and basically optimistic. We see him at the outset, as he really is, making his way to the village priest on what he thought was his wedding day, "in the joyous hurry of a man of twenty, [dressed] in his Sunday best, with plumes of various colors in his hat, . . . with a certain festive air about him which was cocky at the same time." Faced with trickery and violence, he would think of revenge except for the saintly presence of his betrothed and the restraining words of Fra Cristoforo, both of whom recall him to his faith and inborn sense of justice. There is much of the simpleton in him who can be duped or made drunk, and who can react with naive (though never foolishly founded) enthusiasm to a cause, such as the bread riot. In fact, he can rage with blind fury at the crowd which misinterprets his actions and join the devilish antics of the drunken *monatti*. But his peasant instinct for life gives him wit and stamina when it counts; Renzo can discard his optimism and sense dishonesty in someone like Don Abbondio, escape from his pursuers and track down Lucia in the *lazzeretto*. What guides him is not a disposition for diffidence or cunning but a fundamental good-naturedness and a compassion for the suffering. He shares his bread with the hungry, weeps for the victims of the plague, and ultimately forgives his enemies. He is humanity incarnate, and when disabused and disconsolate he finally reaches the banks of his river Adda, his renewed faith has something of the exaltation before the Promised Land. Yet for all this, he continues to be the simple, honest rustic, Renzo Tramaglino, who in the end has learned "not to raise his elbow too much."

His counterpart Lucia Mondella, naturally good like Alyosha in the *Brothers Karamazov*, is a creature of light, as her name suggests, and according to Montano, illustrates how the ideal becomes realized in the real, "the ideal made flesh."[11] Less instinctively active during the course of the story, but more spiritually endowed, she is touched by contrasting effects of divinity, arousing the lustful caprices of Don Rodrigo and engendering the righteous awakening of the Innominato. Who does not understand Lucia does not understand the novel. Losing none of her feminine reality, that of a modest and sensible and pious girl in love, she first appears in a normal state of wedding-day excitement, her headpiece radiating from her hair, and on her countenance "a happiness tempered by slight chagrin, that placid concern one can detect on a bride's face from time to time, which gives her a special character, without distorting her

beauty." Through her, the Virgilian *sunt lacrimae rerum* ("These are
the tears of things") acquires full significance: Lucia weeps before
her abusers, before her comforters, before her friends, and before
the wretched and the sick, and her tears translate into prayer, her
only weapon in the turmoil of evil. Yet she is not the passive Romantic heroine whose pallor leaves only when her feelings are stoked by
love. For all her chaste suffering, when the storm is passed it is she
who appears more self-possessed, more realistic, and more wise
than her husband. Her inner strength and intelligence of moral
principles finally have occasion to emerge. She has worked throughout the ordeal, in her town and in the Monza convent, at the tailor's
and at Donna Prassede's—the honest labor of honest souls—and she
continues to work faithfully as the diligent wife she becomes, and
through it, in her own way, to suggest the noble tenacity of the
species to life. To see her as bland is to misinterpret Manzoni's
intention: to incarnate a moral and artistic ideal in a character with
sufficient human traits to keep her within the framework of realism.
She is Ermengarda and Enrichetta Blondel, but more than they,
that is, more than tragedy and evangelical loveliness; she possesses
some of the enigmatic ambivalences of Leonardo's "Mona Lisa,"
being poetically human as well as humanly poetic. In this sense, she
is not a Madonna, "too much of a saint," as De Sanctis found her.[12]
Her love for Renzo runs vivid and deep, and her vow of chastity, the
only recourse of a simple soul in a state of disarmed terror, creates
an unsettling human tension between promise and desire, until
religion itself intervenes to release her and rectify the balance between the temporal and the eternal. Chateaubriand's Atala, also
bound by a vow, fades before Lucia's spontaneous religiosity. Yet
through her persistent elegiac melancholy, Manzoni wished to
endow her with diffused poetry, with a kind of incantation which
makes her totality exceed the sum of her realistic parts. Apart from
the fact that she was probably his favorite creation, the novel's
internal demands required his making her so: she had to enchant,
stir the special solicitude of Fra Cristoforo, the earthy whim of Don
Rodrigo, the fascination of Sister Gertrude, the attention of Il Nibbio, and the self-doubting of the Innominato, not to speak of the
endless concern of Renzo. Fossi confuses things when he writes
that, Lucia's love not being of the rapturous, springtime, dreamy
variety, "the poetry's song" finds itself hindered.[13] On the contrary,
her "poetry" is all the more radiant since it is compact and contained.

And it need not disconcert us that she is an uneducated girl from the farm. The poetry is not sophisticated. A Lucia is quite capable of profound feelings, as her famous "Farewell" to her native land proves—even though Manzoni is careful to put the poetry not in her mouth but, through the narrator, in her heart.

The ranks of the humble are enlivened by two exceptional portrayals of women, an advising mother and a protective gossip. Lucia's mother, Agnese, is the enterprising woman of the people, affectionate and energetic, endowed with a pointed common sense, whose instinct normally refuses to admit defeat in the face of difficulty. Experience has taught her that life demands shrewdness (she counsels Renzo on how to approach the lawyer Azzeccagarbugli, and devises ingenious plans, such as the secret wedding or the way to keep Perpetua busy to allow others to sneak past Don Abbondio's front door), and, not being subject to excessive scruples, balances her daughter's inviolate sense of honesty. Her typical "Now listen to me" and "Trust in your mother," all with appropriate gestures, and her store of private proverbs or sayings ("It doesn't take much to make poor people look like rascals," she admonishes the Cardinal), cast her in an unmistakably human mold. Her share of personal defects and the usual ineffectiveness of her platitudes, along with her many exclamations ("Oh Virgin Mother!," "That scoundrel from Hell!") reenforce her humanity. If she shows uncertainty about the future, it is only when, tired, she begins to feel the futility of the struggle; but otherwise, when experience does not becloud her natural buoyancy, she moves about live and alert, in her motherly role, "full of a sense of reality, wealthy in perceptions, vigilant through a philosophy of her own somewhere in between pessimism and commonplace stoicism."[14]

In the same village lives Perpetua, Don Abbondio's "governess," or, as Giannessi dubs her, his "*serva padrona*," his "colorful appendix."[15] Faithful to her master, a "perpetual" gossiper otherwise, she struts noisily like the hen in the coop, protecting Don Abbondio at every turn. Critics have generally regarded her as his veritable counterpart (the "appendix"), though, since Manzoni never portrays two-dimensional characters, it is also possible to see her as depending on him for her own identity, "revolving in his halo, without which she would be nothing."[16] All Manzoni's creations have depth and resist reduction to stereotype or easy definability. On balance, however, Perpetua makes up for the priest: when he appears vacuous, confused, and timid, she comes forward sturdy, opinionated, and brash. Flora put it most aptly: Perpetua is "the Sancho of this Don Quixote of fear."[17]

Don Abbondio is indeed fear personified. He fears the *bravi* of Don Rodrigo, their master, the Innominato, but he fears Renzo too, perhaps even his *serva padrona* to whose flow of words he yields repeatedly, as well as the mule that bears him along the precipice-lined mountain road to and from the Innominato's castle. He fears life and his own weakness facing it. Perpetua exclaims: "He's even afraid of being defended and helped!" The portrait is unforgettable, and many believe Manzoni's finest. He has inspired opposing interpretations: to some readers he is a monster of egoism, to others a pitiful weakling. But to all he remains a paradigm of timidity. "You can't give yourself courage," he says as he impulsively slips away from any problem, regardless of his duty. All a *bravo* (one of Don Rodrigo's hired cut-throats) has to do is say "ahem," and Don Abbondio obeys, though he wants no part of iniquity. He calculates feverishly to preserve himself in peace and from trouble, but for all that accomplishes nothing—which then makes him paradoxically the accomplice of what he wanted no part of: evil.

In the sense that Don Abbondio worships the *status quo* and inveighs not against the oppressors but against those who react against their truculence, he arouses indignation. He betrays his mission of charity and love, twists religion out of shape, and pathetically thinks of himself as the victim of his "too good heart." The "roof tiles," he complains, keep falling unexpectedly as he walks by. Part of the reason lies in the way he blends fear into his gnawing awareness of his own weakness, and, of course, into his elemental attachment to life. To the Cardinal, he explains blandly: "I have always tried to do my duty . . . , but when it comes down to a matter of life . . . ." Hence he is more than just a type representing fear. In many ways he performs his role in the historical novel by illustrating a kind of man produced by his society of powerful ruffians, a man for whom the priesthood was not a mission but a way to withdraw and provide for himself. The pronoun "I," Russo notes, with all its oblique cases, is lodged close to his heart.[18] He is the hero of his little ego, the prize of his own self-deception. Chekhov's man in a shell is one of his modern descendants. For in an age of heroism, he comes through as a niggardly villain, while in one of disenchantment and confusion, like the present, he tends to impress us as lamentably human. But with reference to human psychology he cannot be classified as a "period piece," for today Don Abbondio would merely have thought up another scheme not to be broken by life: "probably, rather than join the Church, he would have joined a political party, and kowtowing to this person and then to that one, seeking to set no one against him, he would have attained a tranquil and well nourished position."[19] Don Abbondio himself verbalized his fragility succinctly in Aesopean terms: "[I am] like a terracotta pot forced to travel in the company of many iron pots."

Manzoni's comic art fuses humor and irony, compassion and scoffing, and is therefore an art of indulgence, of condemning Don Abbondio morally but treating him understandingly. The debate over the character arises over the matter of emphasis. For one could say with De Sanctis that though the author elicits our sense of pity for the poor curate, "our sympathetic indulgence is not as good-natured as it seems at first glance."[20] Or we could adopt Sansone's view that he is a vile creature unaware of vileness, the "hero of Manzoni's comicity . . . [born of the author's] superior indulgence and human understanding in the face of such obtuseness . . . [before which] he cannot assume a pensive manner . . . but frees himself in a smile."[21] Indeed, Don Abbondio can be pleasant, expansive, and gay . . . , when no cause for fear exists, as he shows us after hearing of the death of Don Rodrigo. His soliloquies to vent some inner irritation, his clipped phrases and longer metaphors, and his numerous exclamations create true comedy, the highest point of which is reached when he addresses the mule. But there is the reader's irritation, too, before his distorted ethics. While the colloquy with Cardinal Borromeo does bring out the contrast between the latter's noble but almost rigid Christianity and the curate's lax, self-serving faith punctuated by human frailty, we always remain tragically albeit sympathetically conscious of the latter's grotesque deformation of reality and moral norms, to the extent that it would be possible to convert him today into a hero of the Absurd. Manzoni's genius lies in shaping possibly his most attractive character out of not his blackest but his most unattractive material: a small, petty, egoistically defensive man, an absurd little priest, complex because of his very absurdity, and both repulsive and comical because of his very humanity.

The element of humanity enters even Manzoni's blackest material. Don Rodrigo represents evil, that of caprice and vainglory; he is the local tyrant, mediocre in stature by comparison with the In-nominato, and dominated by pique, the petty kind of *pun d'honor* or point of honor bred by his society but identifiable in all societies. When law—in this case, seventeenth century law—is incapable of protecting the oppressed, a Don Rodrigo can get away with his transgressions, "mocking all that noisy fury of screams" coming from his victims. Yet he feels, ominously, an ill-fate hovering over him, a superstitious "distant and mysterious fright" which cultivates an obscure conscience in him, and which is poignantly dramatized when the plague grips him, and, more subtly still, when in the light of the merciless epidemic he realizes he is being betrayed by his trusted bodyguard, Il Griso. Manzoni signifies that no one exists in total unawareness of good and evil—something Don Rodrigo be-trays when in drinking he seeks his vapid comfort. There is, then, an outer story of the man who threatened Don Abbondio and who thought enough of himself to approach the Innominato for assis-tance, as well as an inner one.

He appears mean to the core, from the moment of his ruthless threat to the curate lest he marry Renzo and Lucia, but in effect what we come to despise more essentially is his vain sense of him-self, or sense of caste. The disproportion between the grand, philosophical evil of the Innominato, born of a wish to defend him-self against the arrogance of others and a desire to dominate, and the petty evil of his cheap insensitivities born of a sick, haughty vision of himself, spells the difference between Don Rodrigo and the In-nominato. Therefore Russo may be right: there being no greatness or originality in Don Rodrigo, we feel there exists no "disdainful horror or indignant scorn" on the part of Manzoni, but an attitude of "religious mockery and grave pity."[22] Don Rodrigo's struggle be-tween life and death in the *lazzeretto* amounts to a pathetic transla-tion of the vanity of the deeds of those who pompously spent their lives seeking purely temporal or material satisfactions—something all the easier for a humble soul like Renzo to forgive.

The hero of forgiveness[23] is Fra Cristoforo, who had what Don Rodrigo did not: the rankling of remorse and a vision of something which discards vainglory in favor of altruism. He wears the Francis-can garb, yet his greatness lies not in his practice of Franciscanism but in his devotion to Christianity. His pervasive melancholy may not make him appear "elegiac," as Momigliano describes him,[24] but it does underscore for the reader the continuous presence in his mind of his former life which seeks expiation. The cocky young aristocrat, alias Lodovico, who killed a man in a duel to settle the vain question of a right-of-way by a stone wall, feels the need for perpetual contrition, and ends by outliving in saintliness the dark drama of his past. Through it, he discovers a truth beyond that which is implicit in the rules of social behavior. He had always sensed the validity of the idea of justice, but had known only the use of force to defend it. Now the young swordsman becomes, unarmed, the noble crusader for justice, or better, against injustice. There was no rapid conversion involved, as some have contended, but a catharsis—not totally unexpected in someone whose quick fantasy had hit several times upon the possibility of becoming a monk. True to his past, he remains a man of action, but now of coherence as well, a knightly figure in opposition to Don Rodrigo and at the center of the saga of good and evil. His impulsive nature finds restraint in the Christian religion, though inside him rages a struggle for nobility. Truth translates into a fire of righteousness, and at times, when his central role exalts him, he appears as if he were not of this world, engaged not in a passive but in an active response to the needs of justice and the oppressed. If his impulsiveness is contained by humility, it is not dominated by it: he is the fiery saint whom all must reckon with, and who knows the discipline of ascetic control. One may speak, like Russo, of his moral Jansenism.

He is very complex and fascinating, because his generosity is not conceived in the vacuum of sheer do-good sentimentality. His life is dominated by love, but there is none of the Bishop Myriel in him, just as Manzoni's *miserabili* are infinitely different from Hugo's. Fra Cristoforo has not met with universal critical approval. Carducci tends to make him a moral apologist and an example of resigned Christianity in an historical period of accommodation. Sansone is bothered by his altruistic expansiveness, as if he followed a religious script too closely, as if he preached to command, and as if his fine words were not generated by a deep knowledge of the human heart.[25] Moravia sees him as downright propagandistic, interpreting his "conversion" not as an intimate thing but as a "proud inversion of his inferiority complex" (!) which first draws him to violence and later to humility.[26]

But Fra Cristoforo's humility rings persuasively, and even his offended enemies bow to his charity. Two formidable scenes impress the reader: toward the beginning when, young and vigorous, he visits his rival Don Rodrigo, becomes furious and reaches the summit of prophecy, then regains the self-possession of a tree inside a storm which "naturally recomposes its branches and receives the hail as the sky hurls it"; and the scene toward the end when, comforting the ailing in the *lazzeretto* though ill himself and at the end of his long life of apostolate for the good, he comments to Renzo and Lucia: "Thank the heaven above which has driven you to this point, not by means of turbulent and passing joys but with travail and misery, to ready you for joy which is composed and tranquil." Ill-fortune's providence again provides.

Out of Romanticism's fascination with the legacy of Satan grew the figure of the Innominato, or the Unnamed. His is a titanic existence, an exceptional energy turned evil, through which Manzoni underscores his spiritual view of the world where Providence works out inside man a fated ascension. But for all his Romanticism—or indeed because of it—the Innominato may be viewed as a modern hero: a deeply "conscious" man, his travail and misery are existential when he faces what in today's language is called the negation of the individual and the absurdity of death. His rebellion against society, symbolized by his isolated, inaccessible fortress atop a mountain and peopled with private soldiers, soon reveals itself as metaphysical, and after his life of dispassionate crime it leads to estrangement, to dissociation and self-doubt, and to a lonely dread which opens the door to conversion and salvation. By comparison, the pre-Raskolnikovian anarchistic philosophy of Balzac's Vautrin, the Innominato's great criminal colleague, leads merely to ostracized incognito.

The demonic suggests itself in the way Manzoni seeds the text with epithets and word-symbols which enable us to sense a dimension beyond the purely human: that "man or devil," more likely a *satanasso* who surrounds Lucia with a "reality too similar to a macabre vision of Hell," who reacts violently to the simple mention of God, and who, if we are to believe a chaplain, was "sent . . . [by the Devil]." His being "unnamed" intensifies the terrible mystery surrounding him and enables him to spread more easily the tentacles of his domination "in all corners of the Milanese."[27] From this dark majesty, "one could not remain independent." A good part of his story takes place before we meet him; we learn of his disinterested destruction of everything around him because he saw it as meaningless, absurd. His actions begot an abstract negativism which, through an almost Nietzschean ascension above good and evil, replaced evil with Evil and attained the level of absolute denial: "that man . . . had disposed cold-bloodedly of so many lives [and] in so many actions had paid no attention to the sorrows he had caused." Don Rodrigo's pettiness gives greater relief to the Innominato's magnificent evil, which subconsciously serves his will of self-defense against mediocrity and ugly power and of self-defying justice.

Yet, beneath the surface, we feel what Russo calls "a religious sense, despite his satanism."[28] He is an inner-directed, psychologically oriented man who hears an "imperious *no*" ring inside him as he is about to give orders to Il Nibbio relating to Lucia's abduction. His rebellion gradually abandons its titanic dimensions by being turned subtly against himself and, unbeknown to him, by permitting the concept of infinity, or eternity, to enter his conscience. Abetted by a feeling of "tremendous loneliness"—which Russo interprets not as the solitude of a man who has removed himself from the honest crowd, but as that of a defenseless man before God[29]—he moves toward inquietude and dread. As long as his concerns had remained temporal, he was unmoved by the anguish of thought, but when a sense of the eternal informs the situation, in large part through Lucia's simple, pious words, his world view modulates onto a metaphysical level and he sees himself as dissociated from any vital force. When, during his sleepless night, a series of flashbacks to his countless crimes momentarily makes him raise the pistol to his head, a tragic sense of evil reveals to him the Sartrian dictum: we are the sum of our acts. Of his crimes he thinks: "they were all his, they were he," and the mighty structure cracks. The mystery of death—"To get old, to die, and then what?"—encourages the Pascalian wager, but even more than that: it converts him to a realization that he must make peace with Eternity, "from which he could not escape, not even through death." He fashions a "new *himself*," turning into "that man whom no one could humiliate and who humiliated himself."

To him, God does not say paternally "I am," but sternly "I am, however." And only through such imperiousness can the imperious psyche be daunted. The critics' arguments over the "miracle" of the conversion, divinely understood, and its purely psychological inducement, distort the issue. The Innominato is neither an automaton who acts through mystic stimulus nor a subject whose actions are totally reducible to common human determinants.[30] He is, as many have said, particularly Graf,[31] an indomitably volitional being; the needs of his will introduce his self-examination, and it is his will which cultivates his troubled conscience once questioning sets in and he glimpses the possibility of different dimensions of existence. There is nothing brusque about it, and if "Providence" works the wonder, like the feeling of death which "grows inside," it identifies with the will in its innermost stirring. The Innominato becomes estranged from his old self by acceding to the recognition of a reality outside his own narrow and solitary presence. Being an intimate development, his conversion (brought about during his colloquy with Cardinal Borromeo) constitutes a metaphysical rebirth stemming from existential dissociation and self-doubt. He is the most provocative and overwhelming character in *I promessi sposi* and one of the most psychologically dramatic in nineteenth-century literature. Indeed, he outgrows his presence in the novel and his age, and enters spiritually into our contemporary world of loneliness and dread, self-doubt and religious reconciliation.

Speaking as the voice alongside the Anonymous Chronicler, whose supposed manuscript the author edits and refashions, Manzoni writes: "We have come across a personage whose name and memory . . . through time . . . have been recreated with the placid emotion of reverence. . . ." He is Federigo Cardinal Borromeo,[32] one of the few historical characters in the novel, the incarnation of the best in religious edification, whose life Manzoni can compare unpretentiously with a limpid brook running through many fields and emptying, as limpid as ever, into a river. He stands out as a model of Christian perfection, which means that he condenses and simplifies in a single being the most noteworthy maxims of Catholic morality.[33] But, for this, he has been viewed as an object of hagiography on the part of Manzoni, or at best as a central example of his "oratorical" fallacy.

It is easy to point out the Cardinal's lack of inner torment, of inner psychology, and his exemplary firmness, disconcerting to those who insist that humanity can be measured only in travail and doubt, strikes some as conceptually deficient. He appears the first time as he appears the last: there is no evolution. Yet if he is to represent the security of a humanitarian faith, religiously based, one cannot expect Manzoni to have portrayed him in any other manner. And for all of this, he retains his humanity—that of a noble man, for there are some such men in life. If he is conceptually rigid, he is not artistically rigid; as Momigliano observed, while he impresses through his persuasive serenity, he impresses even more through his penetrating, psychological knowledge of the human condition, and we soon come to understand that his success, fictional and historical, resides in his constant activation of the evangelical principles of existence. No human passion seems a riddle to him, buttressed as he is constantly by the tenets of his faith. For Manzoni, he is that superior individual who understands with assurance the distinction between one of life's paths and another, and who is confident of the goal of being.

We detect this in his four major appearances, which rather than visits we might label visitations: with the Innominato, with Lucia at the home of the tailor, with Don Abbondio, and with those afflicted in Milan by the plague. The word "heroism" does not befit him; his motivating concept is charity, for to him charity is the sole light and hope for life. Russo makes him out to be great reason incapable of admitting anything resembling the small reason of Don Abbondio.[34] Not so: true charity understands, and by its very nature admits, and if the disparity constitutes weakness in any way, it also illustrates a form of poetry, to which Russo also pays tribute. It is only too logical, and human, to confront the curate's paltry self-conservationism with precepts of "rigid" or "oratorical" morality. Otherwise, magnanimity marks his personality. We have only to read his final words to Don Abbondio: "Let us buy back time: midnight nears; the groom cannot be late: let us keep lighted our lamps. Let us present our miserable, empty hearts to God, that it may please Him to fill them with that charity. . . ." A character like this needs no development: he has arrived.

The Cardinal's fulgent aura contrasts with the gloomy shadows of Sister Gertrude, the Nun of Monza,[35] and surely one of the novel's most compelling psychological studies. "She is not a nun like the others." In the first version, she commanded a much longer episode, and some critics point to the counsel of either Tosi or Fauriel or both which helped trim it to its present length and rid it of material which unnecessarily injured religious sensibilities. Other critics would want to crown the passionate tale of the nun with a dramatic denouement.[36] We prefer the more recent view that Manzoni's decision to condense the presentation was made out of a concern for artistic balance more than for religious scruples. The reduction sharpened the psychological presentation of Sr. Gertrude without losing sight of the aesthetic dimension, or of the "sense of painful mystery which increases her tragic greatness."[37] And one wonders how much more drama her compact story could bear: the transformation of an innocent creature into a savage[38] provides its own final drama.

But the savagery is not fierce—she has not an evil soul—because Gertrude's besetting sin is her weakness. Even her pride is weak. And her century nourished that weakness, for the episode constitutes at once an individual and an environmental study. From an early age, her father the Prince conditioned her mind to think of high office in the convent when for toys he bought her nun dolls and cajolingly addressed her as "mother superior." Class interests and an ineradicable family absolutism made him insensitive to her needs as a person with a will for freedom and love and the joy of living, and imposed upon her a false education. Gertrude had no strength to demand or power to sway. She was caught in a world in which religion was an instrument of power, and in which in a struggle between herself and her father (they were spiritually of the same substance, as Russo argues) she was destined to falter and fall, indeed motivate her own failure. She would "withdraw from difficult circumstances with excuses that would place her in even more difficult circumstances, use up future time, as it were, in order to live in present time." The gradual disemboweling of her will caused her perversely to accede consciously to what she recognized as detrimental. Eventually, again trapped by her father in a concatenation of repressive circumstances, she locked herself up in a world completely opposite of her dreams, with hatred in her heart and a bitter nostalgic torment which made her refractory where her faith might have assisted. In the nunnery, where religion was as obsessive as it was oppressive, the pattern continued in the company of "persons who do not think of understanding a soul in order to direct it in its choice, but of fixing it in an already destined choice." The complex nature of her problem—instinctive pride, a vague feeling of a need for good rendered inoperative in a confusion between willing and an inability to will, and a resulting gradual decline to sensual perversion—sought solution, impossibly, in her elevation to the rank of Mother Superior, a role she executed with forbidding sternness, more as a vindictive reaction than as a devotional commitment. If she had not chosen her cloistered imprisonment, she was now to lord in it. Hers became the victim's morality, whereby the evil she had undergone justified the one she committed.[39] If early in life she did not act because others acted for her, now, since any step she took was destined "to descend," she was to jump into situations leading to irreparable crime (the murder of someone who knew of her guilty relationship with Egidio), almost as if under a compulsion of ugliness. Like a tragic heroine, she was pulled down by an undetermined and dark inner force, morbidly attractive insofar as she deemed a return to life in daylight a return to others' domination of her. When the erotic proposition was made to her, she could only answer in the affirmative. The acceptance is merely suggested by Manzoni, who, with the moral qualms of Tolstoy who leaves Anna Karenina's fall suspended undescribed between two chapters, merely writes: "The wretched one responded. . . ."

Sr. Gertrude's story has invited interpretations of determinism, even more specifically of Jansenistic predestination. A century which permitted superstitions and family tyranny, and without enlightened religion, and an individual without strength for responsibilities and predisposed to earthly goods, combine to spell predestination. The nun has been compared with Emma Bovary[40]—both subject to insatiable romantic fantasies, to the "gay and brilliant fancies of days gone by," and both, therefore, seem predetermined. One went from a convent into life, the other from life into a convent ("the only castle which was not in the air, and in which Gertrude could imagine a tranquil and honorable refuge, was the monastery . . ."), but in both cases we can speak of dreams of glittering balls and knights (or pages) and nauseous confrontations with reality. In two chapters, Manzoni did what Flaubert did in a whole novel.

Determinism, however, like absolute Providence, is too strong a word for the Manzoni of *I promessi sposi*.

The psychological penetration of Manzoni, his cultivated and moving humanity, complicate this story of Gertrude with various and different motifs; there is not, and there could not be, in Manzoni a deterministic concept of life, by which Gertrude's fall would be explained only through the machinery of innate instincts and external forces: Gertrude is responsible, and Manzoni knows it and will say so later on; but he also knows how easy it is to fall in certain situations, just as he knows that in each human soul there is an innate need for love and good, and he absolves and condemns, understands and accuses, with a complex and thoughtful humanity which extends his sense of compassion and love over the whole passage. . . .[41]

A spark of whatever was once pure in Sr. Gertrude ignites momentarily with the arrival of Lucia, who provides unknowingly a kind of redemption, but not before arousing the nun's most contradictory reactions: effusiveness and repulsion, reserve and unhealthy curiosity. Yet in the end, wrapped up in her own shadowy self and too proud to seek outside help for her sins and remorse, she sinks back into her Hades, like an emanation, Shakespearean in stature, of Manzoni's most intimate pessimism.

The seventeenth century, which Sr. Gertrude's episode comments on, receives further comment in a number of secondary characters. Manzoni characterized the period with injustice, dishonesty, smugness, and stupidity, with false power and subservience to it. "And perhaps in many ways it stands nearer to us now in spirit than at any time since the novel was written."[42] Dr. Azzeccagàrbugli (literally: fastener of tangled threads, translated as Dr. Quibble-weaver) resembles the crooked lawyer, with his benevolent but false countenance, but his parasitic and cowardly soul casts him differently. He is what would be left of Molière's comic protagonists if one bleached out most of the comedy. Prudence makes him a servant of power, which means a hypocrite. His dispatching of Renzo when he discovers whom the charges aim against gives rise to the kind of humor in which laughter at first erupts and then shrinks into uncomfortable silence.

Another parasite, though more extensively drawn, is the seventeenth-century rationalistic Aristotelian intellectual, Don Ferrante, from whose wife, Donna Prassede, he cannot be considered separately. With their Spanish-like names, they are "a couple of much consequence." Manzoni's irony rarely succeeds more poignantly as when he reveals their grandiloquent spiritual vacuousness. A theoretical premise results in a theoretical conclusion with them. Don Ferrante expatiates on the accidents, substances, and essences of the plague, and dies of it convinced of its celestially influenced provenance. He lives in a book-lined, artificial world, that of the cold litterateur who is removed from life, the "hero and martyr of useless doctrine and formal logic,"[43] and who has memorized his knowledge—like a parasite on the intelligence of others—with which he takes trifles seriously and through which he basks in the infallibility of his method. He would border on carica- ture (and therefore ill fit the novel), had not Manzoni endowed him with a certain honesty and respectability and attractive faith in the importance of knowing. His wife inspires less sympathy. Ultra- Christian because ignorant, presumptuous because of a heavy desire to do good, and pseudointellectual to say the least, she is pretenti- ously diffident of fine qualities—such as Cardinal Borromeo's char- ity, for though a worthy man "he has little experience of the world, and discernment . . . ," or the innocence of Lucia, who must un- dergo her "protectiveness." One critic refers to this protective cus- tody as a "Prassedean inquisition,"[44] something Manzoni spares from his total contempt by gentle, ironic intrusions.

As opposed to their "educated" profiles, one thinks of the modest and affectionate family of the tailor, who hosts Lucia after her libera- tion from the Innominato. Discretion and warmth characterize each of its members, though even here Manzoni refuses bland portraits: the tailor, for example, has read a little, fancies himself competent in letters, and misses no opportunity for an appropriate quotation at the right time, which he pronounces with satisfaction. His naive literature juxtaposes Ferrante's pedantic literature, just as the domestic warmth of the tailor's home counterpoises the coldness of that of the "couple of much consequence." And there are the other good people, generally humble in station, who contribute distinc- tive, however modest, colors to the tapestry. The Father Superior at Monza, cordial and prompt with advice; Brother Galdino, somewhat dense but honest, seeking subventions when nuts are harvested, with his picturesque story of "the miracle of the nuts"; Brother Fazio the sacrestan, hardly intelligent but loquacious; Tonio (and his family), Renzo's friend who attempts to serve with his dim-witted brother Gervasio as witness to the marriage, for with the good food and drink Renzo offers him at the tavern "he would throw himself into the fire": all are priceless little portraits inside the sweeping movement of history. In their own neutral way, the old servant who receives Fra Cristoforo in Don Rodrigo's home with utter amaze- ment, and the innkeepers of the "Luna Piena" and at Gorgonzola, also belong to this category.

These characters have negative, though not necessarily personal, counterparts not only in the niggardly go-betweens like Don Ab- bondio and Azzeccagarbugli, in the dirty old man who rises from the crowd with hammer, nails, and rope to nail the vicar to his door, or in the *cappellano crocifero* (the chaplain) whose pettiness contrasts with the eloquence of the Cardinal, but also in the retinue of Don Rodrigo and the Innominato. The latter has his old lady servant, a dour and hostile creature to whose care Lucia is entrusted, and Il Nibbio, his henchman and conveyor of evil, though not impervious to human promptings before Lucia's anguished crying like the old lady. Around the former is formed a veritable society of dubious, if not despicable, people. There is Count Attilio, the haughty, insensitive, and insolent nobleman, in many ways a boy who cannot brook disagreements with his social standing and knavishly mocks everyone, and whom one critic has found reason to place higher (meaning lower) than Don Rodrigo in viciousness and moral bankruptcy.[45] Then there is the Count Uncle, a man with "the force of his own nullity,"[46] like a *nouveau* in his own way, who wants to appear authoritarian, serious, and wise, and who is none of these. He is nullity become power, vanity become injustice, and pride become egoism. He bests in argument the Provincial Father, another of Don Rodrigo's circle, not because he discusses better but because the Father, though more cogent, acquiesces obsequiously, speaking not for himself but for his role—and that role is to yield to compromise, as the social conditions demanded. Finally—and not to speak of two guests who do nothing but eat while agreeing with everything that is said—there is Il Griso, Don Rodrigo's lurid right arm, who in the beginning fails in his mission to kidnap Lucia, and in the end fails his master by betraying him to the plague, to which, however, he quickly succumbs because he had touched Don Rodrigo's sick clothes rummaging through his pockets to steal his money.

Behind the secondary characters spreads the ominous host of evil which is shaped by oppression, injustice, and violence. The mercenary *bravi* (and the mercenary soldiers called *lanzichenecchi*) prelude the cynical *monatti*, who perform a necessary function but, drunk or sober, remain unmoved by the most abhorrent human plight. This host meshes with the superstition of the *untori* to spread its dark colors throughout the tapestry; its contrastive tonalities— the first fearsome, the second lugubrious—interpret not only the seventeenth century but, by extension, the human condition. Who could not point to their analogues in the nineteenth century, and who could not do the same today? The metaphors of fear and death prevail in all readings of history like invisible forces striking through the unknown.

For this reason, we encounter many characters in Manzoni's novel who stand out dramatically as victims of history, sharply delineated through their anonymity, like the Milanese family of three, united in starvation and returning with bread and flour from the assault on the bakery, or the family with which Renzo shares some buns he had found abandoned upon entering Milan, and through their heart-rending dignity before death, like Cecilia's mother, tired and finally tearless as she delivers her lifeless daughter to the *monatti*, terminating her remarks with the simple words: "when you come by this evening, you will go up to get me too, and not me alone." Only Dante's Pia de' Tolomei condensed such depths of emotion into so few words.

Among the victims Manzoni does not forget are the children, those who agonize and those who die like Cecilia. But other children, of course, provide the seed for the continuation of history: something unobtrusively paternal, even hopeful, underlies the way the author looks at happy little Bettina, alert little Menico, the frightened baker's son, the children in the streets, those of the tailor and of Tonio, those who crowd the Cardinal festively, and those of Renzo and Lucia, who will live on beyond the novel and restore some purity to the world.

Yet the world of a novel whose tone is set by *bravi* and *monatti* is not one of innocence, nor can any sequel to it ever be—not so long as the powerful offset the humble, and even less schematically, not so long as human beings remain their frail, imperfect selves. On this side of eternity, despair dictates to us more than hope, but hope there is too, albeit in limited measure. Frailty and imperfection obviate purity, which means that just as total despair is as rash as total hope, ultimately "no one is guilty, no one is innocent." Even Il Griso (who in the end cannot look his master in the eye), even Don Rodrigo (who fears Fra Crostoforo's prophesy), harbored a notion of good, insists Momigliano[47] as he cites Manzoni's dictum about duty "which lies like a germ in the hearts of all men." For, to quote from the beginning of *I promessi sposi*, "right and wrong never divide up so neatly that any one side can lay claim exclusively to one or the other."

So considered, the characters (even without the author's commentary) bespeak a view of the century and of the world. Because of its universality, the tale of sorrow and violence could be told by anyone—and indeed this is the case. The Anonymous Chronicler not only serves Manzoni's moral purpose of condemning the seventeenth century's poor taste, bad customs, horrible violence, and worse rhetoric, but his artistic purpose as well of gaining through the distance of a split author's personality the double-edged advantage of narration and criticism. One can comment while the other recounts. The interaction of the two generates a dialectic of irony, like a variation of Romantic irony, indulgent to be sure, which evolves into a world view no less fictionally inspired than historically ascertained. And in his role as commentator with the benefit of special distance, Manzoni can interpret the actions described by the narrator, penetrate deep down into the motivations of behavior. Among other things, his talent is profoundly psychological, and his inquiry accurately human and persuasive. The cold analyses of so-called psychological novels, which border on the clinical in order to compel attention, remain foreign to his creative process. Not the mechanical formulations of case studies obtain, but the revelation of feelings we all know we have and understand vaguely but cannot unravel.

All humans have secrets, of course, and the deeper the secret the more travailed the life, and the more unusual, even surprising, the inner motivations when at times they surface. Some of Manzoni's characters exhibit startling developments, which he prepares commensurately with their unexpectedness. A few of the obvious questions we can extract from the text, without presuming that he asked them of himself *in abstracto* (Manzoni's intense sensibility shaped his characters organically without the distortions of imposed psychological speculations), would be: What happens when a man becomes a priest, because he lives in an age when priesthood is a privilege, and brings into his ministry the same narrow preoccupations he would have as a man, that is, the same fears which made him consider the priesthood in the first place? What happens to an impetuous, self-centered youth who needlessly kills another human being in accordance with a snobbish code, and who chooses expiation in the most altruistic mode of existence possible? What happens to the weak will as it keeps acquiescing to unfeeling authority, and then succeeds in attaining authority in a context totally inimical to its most natural instincts? What happens to the strong will when it has no higher level of evil to ascend to, and which then is turned to questioning all the premises of its previous existence? What happens to the petty criminal, whose villainies made him feel he controlled the lives of others, when, no different from the many, he is afflicted with a slow death?

Mass movements particularly claimed Manzoni's attention: the rioting crowd when it seeks to locate the blame for its disturbance, or the hungry crowd for its suffering. How serious is the clash between contradiction and ingenuousness stirring inside the angry masses, and how do unverbalized urgings and instinctive needs set in ruinous motion whole multitudes of people who, as individuals, would not agree to the same action?

But even more penetrating is Manzoni's power of depicting not pronounced psychological travails, of which he is a master, but the human, common, every day reactions to given situations: the words, the gestures, the feelings, the actions—unplanned moments, perhaps, suddenly disclosing through their astonishing, simple truths whole private worlds of being. Manzoni's delicacy of understanding is matched by his subtlety of expression. All individualization assumes a kind of psychological uniqueness, a particular profile emerging from a network of motives, some of which grow independently out of a person's intimate psyche, some of which relate to this psyche but are shaped by outside contacts. These the author amply illustrates. But more significant from the standpoint of an epical novel becomes the interactive psychology of the characters, who finally cannot be isolated from each other because one offers the other the occasion for self-revelation, an occasion the commentator repeatedly welcomes as he digests the words of the narrator. Psychologically, Don Rodrigo is a function of the presence of Fra Cristoforo, just as Don Abbondio and Donna Prassede are of the Cardinal, Perpetua of Don Abbondio, the Innominato and Sr. Gertrude of Lucia, Renzo of Azzeccagarbugli, and so on. The way one illumines the other has been called the "choral" device in Manzoni's scrutiny of human motivation (the writer's task is "to consider how men behave in reality"[48]). He conducts his inquiry with such naturalness that Hofmannsthal's saying comes to mind: the art is concealed on the surface. There may be some pages in *I promessi sposi* which read more roughly than others, where the Anonymous Chronicler and Manzoni do not work things out between themselves too smoothly, but on balance the saying applies. Effortlessness is the mark of this "extraordinary designer."[49]

CHAPTER 8

Those Words One After the Other

WHEN the Innominato has spoken with the Cardinal and changes his way of life, he recalls easily his long-silent prayers: "and those words, which had remained there bunched together for so long, came out one after the other, as if they were unraveling." Manzoni's style exhibits the same characteristic of flowing ease in what is, however, a highly sophisticated and precise use of words. Apart from the shifting point of view between the author and the Anonymous Chronicler, Manzoni made no use of devices. His primary interest was style, a finely honed language of narration, commentary, soliloquy, and dialogue; his goal was the compound beauty of description, portrayal, analysis, humor, irony, and moral example. The whole gamut being present, one critic has referred to the language of *I promessi sposi*, primarily because of the variety of dialogue tonalities, as "rather a chorus, a concert of languages."[1] This interest became a veritable preoccupation, as his many linguistic writings throughout his life clearly evidence. The problem was communication, that of working out a language "capable of live affections and feelings," widely understood and not regional or heavy with pretentiously literary locutions (the Academies still lorded over written Italian). *I promessi sposi* would become Manzoni's way of putting his linguistic theory into practice, which meant to evolve a living language by abolishing the distinction between educated and popular or daily idiom, written and spoken.

To Fauriel he had said that he did not want "a language never written as it is spoken, . . . lacking a feeling of communion with the reader," but one look at *Fermo e Lucia/Gli sposi promessi* convinced him that he had not achieved his goal. He deplored the "miserable state it was in in its first edition with respect to style."[2] Language was a social fact to him, demanding a communality between the one who writes and the one who reads, and his readers, if only for the patriotic possibilities of his story, resided throughout the Italian peninsula. Yet *Fermo e Lucia* contained hybrid forms, solecisms, and Lombard dialect in the area of dialogue, and elevated expression in those of exposition and digression (historical accounting). To expunge the archaisms, the local idiom, and the pedantry, he worked in Florence, in 1827, with Niccolini and Cioni, and then in Milan with Florentine Emilia Luti. The purpose was to "unlyricize" himself *(siliricarsi)*, not only to rid himself of stylistic residues from his poetic period, but also by example to lower the pompous, near fatidic tone of traditional prose, for the flowery style of Italian had resulted in the word losing its communicative vitality. In canceling the subjective in favor of the realistic, he prepared modern Italian, placing it in the mainstream of the modern aesthetic of style anywhere. The language of *I promessi sposi* enjoys flowing felicity and agility, cordiality and graceful familiarity, that is, truthfulness, here and there punctuated with syntactical and lexical originality; there is a sense of reverence for the word as it "unravels," everywhere fresh and natural, even in some of its denser, historiographical passages. Manzoni's respect for language seems almost religious, and as such contributes a reverent tone to a novel whose substance is already ethico-religious.

The prose has a psychological quality, too. It is contemplatively calm and limpid, expressively simple but with a minutely analytical gait. Lucia's "Farewell" remains its finest example. It has been observed that this kind of style, devoid of the exaltations of a Wergeland or the mysteries of a Poe, results from the inner equilibrium of the author, for whom the French dictum, "style is the man," obtains. The opening paragraph of the novel is symphonic, a subdued prefiguration of the story which like a modest "stream" empties into a large "lake": from the two mountain ranges and the two shores beneath them destined not to meet, like Renzo and Lucia; to the Adda river, the symbol of home, safety, and "return"; to the ambiguous pinnacle of the Resegone, like the Innominato inaccessible, fearsome, and dominating at first, yet protective in the long run; to the walls of Milan and the "vast [yoking] chain of mountains" and the oppressive connotations of the word *(giogaia)*, repeated almost immediately twice as "yoke" and "yokes," as if to hint at the many complications that will stem from the original one concerning the wedding; and finally to the nature of the original complication, namely, Don Rodrigo's dishonorable intentions over Lucia, subtly suggested by an ironic reference to the Spanish soldiers "who taught modesty to the girls and women of the countryside."

The "Farewell" finely blends feelings and landscape, the placid sorrow of a pious young lady forced to flee her home and the quiet loneliness of the mountains and moon. There is nothing vague about it, nothing resembling the typically Romantic *vague des passions* (vagueness of feeling) of Chateaubriand, or the sentimental meanderings of Wordsworth in Grasmere, or the misty *Sehnsucht* of Novalis. Lucia's elegy is permeated with specific dreams and remembrances, as specific as the particular hills and lake and houses she identifies in flight. There is pain but not despair; only her faith sustains her, somewhat like the water floating her boat which also corroborates the fluidity of her unfolding feelings. Realism sacrifices nothing to lyricism. In Momigliano's words, "There murmurs even beneath the most defined particulars a subdued music of sorrow; the sentences run almost silently, as if over a base of grass, and Lucia's final attitude . . . seems to be gradually delineated in the painting of the landscape. . . . Her farewell has the serene lines of that moonlit night. The sky, the mountains rising from the water, and Lucia are but a single thing: a solemn breath of melancholy. The words are Manzoni's, but the breath is that of the resigned and confident soul of Lucia."[3]

Farewell, mountains springing from the waters and rising to the sky; rugged peaks, familiar to any man who has grown up in your midst, and impressed upon his mind as clearly as the features of those nearest and dearest to him; torrents whose varying tones he can identify as easily as he can the voices of his family; villages scattered white over the slopes, like herds of grazing sheep; farewell! How sadly steps he who was reared among you, as he draws away! . . . . Farewell, home where, sitting among her secret thoughts, she had learned to pick out from all others the sound of a footstep awaited with a mysterious awe. Farewell, house that was still not hers; house at which she had so often glanced hastily in passing, not without a blush; house in which her imagination had pictured a perpetual calm, an unending life of married bliss. . . . Farewell, church . . . : farewell! He who gave you so much happiness is everywhere, and never disturbs the joy of His children, except to prepare for them another one, greater and more certain.

Through passages such as this, Manzoni situates the humble centrally in his spiritual view of the universe.

The tranquil tone of such descriptions becomes austere when historical material is used. The plague which struck Milan in 1630 is one of the most powerful presentations in literature. Manzoni dramatizes it, relying on a crescendo of events and fear to produce the needed effect of horror. The first symptoms after the passing of foreign troops are not noticed quickly enough; it lies dormant during the winter months, then aided by a general unwillingness to admit what is happening, it serpents through the city until the mounting number of dead nullifies rationalizations. Superstitions regarding the yellowish grease of the *untori* (greasers) further complicate matters, and before long the city is turned upside down with confusion, fear, arrests, inquisitions, trials, and torture (as the *Storia della colonna infame* also informs us). And death, for the disease fills the *lazzeretto* with fifteen hundred sick daily, at one point, and in the face of a dearth of beds, medicines, doctors, and food. Misfortune breeds perversity: knaves take advantage of the confusion, *monatti* and *apparitori* (who were subordinate officials) become bosses and with their filthy hands touch women and children indiscriminately, thieves loot, and everything is "an enormous and confused mass of public folly." Along with Renzo, we witness one tragic vision after another, but none leaves its imprint on the reader so deeply as the sculpturesque pair of Cecilia held by her mother. Ultimately better than a thousand words, the single vision synthesizes the historical moment by suddenly changing the prose rhythm. The stylistic crescendo culminates in this disconsolate downbeat. Manzoni's expository power of language here encourages few challengers.

The stylistic mood changes again with dialogues, when it becomes compact, and with monologues, when it becomes wordy, sometimes fitful or convulsive. Renzo is "pluriexpressive," according to Petrocchi,[4] with the frank language of a frank man, but also with the adaptive prose of one who tries to discuss in the manner of his interlocutor. Manzoni modulates his dialogue accordingly. And when Renzo gets drunk, a stream of sprightly words and images slowly gives way to a sluggish set of repetitions and confusions. Each character is individualized through his speech. Perpetua's rapid, spontaneous, gossipy rhetoric of a woman of the people differs from Lucia's composed, reserved expressions of someone less familiar with (and therefore more fearful of) the ways of the world but more expressively coherent. Fra Cristoforo's sermonizing idiom, a rhythmic mixture of impulsive and willfully controlled speech, contrasts with the pontifically serene locution of Cardinal Borromeo, but even more so with the haughtily self-assured verbal gait of Don Rodrigo as well as with his vulgar outbursts. Russo calls Agnese's popular syntax, its clarity, exuberance, and superfluousness which befits a talkative, basically good busybody, linguistic *verismo* before its time. Indeed, this kind of naturalism applies to all the humble in *I promessi sposi*, if by it we mean the way in which popular thoughts and emotional states unfold through words.

At times, Manzoni couples adjectives, to render better the familiar flavor of the situation (Lucia, her apron full of nuts, holds it with arms "stretched and outstretched"). At other times, he strings verbs to enhance the picturesqueness of the event (Don Abbondio "saw confusedly, then saw clearly, got frightened, became astonished, became furious, thought, and came to a decision"). The language is further enlivened by proverbial sayings ("Tell me whom you go around with and I'll tell you who you are"), juxtapositions ("The governor came to spend well his badly earned popularity"), and by more pronounced humorous and ironic traits. For reasons like these, it tends to resist translation; the relation of gesture to the language describing it, the vocal inflexions that come through naturally to the Italian ear, the peculiar glances, monosyllabic utterances, and quaint similes all demand enormous linguistic suppleness on the part of the translator.

Dialogue dominates. It manipulates the tonal and modal variations in *I promessi sposi*. We think of the chorus, or the concert of languages, leaving us with the impression that the novel is a "dialogued narration."[5] Yet it is itself also a narrated dialogue, in the sense that Manzoni in effect converses with the Anonymous Chronicler and with the reader, so that we might conclude that the whole novel is "spoken." But it is the direct discourse that sets the tone. The story of *I promessi sposi* "finds its most immediate expression in the voice of its characters: what is 'spoken' creates openings, 'zones' in which the narrator disappears and only the persons and the events remain in the foreground."[6] Manzoni establishes a living pattern of narration and dialogue, dialogue and commentary, commentary and narration, enabling his work to breathe internally with its own organs and at its own rate, and making it to that extent all the harder to be spoken by a different tongue.

Humor and irony pervade Manzoni's style. They are substantive

elements, not sporadic injections or simple mood-changing digressions from point of view, for they form an integral part of his
ethico-poetico-religious interpretation of human history. Humor establishes a balance between moral judgment and human understanding. It is good natured and has indulgence, that of a writer who
likes his characters, often because of their very frailties. He does not
"use" his people for comical ends; rather, he reveals their imperfec-
tions with an eye not to bludgeon their identities with rigid
moralism but to dent their consciences a bit, introduce an ironical
touch, show the relativity of all things human and the ultimate
weakness of our temperaments in dealing with our major problems.
"Manzoni's humor is the fruit of a singular capacity to feel the discordances, bizarreness, absurdities, pettinesses, poor cunning, and
instinctive hypocrisies of our spirit, accompanied and deepened by a
pitying and religious awareness of man's fragility."[7] Such a view
unites the humble and the powerful as humans. It equalizes before
God. It attenuates the bitterness and tragedy, and it regulates the
complexity of grave situations. When, for example, Renzo is mista-
ken for an *untore* and manages to escape the frenzied, murderous
crowd by jumping onto a passing wagon heaped in the most macabre
of fashions with cadavers, even the *monatti* take amused pity on the
untorello who could not possibly cripple Milan on his own, and
invite him to drink. The final humor of the deathly situation tempers
the mood without whittling its severity.

Humor is used psychologically, too. Manzoni chooses words and
phrases from familiar speech which of themselves describe the
psychology of an individual or a group. It is difficult to forget, for
instance, the scene of the farmers marching toward Lucia's house, in
shouting consultation, then dispersing to return home trium-
phantly, only to conclude their tales of adventure yawning at their
wives. At times Manzoni "grazes buffoonery," but he never falls into
it.[8] It would have been a mere matter of momentary carelessness to
make burlesque of Renzo's drunkenness at the inn, or of Azzeccagarbugli's panicky restitution of the two capons like rejected victims, or of Perpetua's perpetuous patter. Similarly, it would have
been tempting to stress to the limit Don Ferrante's ridiculous intellectualism, or Agnese's total confidence in her sagacious plans and
total blindness to that "Achilles' heel" in each of them. But Manzoni
is vigilant, and his vigilance is abetted by the subtle temperament of
an artist whose mortality precludes extremes and accepts man,

whatever his foibles or manias, with a smile. By limiting the ideal, he uncovers the opposite, "objectified and living," as Pirandello said, and inside this zone lies what is "not only comical, but frankly and profoundly humorous."[9] Manzoni's brand of humor blends the ideal and the real.

The masterpiece of "counterideal" humor is Don Abbondio. Whether contrite in his apologetic egoism before Cardinal Borromeo, or incapable of containing his elation at the news of Don Rodrigo's death, or haunted by falling tiles, or feigning normalcy at the sight of the *bravi*, or screaming like a demon when he suspects he is being trapped into performing the wedding, he is treated with gentle malice by the author, who is at his best in showing the comical martyrdom of a priest, rent in the disparity between duty and fear, whose body is far too large for his soul. "That's enough! Heaven *has an obligation* to help me . . .": this seems his most natural utterance. His journey on muleback down the mountain from the Innominato's castle remains a monologue classic of humorous style:

. . . He was feeling the discomfort of this mode of travel to which he was little used; he felt it much more now than on the outward journey, particularly at the beginning during the descent from the castle to the bottom of the valley. The postilion, urged by signs from the Innominato, was driving his animals at a smart pace; the two mules were following close behind at the same pace; so that in some of the steeper parts poor Don Abbondio would be pitched forward, as if pushed by a lever from behind, and he would have to steady himself by clutching at his pommel. He did not dare to ask them to go slower, but on the other hand was longing to get out of that neighborhood as soon as possible. Moreover, whenever the track ran over a bank or ridge, the mule, according to the habit of its kind, seemed to take a spiteful pleasure in always keeping to the outside and planting its hooves on the very brink; and Don Abbondio would see almost perpendicularly beneath him a drop, though to him it appeared a precipice. "You too," he muttered to the animal in his heart, "have this cursed craze for going out of your way to look for danger when the path's so broad!"—and he would pull the bridle in the opposite direction, but in vain; so that in the end, grumbling with rage and fear, he let himself be led along, as usual, by the will of others. . . .

We smile at the Don Quixote in all of us when we display our contradictions, like a five-year-old trying to swing a calvalry saber, and do not live up fully to the ideal of wisdom or energy we have chosen for ourselves. And "that smile is a testimonial of sympathy."[10] But the other side of the smile is irony: the blade cuts two ways. It is complex irony, one which grants eternal humanity its transcendental value, but at the same time satirizes historical humanity in its particular society and civilization as well as in its ubiquitous incongruities.[11] Manzoni's irony is a function of his temporal pessimism, tempered by his Christian idealism. The action of tempering may be followed simply by confronting textually the acid sarcasms in *Gli sposi promessi* and the gentle irony (so far removed from anything resembling Jansenistic dispositions!) in *I promessi sposi* with the more salient role accorded to Providence. In a vibrant and nonplatitudinous way, "Love thy neighbor" checks the ironic style which otherwise would have run rampant—which does not mean that through excessive gentleness it remains bland. It can become quite trenchant, commensurate with the degree of condemnation the human action elicits, and it borders on the black in describing how man's stupidity caused the plague to spread. Irony, high and low, indulgent and cutting, provides the various dynamic emotional levels in the symphony, and, like humor, like dialogue, becomes part of the tonality of the whole novel.

It is diffused throughout the texture of the work in such a way as to become a vital ingredient of style. It is compassionate with small defects, like the inconsistencies of the humble, and stern with large ones, particularly with the intrigues of the powerful and with their casual way of deciding issues of import for whole societies which may shove the anonymous masses irresponsibly in the direction of destruction and death.[12] Rather than bland, then, we must recognize Manzoni's irony often as veiled bitterness, albeit indulgently composed and controlled through a stylistic expressiveness which makes us smile sadly at the world of ferocious passions and historical clashes the novel portrays. The sadness sounds through the all too frequent ineffectualness of charitable feelings, simple humility, and religious structures. But because the language is subdued, the irony, like the humor, moves constantly and inwardly, never allowing the reader to forget, humming in his ear. In this way it becomes constructive, seconding the working of Providence. Manzoni is serious when he smiles.

CHAPTER 9

Angelic Goodness and Diabolic Machinations

THE "tapestry" (Manzoni uses the word in his preface) of *I promessi sposi* contains many threads which can be traced throughout the various planes of the novel in such a way as to bind its fabric and give it unsuspected artistic depth. They structure the novel expressively,[1] relating to one another through images and words, planted here and there to create a desired tonality. When the frequency and concentration of their appearances are calculated, they become word-symbols which interrelate structurally any number of aspects of the novel, pointing to its expressive coherence, and stimulating the reader's associative process through a cross-weaving of images.

Even if Manzoni left no precise indication of how he saw the chapter-by-chapter arrangement of his work (and the earlier version yields only modest information on this score[2]), it is still true that the "architecture" of *Gli sposi promessi* is "almost always baroque" and that of *I promessi sposi* is "solid and symmetrical."[3] A plan for artistic reorganization was clearly put into effect between one version and the other. The story is introduced on a plane of definition and presentation (chapters 1–8), and subsequently we see the tapestry expand in three successive planes, each linked to the next symmetrically by a few transitional chapters. Plane two (12–17), then, recounting the peripeteia of Renzo in and around Milan, is preceded by three chapters (9–11) introducing Milan, including Sr. Gertrude's episode. Similarly plane three (20–24), the Innominato's section, is preceded by two bridging chapters (18–19) leading out of plane two (with the events at Renzo's home and Agnese's return) and into three (through Don Rodrigo's request for help from the Innominato). The final plane (28–37) concerns the famine, the invasion, the plague, and is introduced by three more transitional chapters (25–27: the events which resulted in the plague). The last chapter (38), with the marriage of Renzo and Lucia, constitutes an epilogue, just as the preface, in which Manzoni presents the manuscript he has discovered, constitutes a prologue. The tapestry broadens continuously, from bottom to top, from the foreground with the private human affairs of Renzo and Lucia, to the wider vista of their experiences with the world's evil, to the forces behind the evil, and to the background with its vast representation of the public and social calamities resulting from that evil.

Pellizzari notes that Manzoni revamped his novel "for reasons of order, measure, artistic balance."[4] This last reason is important, for artistic balance underscores the content of the novel which finds organic unity through a series of juxtapositions adumbrated in the "prologue": "virtuous deeds and angelick goodness opposed to diabolick machinations." Otherwise stated, the forces of good and evil, standing like Fra Cristoforo's convent of Pescarenico and the mansion of Don Rodrigo which oppose each other across the valley in which lies the village of the protagonists. Rather than spark Manzoni's optimism, based on the notion of Providence, the forces encourage his pessimism: "[His] vision of life is not one of fatalistic optimism, as we have been tempted so often to suspect by looking at the working of Providence, in which vision comes to rest; indeed, in a certain sense, Manzoni may appear rather a pessimist, for whom any human virtue or any good-will effort does not succeed in freeing men from sorrow."[5] The ubiquitous theme of Providence does not make the novel a "poem of Providence" (as many have held) in the sense of a Christian God or external force ordering human history. Providence is a factor in Manzoni's profound view of reality, "felt not like the absurd moving about of contrasting elements, but like the eternal, holy blending of necessary oppositions."[6] Thus the "Renzo plane," where good is buffeted by the forces of evil, stands in opposition to the "Innominato plane," where the archmaster of evil comes face to face with the powers of good. The opposition results inevitably in a harsh, expiatory conflict: the plane of the plague. There is something of Van Gogh's bold distribution of masses in Manzoni's contrastive grouping of tone-colors. The effect is dialectical; Providence is a working-out of life not from without but from the necessary inner nature of things, and for this reason we can speak aesthetically of an expressive structure which is simultaneously a moral structure.

Manzoni often sets the tone by an unobtrusive repetition of words.

"Wall," for instance, along with its corollary in the natural world, "mountain" (both logical enough in the story's setting and period), punctuates the novel from the opening paragraph, connoting an atmosphere of oppression, a sense of confinement or obstacle. A close look reveals that the first scene in the book, Don Abbondio's encounter with the *bravi*, takes place by two walls, and the last word of the last plane (that of the plague), which is also the last time the word appears, is "low walls" (*muriccioli*), where the diminutive seems to suggest that the catastrophe is ending, that the obstacles are finally being surmounted. If we follow the thread of this word-symbol, we come across Ludovico's (Fra Cristoforo's) duel-provoking confrontation with the nobleman which changes his life because of the honor code's right-of-way by a wall; the wall that Renzo's group and Il Griso's men scale during the "night of schemes and subterfuges," or the one along which Lucia flees after being betrayed by the nun; the enclosing convent walls of Sr. Gertrude, the *lazzeretto* walls, plague-ridden Milan and its "greased walls," the bakery walls assaulted by the hungry crowds—for the wheat was "immured" and the hungry mob reduced the walls to a few *muriccioli*. Manzoni gently presses the symbolic value of this word, in relation both to "that natural repugnance to enclosure" common to all men and often a fact of life, and to the final crumbling of the obstacles that obstructed the marriage of Renzo and Lucia. In its way, the thick fabric of this word-symbol becomes the inner substance of the narrative structure.

The word-symbols themselves interrelate. Associated with the famine and the "immured" wheat is the word *bread*, which is in turn juxtaposed to *wine*. The opposition parallels the massive architectural disposition of the Renzo and the Innominato planes, so that if we follow the prologue's clue we have to speak of the bread of angels and the wine of demons.[7] The traditional symbolism of bread as life and salvation, both physical and spiritual, obtains. Renzo exclaims: "they would have supported me against the devil. Had I had an enemy, . . . all I needed was to let him know where I stood: he would have stopped eating bread in no time." Bread is in Agnese's proverbs, which anticipate the bread crisis to come; in Milan, Renzo gathers buns left by rioters, symbolically by a column with a cross, and later refers to it as "the bread of Providence." Bread, he suggests, is God's gift to man; he buys some to stay alive, and when he innocently observes during the famine—which led to the plague—that "bread was falling," he says more than he thinks. But the thread that unifies these allusions is the one we follow with Fra Cristoforo. When he presents himself penitently at the home of the aristocrat whose brother he has killed, his noble repentance moves even his host, who offers him anything he wishes; he asks merely for some "bread of forgiveness," keeping a piece of it on his person in a small wooden box, until he offers it as a spiritual memento to Renzo and Lucia just before dying: "in here is the rest of that bread . . . the first I asked for as charity; that bread you have heard me talk about! I leave it to you; save it: let your children see it." Lucia accepts the holy bread of angels.

With the wine thread we shift from the Apollonian to the Dionysian. Don Abbondio drinks it "like a medicine" to settle him after his experience with the diabolical *bravi*, and from that point it is associated with negative forces. Don Rodrigo offers it, appropriately enough, to Fra Cristoforo: "bring Father something to drink . . . ; let it not be said that a capuchin leaves this house without having tasted my wine." Then later at the table, it mingles with thoughts of killing; after toasting the wine's excellence, the guests' gay voices blur in a din, over which the only audible words are "ambrosia" and "hang them [the bakers]." If Fra Cristoforo sips some wine, it is only out of politeness, after attempting to refuse it. After this episode, all subsequent references fall into perspective, like Lucia's refusal to have some wine at the Innominato's castle, "the kind that the master drinks with his friends . . . when one of those people happens to come by . . . !" Wine is almost fatal to Renzo, who despite his "bread of Providence" gets drunk in Milan, talks too much, is arrested, and his escape makes him a hunted man through two-thirds of the novel. He too later refuses the brew, offered by the bedeviled *monatti* who heaped cadavers on their carts. "He came to hate wine," and the lesson he learns is "not to raise his elbow too much."

The repeated use of the word *devil* enforces the tone set by wine. Here again, the recurrence of a word-symbol moves from the common, literal, objective allusion to the inner reality of the novel, so that any mention of "devil" becomes a subjective experience for the reader, an interiorization of the facts of the narrative or a deepened dimension of meaning whereby even a simple exclamation like "What the devil!" looms larger than itself. The pages concerning Don Rodrigo are seeded with allusions to the word, or its derivatives; he is described as having "the devil on his back," and Renzo exclaims he will find him "in the house of the devil." But an even more profound association, mixed with references to fire, develops in the pages concerning the Innominato, the "old satan," where the word is used in heavy concentration, whether the author is describing or quoting his characters—particularly the gossipy client at the Gorgonzola inn, whose speech is aided by tall glasses of wine. In the Innominato's castle, the angelic Lucia sees herself surrounded by a "reality too reminiscent of a funereal vision of hell," for the master is "either a man or a devil." But the ambiguity of him who has "a demon hidden inside his heart" quickly dissipates; the old lady who surveils Lucia is herself one "in whom Satan would have recognized his will," and the Innominato proves his spiritual identity when he reacts violently to any mention of God. When he reforms, he says it is to "unload this devilry from his shoulders," to remove "the hell in [his] heart." All leads the reader to sense that his warm welcome by Cardinal Borromeo suggests how God might some day welcome Lucifer's return.

This demonic thread is enforced in three places by the almost surrealistic appearance of diabolical figures that emerge from the *interior* of the narrative. There is the "bedeviled" old lecher, with "sunken, fired eyes, contracting his claws with diabolical countenance," who leads a crowd against Renzo when in speaking to it the latter has associated bread with God. Later, during the plague (and the next concentrated use of the word *devil*[8]), a story circulates in connection with the people's fear of ointments, involving a similar figure "with fiery face and lighted eyes, . . . and lips formed in a threat." And finally, as Renzo seeks information regarding Lucia, he comes upon a woman expressing "malice, with twisted eyes . . . and two clawed hands bent like pincers." Through these near apparitions, related by common physical features, and by repetition and variation, Manzoni converts something relatively marginal into a metaphor of lifeblood.

By the end of the fourth or top plane, the allusions to wine and demons have formed a pattern of complementary forces, spelling each other out, as it were, to sustain our sense of the presence of evil. The allusions are alternating dark tones in the tapestry, differing only in intensity and placement. Then, after the plague has been submitted to diabolical (as well as historical, social, political, and medical) analysis, and abetted by the fears of the "infernal" *untori* and the actions of the "diabolical" *monatti*, the wine and demon threads converge to produce the most chilling scene in the tale, which only Manzoni's philosophical serenity and delicate humor could keep from becoming gothically macabre: the last pages of chapter 34, with its black *monatti* bearing cadavers in carts, each not unlike the one who stands out with an "atrocious and cursed snicker," singing their "infernal dirge" and drinking with abandon wine stolen from the cellar of a man whom, with Mephistophelian wit, they claim to have "put in a carriage to take him on a holiday." As Renzo had said, "if he's a devil there, he won't want to be an angel here." The word symbols translate into inner substance.

Perhaps the best example of this process of interiorization[9] is the image of light with which the author opposes the satanic forces of darkness. Marcazzan has noted this process when it comes to nature descriptions, which are, for him, "more than aesthetically or estatically contemplative delays"; Manzoni fashions them by "assimilating external material into inner existence."[10] But he does more: he extends his descriptive ingredients, like light, beyond themselves, so that they too become threads. Through its association with them, light interrelates the honest characters (Renzo, Lucia, Fra Cristoforo) in their struggle against Don Rodrigo. Renzo finds himself in a climate of "dawning" and "light" when he flees Milan and reaches the Adda river (another thread in the tapestry). Lucia first appears in saintly radiance, silver hairpins in her hair splaying out "almost like rays," just as her inner radiance shines out when she falls asleep in the Innominato's castle. Not coincidentally, the latter first sees her "by the light of a lantern." The previous chapter, describing the gloomy castle and its fearsome setting, was filled with words like "precipices," "lairs," "harsh mountain range," "dark corridors," and "three mouths of hell." Now nature responds differently, symbolically supported by the ringing of bells: "the rather cloudy sky was all a grey cloud, but brightness . . . grew little by little. . . ."

Fra Cristoforo, too, first appears with saintly radiance, except that his spirituality is broader, nobler, and more diffuse, because nature corroborates it immediately in the form of the rising sun. Indeed, the chapter introducing him begins with the words "The sun," and proceeds to describe how it gradually brightens the valleys and slopes. The capuchin, too, brings light into inimical surroundings, into the clefts and fissures, one might say. And the feeling of light intensifies around him during the final days of his life as he succors the sick in the *lazzeretto*. Momigliano speaks of a "spiritual ascension" in these pages, of a "crystalline pureness" after which death appears as a "luminous mystery."[11] The splendent soul is about to leave mortality behind: his body shines "alive . . . splendid . . . , a pure fire in his eyes." We are thus prepared for the lightnings that flashed while the monk was reuniting Renzo and Lucia, and when the former asks when they will see each other again, the response is laden with brightness and serenity: "Up there, I trust." It is at this point that Fra Cristoforo's "luminosity" compels us to recall the dream of his antagonist, Don Rodrigo: a dream about none other than the monk with his "flashing . . . look," set between two symbols of light—the "damned light" of a candle before he falls asleep, and after he awakens "the light of day . . . which bothered him, like that candle the night before." The image of light is now completely interiorized, while living out simultaneously its thematic role in the novel and allowing us to make an expressive series of spontaneous identifications. Through the process of crossweaving images, we see characters like Renzo (before the demonized crowd or guzzling *monatti*) or Don Rodrigo (before the "luminous" Fra Cristoforo) standing in relationship with a reality higher than their individual selves.

In his dream, Don Rodrigo sees Fra Cristoforo in the exact attitude he had assumed during their first meeting in his mansion, when, speaking in the name of God, the latter had annoyed his interlocutor with what becomes another cogent yet subtly woven symbol in the fabric of the novel: the skull. As he spoke, he waved the little wooden skull at the end of his rosary in front of Don Rodrigo's nose. If we look back, we recall that two great vultures, "their skulls hanging down," were nailed to each of the double gates through which Fra Cristoforo had entered the mansion. And if we look ahead, we see that these two instances anticipate Don Rodrigo's death and its cause. For the plague, too, or rather its deathly intensity, is foreshadowed by the general misunderstanding of the seriousness of the situation that led to it, when the procession is held bearing the mutilated, decayed relics of St. Charles, "his skull mitered." Thus we are prepared, when in the *lazzeretto* Fra Cristoforo takes Renzo to see Don Rodrigo breathing his last: "The miserable man was motionless, his eyes gaping but lifeless, his face pale . . . : you would have said it was the face of a cadaver." The underlying skull is suggested, and with this image ends the long confrontation between the two rivals.

The juxtaposition of light and dark, which gives relevance to their relationship, is summarized in the character of the Innominato, the satan who becomes saint. Word-symbols help Manzoni prepare this conversion: the clouds and the sun become the identifying images of his character's inner struggle, even as they externalize the gloom one experiences in the presence of the plague, and the Providential hope for renewal after it passes. The sky is first "totally veiled by a cloud . . . , denying the sun," and then "huge clouds . . . suggested a stormy night, except that . . . the sun pierced through, as if from a dense veil." We must recall that nature descriptions are relatively rare in Manzoni, so that each calls special attention to itself. There are several on the Innominato plane. Pellizzari judiciously singles out Manzoni's reference to him as a man with a heart concealing a demon, in order to underscore the character's basic, though at first indistinct, dualism of evil desires and good instincts: "and we feel in advance the great struggle of passions which will take place in him."[12] The dualism takes visible form with the interplay of sun and clouds above the Innominato's landscape, which Marcazzan calls "a psychological introduction."[13] For we read of the sun hiding behind a mountain, of clouds glowing with fire, of angry light and dark cold—each item assuming a special significance. And we are thrown back to an early symbol at the beginning of the Innominato plane, the sign over the tavern guarding the access to his estate: "On both sides of an old sign which hung from above the door was painted a radiant sun; but the public . . . called that inn only by the name of Evil Night [*Malanotte*]." By retracing this particular thread of the tapestry, we become not only more conscious of our original impression of the mood-setting nickname of the tavern, but also aware of the meaning of the blazing suns on the sign, given the denouement of the Innominato episode. We are forced to imagine that the nickname does not endure.

Thus we see that through an intricate crossweaving of word-symbols the structure of *I promessi sposi* achieves that special coherence existing at the base of what most critics have called Manzoni's "lyricization" of reality. Surely, as Montano asserts,[14] Manzoni was not an artist to play the intellectual game of correspondences. From their metaphoric depth, images and symbols grow organically out of the inner stuff of the novel while relating to it spiritually. At work are both a process of interiorization, by which the images become the lifeblood of the novel and its characters, and a process of exteriorization, by which the human situations find artistic dimension in symbols which integrate, and thereby structure, the novel. Symbolic counterparts weave a dialectical fabric.

CHAPTER 10

The Juice of the Whole Tale

A BOVE the irony and through the humor there dominates a sense of life's seriousness and of its intrinsic and potential beauty. An inner glow of understanding serenity, which not without reason commentators have labeled faith, makes Manzoni communicate with the reader with tacit directness. Despite the "personal" interventions in the play between author and Anonymous Chronicler, Manzoni does not beckon our attention; hence the word "faith," which describes well Manzoni the man, poet, and essayist, is too concentrated to describe a suffused ethico-religious attitude which warms the novel inwardly but does not point to itself as the work's condition of being. His focus is more on people and how they are than on humans and why they are.

We can speak of both his Romanticism and his Realism. The mixture may be observed in his nature descriptions, however few in number. They stand out in sober style; landscapes are not worded effusively. With the attitude of a Classical realist, Manzoni delights in them not out of sentimentality in the manner of Werther but more in the manner of Keats, out of joy in the contemplation of beauty. Hence his glance was more topographical than ecstatic. Surely the vision of home the exiled protagonists keep experiencing is a topographical vision,[1] like the houses and hills Lucia sees during her "Farewell," or, less poignantly, like the setting Fra Cristoforo observes when he leaves his monastery in Pescarenico to visit Lucia:

The sky was completely serene. As the sun rose gradually behind the mountain, its rays could be seen descending from the summits of the opposite mountains and spreading rapidly downward over the slopes and into the valleys below. An autumn breeze was shaking the dead leaves from the branches of the mulberry trees, blowing them about, and falling a few feet from the tree. To the right and left, the vineleaves in the vineyards sparkled

in varied shades of red on festoons that were still taut; and the freshly
turned furrows stood out in vivid brown amid the fields of stubble, white
and glistening with dew. The scene was cheerful; but every human figure
that appeared in it saddened the eye and the mind.

Someone has said that for the most part his landscapes are implicit
in the story rather than described, and where they exist they relate
to inner life,[2] but not as Romantic extensions (*à la* René) of the
individual character's psyche. The sun rises when Fra Cristoforo
moves about, and it is clouded over when the Innominato looks out
of his window. But these natural occurrences are not projections of
an inner state, as we have seen. They relate aesthetically to the
totality of an ethical situation.

   Manzoni's "Romanticism" contains eighteenth-century proto-
Romantic elements of sensibility, philanthropy, and popularism,
but also more immediately Encyclopedic attitudes, such as a
"philosophic" critical intellectualism which, as a result of its acuity
and his moderate temperament, expressed itself in irony against
society and against judicial and religious abuses. His whole manner
exhibits that *philosophe* tendency, extended by the Romantics, to
educate the masses away from superstitions and errors, and to correct the elite's prejudices and intolerances. It is not the poet Manzoni who exhibits this, but the historian, the political and social
critic who wrote an historical novel,[3] one which reflects sadly on
man's ability to govern himself. His pessimism vis-à-vis human history, assuaged by his ironic smile, becomes Romantic through the
overlay of Christian sentiment imposed upon it by his deeply ethical
conscience. Hence his most genuinely Romantic trait, which ac-
cords with principles enunciated by one of Italy's first Romantic
voices, Giovanni Berchet: the popularization of art, its democratiza-
tion through choice of subject, use of language, and sense of mission. Arturo Graf properly agrees to the label "Romantic" for Manzoni, and admits that he headed the Italian school, but cautions us
with many reservations about the full applicability of the label.[4]

   Indeed, if labels are to be sought, that of Realist suits him better.
He said it well in talking about plot in a novel:

As for the course of events and plot, I believe that the best way to do things
differently from others is to focus one's attention in reality on the way men
behave, and above all on what about it is contrary to the romanesque spirit
[*esprit romanesque*]. In all the novels that I have read, I seem to notice an

effort to establish interesting and unexpected relationships among different characters, to give them prominence, to find events which simultaneously and in different ways influence the destiny of everybody—in short, an artificial unity which one does not find in real life. I know that this unity pleases the reader; but I think that this is because of an old habit. I know that it is considered a virtue in some works which derive a true benefit of the first order from it; but I am of the opinion that some day it will become an object of criticism, and that one will cite this way of tying events together as an example of the sway which custom exerts on the best and loftiest minds, or of the sacrifice one makes to establish taste.[5]

Manzoni's realism, more particular than Jane Austen's (whose temperament was also largely unsympathetic to the Romantic movement, who wrote more about human than external nature and not about heroic passions but about everyday details of living, and whose subtle wit and worship of calm sense and level-headedness remind us in many ways of Manzoni), comes closer to Gottfried Keller's in that it pays attention to human facts in their natural habitat, as it were. It also reveals an awareness of the shock value of horrific occurrences at certain times in history, such as the macabre spectacle of the "convoy" of the dead being carted away to the *lazzeretto*, an episode whose trenchant realism provides a climax for human stupidity. But at no time can it be said that the author engages the lugubrious, or the gothic, for its own sake.[6] In fact, the gothic repulsed him because it is unrealistic; his classical nature preferred daylight to darkness. Along the same lines, he avoided the presentation of stormy passion and fiery love: a Heathcliff and a Lelia made him turn the other way. In *I promessi sposi*, love is not declared; it does not magnetize attention to itself, and on no page does it tell its story exclusively. But it is interiorized in almost every page, so that it is hard to conceive of any action of Renzo, for example, divorced from its context. There is sentiment in the novel, but no trace of sentimentalism, as there is no dream-world emotionalism. Similarly in the question of language, as we know, Manzoni's aim was not inflation, or, more acceptably, the picturesque enrichment which Romantics in other parts of Europe strove toward, but clarity and realism, words in their educational and pervasively social or national context.

Identification of Manzoni with his characters—possibly with the humble—is possible only on a "religious" level, that is, on the level of their intimate affinity with his own spiritual qualities. If he had not been detached from them (the Marxists would say paternalistic) and had identified with them on the social level as well, *I promessi sposi* would have stood out as a case of Verismo, or Italian Naturalism, long before Verga and Capuana gave it form. But as it was, Manzoni still opened a window in its direction by intuiting the need to interpret the psychology of the lower class, to scrutinize its motivations, its special logic, its linguistic mechanisms oiled with proverbs and exclamations and interjections, and its confidence in its own perceptions as sources of common sense. An Italian critic writes: "Having known how to strip our literature from humanistic and literary postures, having directed the artist's interest onto the humble classes, having elevated their prestige and human significance in history—this clears the field and opens up our view to this world which is dark but full of a characteristic truth and psychology which the *verist* writer will attempt to reveal by the use of dialectical expressions."[7]

Manzoni's realism embodies a philosophy. More than "Catholic" or "social," as this philosophy has often been classified, it is simply humanitarian, and the humanitarianism is anchored in a realistic view of life. It is not accurate to say that "Manzoni expects the reader to sympathize with his own outlook, a position possible in his age but not in ours,"[8] though, to be sure, his judgment of men's actions is rendered in the light of eternal Christian morality. If *I promessi sposi* represents his statement of his view of life, the statement is not theological because the morality relates to all human existence and is not bound by dogmatic precepts. That he is an artist who espoused a Christian outlook on the world does not permit us to consider his cult the sole determinant of his art, any more than we should claim that Dante's art is totally dependent on his medieval beliefs. Similarly, Manzoni's compassion for the humble does not permit us to see a kind of socialism as the inspiration of his novel. Ideology and art do not mix when an author proselytizes. This is not the case with Manzoni, whose ideology remains private and contained in an intimate vision which may become a fictional objectification of his personal moral world, but which, for all that, does not force itself upon the reader. It has been observed that the Catholic conscience was being eroded by libertarian thinking in his day, the way Reformation and Counter-Reformation had shaken many tenets of faith in the early seventeenth century, when the novel takes place. However, Manzoni's attempt to blend faith and reality was made without propagandistic overtones, if only because the blending outlined for him the parameters of a realistic moral cosmos.

This point cannot be overemphasized, for many a warped perspective has arisen about Manzoni, whose "juice of the whole tale," as Lucia says in the end, becomes a veritable "message," and as such is not just explained but explicated by a rigid application of what a social and confessional religion maintains. Some have asserted that the novel stems directly from the *Osservazioni*.[9] Others have asserted that Providence directs the course of all action, from falling tiles to plague and from rising dawn to rain, and that even Fra Cristoforo's efforts count little in the outcome of things.[10] This view, subject as it is to entirely religiously based assumptions, emasculates the novel. For *I promessi sposi* is about people, which means about life, and was not written with preordained pedagogical ends of the sermonizing kind. Montano put it well, in reacting to the Crocean stress in the work's "oratory":

This is a Christian society. The poet believes in the same values in which it believes; in some way, he is inside it. Men and things are portrayed by one who belongs to that same world, who clearly recognizes the good people and the bad in the same way those living in that world could recognize them. . . . The author has not the slightest interest in altering things and in presenting things in a different light. He knows well that the good and the bad exist in the world; he knows that quite often the bad succeed in the world and that the good succumb. Manzoni . . . is the last person to believe that virtue wins out and is rewarded by God in this world. . . . Manzoni wants to reveal the world as it is; he needs only remain faithful to the Christian view of the society portrayed for which Don Rodrigo is a scoundrel and Fra Cristoforo . . . a generous and fiery man of religion. The poet is like the conscience of the world. The portrait we get is that of a man who believes in the same values. Those are the proportions; there are no prejudices, no distortions. This fact contributes immeasurably to the naturalness, to the realism. The poet undoubtedly has a more elevated conscience; he is in a position to see the superior humanity of Borromeo as well as the cowardice of Don Abbondio or the profound moral beauty of Lucia; but his judgment coincides with the most concrete and objective premises of the society portrayed.[11]

This accounts for the fact that no mysticism enters Manzoni's work. If anything, his interest lies in eternity as actuated by history. Mysticism is tantamount to excess; so is effusive love. And death, as the novel implies, emerges not as the horrid mystery or absurdity of disturbed imaginations, but as a form of terrestrial life, its culminating reality. Like Cardinal Borromeo, to "take things seriously" means to see life realistically as well as with a sense of mission— something ego-bound creatures like Don Abbondio and Sr. Gertrude cannot do. To distinguish abstract moral norms from pragmatic action in our personal conduct amounts to a form of hypocrisy. Yet history reveals how often the hypocrisy is practiced. Injustice and violence characterize the children of Adam and Eve. Hence the pessimism, as the end of *Adelchi* clearly illustrated. Manzoni's finest poetic moments in *I promessi sposi* come when he contemplates universal suffering. He is like Pascal minus the open anguish, and more like Tolstòy; he is "the poet of human misery consoled by divine mercy."[12] Man wanders astray because he does not see well, and because he hears prejudices echoing all about him; and he wanders in a world which has lost its taste for simplicity and intimacy.[13] "*Vanitas, vanitatum, et omnia vanitas,*" Manzoni too could exclaim toward the end of his life.[14]

But to deduce from this that his portrayal of evil confirms "the insufficiency of the religious criterion before characters and situations of the modern world"[15] misinterprets the ethical component of his poetic inspiration, that intimate vision of life. Lay pessimism and spiritual optimism hallmark the philosophy of Manzoni. There is something in this vision of that pomegranate bush he had in his garden in Brusuglio: "I have here in a little garden of mine a young pomegranate which has blossomed richly this Spring, and the flowers have fallen in part, and in part they have held; together, the rankness of all of them and the vigorous health of some announce that this little tree is destined to yield copious and select fruits."[16]

In the fact of poetry, Providence emerges less a faith than a reasonable hope, like the fruit on that tree, less a dogmatic certainty than a universal need, and not a matter of blind, facile belief but of rational desire. Theology emerges simply as moral philosophy, religion as natural morality. Man's heroic measure is taken not in accomplishing great deeds in the mouth of danger but in unassuming strength of character in the midst of human suffering. In this chaotic scenario of life, Manzoni does not turn subserviently to the Gospel's philosophy of suffering but to the conquest of inner man acting freely, and hopefully with the support of his faith. Every chapter of the novel leads to this conquest, and it takes a long time to reach the inner peace of temperance and justice, fortitude, prudence, and charity; it is a long novel, an epic, at the end of which Renzo and Lucia offer us a simple conclusion: ". . . that troubles often come to those who bring them upon themselves, but that not even the most cautious and innocent behavior can ward them off; and that when they come—whether by our own fault or not—confidence in God can lighten them and turn them to our own improvement." This simple conclusion, this "juice" of the tale, discovered by a humble man and woman, is a discovery of God, however defined. It is a conquest far greater than the embattled conquests of powerful rulers and potentates who think they have accomplished great things and who make no discovery. And Manzoni's is a discovery through art, which is a form of moral life, limited, as Galletti says,[17] only by life itself, yet propelled by the aspirations of beauty and purpose, and endlessly struggling against the base instincts of our human nature.

Notes and References

Chapter One

1. Attilio Momigliano, *Alessandro Manzoni* (Milano: Principato, 1966), p. 3. As stated in the Preface, all translations appearing in this study, from both primary and secondary sources, are the author's.

2. In short order, Lombardy and almost all the Papal States (after Pius VII's departure from Rome in 1809) were incorporated in France, and Ferdinand I was driven from Naples by Joseph Bonaparte (in 1808 he was succeeded by Gioacchino Murat).

3. Some have raised doubts as to his legitimacy, suggesting Giovanni Verri as his possible father. Giulia, who was twenty-six years younger than her husband, had known Verri prior to her reluctant, family-induced marriage to Pietro, and even Tommaseo suggests that the relationship did not stop there.

4. As he referred to her in a letter to Giovambattista Pagani, Paris, May 29, 1807, *Espistolario di Alessandro Manzoni*, ed. Giovanni Sforza, 2 vols. (Milano: Paolo Carrara, 1882), I, 47.

5. See Archibald Colquhoun, Introduction to *The Betrothed* (London: J. M. Dent & Sons, 1959), p. vii.

6. *Sermone* I, vv. 9–10.

7. Quoted from *Epistolario*, I, 5.

8. The poem was circulated in manuscript form among his friends, but was not published until five years after his death, in 1878.

9. Some say that it was Claude Fauriel who asked Alessandro to join his mother right after Imbonati's death. He also inherited property from his father, who died in 1807.

10. Manzoni, incidentally, later liked to add the name Beccaria to his own. A letter to Pagani (Paris, March 12, 1806), referring to Pagani's publishing the *Carme* in Milan, contains the following: ". . . I should like you to add to my name a title I'm most proud of, and to place 'Alessandro Manzoni Beccaria' on the frontispiece" (*Epistolario*, I, 15).

11. Letter to Fauriel, Milan, June 4, 1808, *Epistolario*, I, 73.

12. Letter to Fauriel, Milan, March 3, 1826, *Epistolario*, I, 338.

13. Letter to Pagani, Paris, September 14, 1806, *Epistolario*, I, 26.

14. See Elena Gabbuti, *Manzoni e gli ideologi francesi* (Firenze: Sansoni, 1936).

15. *Carme* "In morte di Carlo Imbonati," vv. 631–33.

16. Letter to Fauriel, Brusuglio, April 20, 1812, *Epistolario*, I, 124.

17. Letter to Fauriel, Milan, January 27, 1808, *Epistolario*, I, 62.

18. Letters to Fauriel, Belvedere on the Lake, n.d. (October, 1807?) and March 7, 1808, *Epistolario*, I, 55, 67. The ceremony on February 6, 1808, was performed by Minister Giovanni Gaspero Orelli.

19. Letter to Fauriel, Milan, January 27, 1808, *Epistolario*, I, 64.

20. By Manzoni's later marriage to Teresa Stampa.

21. Symptomatic of his dislike for Jesuits is the statement in a letter to Luigi Tosi (Paris, December 1, 1819, *Epistolario*, I, 168): "The Jesuits own eighty homes in France. The sorrow a Catholic experiences seeing respect for religion diminish daily in such a glorious and important sector of the Church is all the more bitter . . ." etc.

22. Another simultaneous influence was that of Count Jean-Baptiste Somis, a fervent Catholic, with whom they often conversed.

23. See Alfredo Galletti, *Alessandro Manzoni* (Milano: A Corticelli, 1944), particularly pp. 81–100, and Achille Pellizzari, *Studi manzoniani* (Napoli: F. Perrella, 1914). Galletti also brings out Manzoni's appreciation of Bossuet's thoughts on the eternal vicissitudes of human life.

24. Apparently the ceremony took place in the Chapel of the Italian Embassy, the blessing being administered by the parish priest of the Madeleine in Paris, Fr. Costaz.

25. Letter to Gaetano Giudici, Milan, June 29, 1810, *Epistolario*, I, 94. Manzoni asked Giudici to intercede.

26. Momigliano, pp. 15 and 23–24.

Chapter Two

1. See Letter to Fauriel, Milan, March 25, 1816, *Epistolario*, I, 139.

2. Letter to Giuseppe Acerbi, Milan, August 26, 1815, *Epistolario*, I, 134.

3. Letter to Fauriel, Milan, October 17, 1820, *Epistolario*, I, 186.

4. Letter to Countess Diodata Saluzzo, n. pl., October 30, 1829, *Epistolario*, I, 411. We know, of course, that Manzoni expressed many literary judgments—but never polemically or with partisan feelings. See also his letter to Luigi Fratti (Milan, [month missing] 25, 1830, *Epistolario*, I, 415), in which he declares his habit of "staying completely away from any dispute on Italian literature."

5. Letter to Antonio Marinovich, quoted from *Epistolario*, I, 333.

6. See the beginning of his *Carme* "In morte di Carlo Imbonati," vv. 5–8: ". . . I should not wish to stir / The fetid slime of my filthy century / If I but saw a ray of virtue on earth."

7. See letter to Fauriel, n. pl., May 29, 1810, *Epistolario*, I, 90: "There is really only *you* through whom I am still attached to that Paris which I do not like at all in other respects."

8. Manzoni, it seems, hoped to write even more than twelve poems for the series. We have only fragments of some.

9. Letter to Professor Pier Alessandro Paravia, Milan, July 23, 1855, *Epistolario*, II, 251.

10. Letter to Fauriel, Milan, February 9, 1814, *Epistolario*, I, 129.

11. Not that Manzoni ever gave the impression of being exaggeratedly humble. Momigliano correctly gives an example of "correct pride" (p. 68): when he was elected "foreign member" of the Royal Academy of Sciences of Turin, he subtly criticized in his thanks to Prospero Balbo the formality of the near obsolete title: ". . . such an honor would be dearly paid if I could only obtain it with the title of 'foreign academician,' since closer to my heart is the fact of being your compatriot and that of the other illustrious men of whom this Academy boasts than of being their colleague; for if the latter is an effect of their designation, the former is a gift of God, who made me be born in this Italy which is proud to call them her own."

12. See his letter to Marco Coen, Milan, June 2, 1832, *Epistolario*, I, 441–51, and the analysis offered by Giorgio Petrocchi, "La lettera manzoniana al Coen," *Critica Letteraria* 1, no. 1 (1973), 44–56.

13. *Epistolario*, II, 241. A number of biographers have spoken of Manzoni's precise knowledge of agriculture and of how he aided the development of Italian agriculture. His correspondence refers frequently to his interest; "I am in projects of agriculture up to my neck" (letter to Fauriel, Brusuglio, September 21, 1810, *Epistolario*, I, 104). The first to pay tribute to this side of the man was A. Galanti, "Alessandro Manzoni agronomo," *La Perseveranza* 15, no. 4907 (1873). Three paragraphs of this article are quoted by Ercole Gnecchi, ed., *Lettere inedite di Alessandro Manzoni* (Milano: L. F. Cogliati, 1900), p. 89. A fuller account is given in *Epistolario*, II, 240–43: "Nor did he lack exact biological cognitions, as if he knew by heart the dictionary of the common names of plants. . . . It was often Manzoni to first experiment with the groundnut and many other technical plants, and this permitted many of his friends to learn the unknown virtues of cultures which are useful and used in foreign lands. This is exactly what happened with French vines—so called erroneously, since the methods and vines were used in Italy for some time—a plantation of which he laid as early as 1829, using Burgundy grapes; and he adopted the precise Levantine pruning method which, being quite economical, was imitated by other progressive viticulturists of that day." Manzoni read at length the works of Filippo Re, the noted agronomist, as well as the *"Bon-Jardinier* [an almanac], Dumont-Courset, and Miller" (letter to Fauriel, n. pl., February, 1811, *Epistolario*, I, 111, 210 [n.d. 1821?]).

14. See Larry H. Peer, "Schlegel, Christianity, and History: Manzoni's Theory of the Novel," *Comparative Literature Studies* 9, no. 3 (September, 1972), 266–82. In a letter to Countess D. Saluzzo (Milan, September 16, 1827, *Epistolario*, I, 355), Manzoni wrote: "I am deeply convinced of the truth of that principle expressed the first time, as far as I know, by Mr. A. G. [W.] Schlegel, that the form of compositions must be organic and not mechanical. . . ."

15. Letter to E. De Amicis, Milan, June 15, 1865, *Epistolario*, II, 314.

16. See Momigliano, p. 62.

17. See Letter to the President of the Society for Comic Theater, Milan, February 28, 1871, *Epistolario*, II, 383. See also Letter to Countess D. Saluzzo, n. pl., October 30, 1829, *Epistolario*, I, 411.

18. See Letter to Giorgio Briano, Lesa, October 7, 1848, *Espistolario*, II, 176–77.

19. Quoted from *Epistolario*, I, 374.

20. In *Gespräche mit Goethe*, quoted from *Epistolario*, I, 354. Goethe admired Manzoni's characterizations, but was less taken by his historical digressions, which he found tedious.

21. Quoted from Colquhoun, p. xiv.

22. See *Epistolario*, I, 475.

23. A fuller summary of these facts relating to reaction to the novel may be found in Colquhoun, pp. xiv–xv.

24. Letter to Fauriel, Milan, November 3, 1821, *Epistolario*, I, 215.

25. Other writings on this general subject include another letter to Bonghi on Dante's *De vulgari eloquentia* and a *Lettera al Casanova* of 1871.

26. Letter to Marco Coen, Milan, May 20, 1834, *Epistolario*, I, 478.

27. Raffaelo Barbiera, *Il salotto della contessa Maffei* (Milano: Fratelli Treves, 1925).

28. While no one could replace Enrichetta, he loved Teresa too, though this second marriage came about in large part because his health demanded a constant companion. We might also note that Manzoni survived many of his friends, thus intensifying the growing solitude of his later years: for example, the chemist Gaetano Cioni (died 1851), the archaeologist Domenico Sestini (1852), Tosi (1845), Vieusseux (1863), the nobleman atheist Visconti (1841), the lawyer Pagani (1864), Cuoco (1823), Somis (1826), Dègola (1826), Monti (1828), Carlo Botta (1837). Manzoni's father died at the age of 71 in 1807, and his mother at 79 in 1841.

29. Letter to Louise Collet, n. pl., 1860, *Epistolario*, II, 282–83.

30. Letter to Biagio Giuccioli Valentini, Brusuglio, September 26, 1829, *Lettere inedite*, p. 60.

31. Letter to Fauriel, n.d. 1821?, *Epistolario*, I, 209.

32. Letter to Fauriel, Milan, September 12, 1822, *Epistolario*, I, 254.

33. Letter to Count Gabrio Casati, Lesa, March 10, 1850, *Epistolario*, II,

189. See also Letter to Professor Pier Alessandro Paravia, Milan, July 23, 1855, *Epistolario*, II, 251.

34. Letter to Professor Giovambattista Giorgini, Stresa, June 27, 1855, *Epistolario*, II, 248.

35. Ibid., p. 249.

36. Quoted from *Epistolario*, I, 370, 373.

37. To Cesare Cantù in 1867, *Epistolario*, II, 93.

38. See again (note 11, above) the subtle words used to the President of the Royal Academy of Sciences of Turin, Prospero Balbo, in which he places matters of national conscience above those of academic organization.

39. This he did despite the fact that his son, Filippo, had been captured and made prisoner by the Austrians during the street fighting of the Five Days of Milan, during which the Milanese drove out the aggressors.

40. See *Epistolario*, II, 35–38.

41. Letter to the President of the Piedmontese Assembly, Lesa, October 13, 1848, *Epistolario*, II, 178.

42. Bernard Wall, *Alessandro Manzoni* (New Haven: Yale University Press, 1954), p. 13.

43. Letter to Victor Cousin, Milan, June 8, 1840, *Epistolario*, II, 37.

44. "All'Offertorio," in *Strofe per una Prima Communione*, stanza 2, v. 6.

45. Colquhoun, p. v.

Chapter Three

1. C. F. Goffis, in *La lirica di A. Manzoni* (Florence: La Nuova Italia, 1964), establishes a link with the *Ultime lettere di Jacopo Ortis* (pp. 31–32).

2. See Ferruccio Ulivi, *La lirica del Manzoni* (Bari: Adriatica Editrice, 1967), pp. 22–23, for example, where the author wants to show how Manzoni's preconversion poetic manner often adumbrates aspects of future poetry—of the Choruses, or the *Inni sacri*. Luigi Russo, too, sees in the *Sermoni* a foreshadowing of the Catholic view of evil and sin (*Ritratti e disegni storici*, series II [Bari: Laterza, 1946], p. 139–141).

3. Mario Sansone, *La poesia giovanile di A. Manzoni* (Milano: Principato, 1941), p. 40–43. See also, by the same author, *L'opera poetica di A. Manzoni* (Milano-Messina: Principato, 1947). It might be noted at this point that, as a comment on his artistic self-evaluation, Manzoni only published three of his early poems: "A Francesco Lomonaco," "In morte di Carlo Imbonati," and "Urania," which reflect his three principal concerns: patriotism, parent, and poetry.

4. Milan, February 19, 1836, in *Lettere inedite*, p. 75. He further speaks warmly of the elementary, common, and fixed qualities of the language of the Catholic church.

5. See Giosuè Carducci, "A proposito di alcuni giudizi su A. Manzoni," in *Prose* (Bologna: Zanichelli, 1944).

6. Ulivi, p. 54.

7. Pietro Paolo Trompeo, *Vecchie e nuove rilegature giansenistiche* (Napoli: Edizioni Scientifiche Italiane, 1958), p. 44.

8. Goffis, pp. 117–18.

9. See Aurelia Accame, *La formazione del linguaggio lirico manzoniano* (Roma: Edizioni di Storia e Letterature, 1963), p. 84–86.

10. Momigliano, p. 192.

11. See Umberto Bosco, "Lettura degli *Inni sacri* manzoniani," *Aspetti del romanticismo italiano* (Roma: Cremonese, 1942), p. 187.

12. Giuseppe Petronio, *Formazione e storia della lirica manzoniana* (Firenze: Sansoni, 1947), pp. 39–40.

13. Giovanni Battista De Cristoforis, in no. 88, 1819, p. 355.

14. Quoted from *Epistolario*, I, 131.

15. See Natale Busetto, *La composizione della "Pentecoste"* (Milano-Roma-Napoli, 1920). See also I. Sanesi, "Il codice autografo degl' *Inni sacri*," *Annali manzoniani*, vol. 4, Milan, 1943.

16. We must note, however, that the fifty-six verse fragment of "Ognissanti," begun in 1847, contains poetry of rare beauty:

> To Him who once again placed
> The vital stalk in the grass of the field,
> Mended the threads of your garment,
> And tempered the pharmacist's brew;
>
> Who made pines inflexible to south winds,
> Who made the willow soft to the hand,
> Who made the larch endure the winters,
> And the alder endure the water. . . .

17. Ulivi, p. 61.

18. Momigliano, p. 193.

19. Ibid., p. 195.

20. Niccolò Tommaseo, "A. Manzoni," *Inspirazione ed arte* (Firenze: Le Monnier, 1858), p. 341.

21. Koerner actually died on August 26, during the battle of Gadebusch. Caution being the better part of valor, as Rabelais among many believed, Manzoni withheld publication until 1848, when he released it on the occasion of the Five Days of Milan, along with his *Proclama di Rimini*.

22. As early as 1806 (February 9, Manzoni had observed: "I believe that meditation on what is and on what ought to be, and the bitter feeling that is born from the contrast—I believe that this meditating and this feeling are the springs of the best works of our time, in verse or in prose" (Letter to Fauriel, quoted in Eurialo De Michelis, *Studi sul Manzoni* [Milano: Feltrinelli, 1962], p. 106).

Chapter Four

1. Letter to Attilio Zuccagni Orlandini, January 4, 1828, quoted from *Manzoni: tutte le opere* (Roma: Avanzini e Torraca, 1965), pp. 66–67.

2. Giovanni Orioli, in ibid., p. 67.

3. Letter to Fauriel, March 25, 1816, *Epistolario*, I, 140.

4. Galletti, p. 384.

5. Letter to Fauriel, March 25, 1816, *Epistolario*, I, 140.

6. Letter to Gaetano Giudici, February 7, 1820, *Epistolario*, I, 172.

7. Momigliano, p. 177. To the contrary, Francesco Flora sees in Carmagnola's "religious acceptance of death" the culminating sign of an essentially "poetic" character (*Storia della letteratura italiana* [Milano: Mondadori, 1940], III, 204–6).

8. Galletti, pp. 389–90.

9. See Orioli, p. 67.

10. The Chorus is in sixteen octanes (seven decasyllables and a final nonasyllable) and in rhyme: abacbddc.

11. Letter to Gaetano Giudici, February 7, 1820, *Epistolario*, I, 172–73.

12. Alberto Chiari, Introduction to *Il Conte di Carmagnola* (Firenze: Le Monnier, 1947), p. xxxvi.

13. Foscolo actually despaired: "Poor us! Poor *belle lettere!* . . . What a sacrilege!" The *Biblioteca italiana* (February, 1820) said scoffingly: "We have hundreds of such tragedies . . . ," and the *Quarterly Review* urged Manzoni to stick to splendid odes and not disgust the public with weak tragedies (December, 1820). See *Epistolario*, I, 193–96.

14. Used for *Adelchi*, though in his mind the epithet applied also to *Carmagnola:* letter to Fauriel, March 6, 1822, *Epistolario*, I, 228.

15. Letter to Johann Wolfgang Goethe, January 23, 1821, *Epistolario*, I, 191. In this letter of gratitude for the German poet's "favorable judgment," Manzoni expresses surprise that critics "saw almost everything differently from the way I had imagined it; they praised those things to which I had given less importance, and took as oversights and inadvertences . . . those parts which were the fruit of my most sincere and persevering meditation."

16. *Epistolario*, I, 194. Goethe's long analysis was in *Über Kunst und Alterthum* of that year. Manzoni admitted to Goethe that the character distinction was due to "too scrupulous an attachment to historical accuracy" (*Epistolario*, 1, 192), and of Fauriel (March 6, 1822, *Espistolario*, I, 231), who was preparing a French translation, he requested a deletion of the distinction. A German translation was readied by one Arnold.

17. See *Epistolario*, I, 194.

18. Letter to Fauriel, December 3, 1821, *Epistolario*, I, 218.

19. Letter to Fauriel, March 6, 1822, *Epistolario*, I, 228.

20. Quoted in *Epistolario*, I, 197.

21. See Chiari, p. xxxiii.

22. Letter to Fauriel, October 17, 1820, *Epistolario*, I, 187–88.

23. Letter to Luigi Paroletti, 1820(?), *Lettere inedite*, pp. 6–7.

24. Filippo Piemontese, "L'ispirazione storico-religiosa dell'*Adelchi*," *Convivium* 1 (1949), p. 4.

25. Galletti, p. 391.

26. Manzoni later asked Fauriel, when translating into French, to leave the historical names as they were, for even if they sounded coarse that could not be helped, but to make the fictional ones "less baroque and closer to their Germanic root . . . since I have had to distort them in order to Italianize them" (Letter to Fauriel, March 6, 1822, *Epistolario*, I, 230).

27. While the whole play, like *Carmagnola*, is in endecasyllables, the two Choruses stand out rhythmically through their change in meter. "Italy's Chorus" (the first) contains eleven stanzas of six 12-syllable verses each, rhymed aabccb. It has a slow, deliberate cadence, creating an effect of sad solemnity. "Ermengarda's Chorus" (the second) is made up of twenty stanzas of six 8-syllable lines, with only 2 and 4 rhyming, and 6 with the previous 6. The effect is totally different: it moves along effortlessly, and more lyrically and more serenely than the first.

28. See the study by Cesare De Lollis, *Alessandro Manzoni e gli storici liberali francesi della Restaurazione* (Bari: Laterza, 1926).

29. Bollati, quoted in Orioli, p. 69.

30. Benedetto Croce, "Alessandro Manzoni," in *Saggi e discussioni* (Bari: Laterza, 1952), p. 118.

31. Francesco De Sanctis, *Letteratura italiana nel secolo XIX*, ed. L. Blasucci, 2 vols. (Bari: Laterza, 1953), I, 101.

32. Croce, p. 120.

33. However, we are not of the opinion, held by some, that the characters in *Adelchi* in the long run become rigidified into symbols of Manzoni's thought. In varying degrees, each has his own complexity which precludes the vagueness of abstraction or the neatness of allegory.

34. Ulivi, p. 101.

35. See Emilio Santini, *Il teatro di A. Manzoni* (Palermo: Palumbo, 1940), pp. 79–87 passim.

36. Letter to Coen, May 20, 1834, *Epistolario*, I, 479.

37. Quoted in Galletti, pp. 394–95.

38. Filippo Piemontese, *Manzoni* (Brescia: La Scuola Editrice, 1953), p. 161.

39. Galletti, p. 395.

40. Momigliano, p. 188.

41. Letter to Fauriel, March 6, 1822, *Epistolario*, I, 228.

42. Russo, pp. 19–20.

43. Momigliano (pp. 186–87) suggests that the reason Martino does not reappear in the play after scene 3 of Act II is that he represents the great hope for Italian liberation, to be executed by the Franks, and when this

hope is crushed (as Italy's Chorus tells us) by subsequent disillusion, there is no need for him to return on stage. He vanishes with the hope. Russo stresses too heavily the "presence of God" and the "poetry of faith" in this description of nature's wonders (*Alessandro Manzoni: liriche, tragedie, e prose* [Firenze: Sansoni, 1951] p. 180). We see it primarily as a structural device.

44. "M. Fauriel," in *Portraits contemporains* (Paris: Calmann-Lévy, 1889), IV, 206.

45. Nino Borsellino, "Panorama della letteratura critica sull'*Adelchi*," *Quaderni del teatro popolare italiano*, no. 1 (Torino: Einaudi, 1960), p. 147.

46. See a brief discussion along some of these lines in Luciano Codignola, "Aless. Manzoni: *Adelchi*," in ibid., p. 142.

47. Ulivi, p. 89.

48. Russo, "Parere sull'*Adelchi*," in *Ritratti e disegni storici*.

49. Galletti, pp. 405–6.

50. Ibid., p. 396.

51. See his *Opera poetica di Alessandro Manzoni*, the discussion of *Adelchi* which centers around this point of view.

52. Croce, p. 117.

Chapter Five

1. As well as of the seventeenth-century French orators: Bossuet, who is more eloquent, Bourdaloue, who is more arid; and Massillon, who is more maudlin.

2. Mario Sansone, in *Letteratura Italiana: I Maggiori*, (Milano: Marzorati, 1956), II, 969.

3. Letter to Countess D. Saluzzo, Milan, September, 1828, *Epistolario*, I, 362–63.

4. See, for example, Momigliano, p. 89; B. Croce, p. 58; and Galletti, p. 161.

5. Cesare Angelini, *Invito al Manzoni* (Brescia: La Scuola, 1960), p. 49.

6. Letter to E. Dègola, Milan, February 27, 1812, *Epistolario*, I, 114. The "praise" is psychologically consistent with Manzoni's desire to "shake my slowness in the service [of God, since I] not only forgot God but had the misfortune and brashness to deny Him" (Letter to same, n.d., *Epistolario*, I, 120).

7. See Giuliano Manacorda, in *Manzoni: tutte le opere*, p. 611.

8. See Momigliano, pp. 89–90, and his discussion of the latter point, p. 92. Manzoni, he says, makes belief a moral duty, but the fact still remains that spiritual purity can exist without faith, and the will might be able to enlighten, correct, or modify a feeling, but it cannot give birth to it. The argument is coldly intellectual, and does not take into account how, after novel and dispassionate examination, emotions and attachments arise which were never dreamed possible previously (understanding is the first step

toward acceptance), so that it may indeed be possible to acquire faith through will.

9. Momigliano, p. 94.

10. Ibid., p. 100.

11. Galletti, chapters IV and V, and "Le idee morali di Alessandro Manzoni e le *Osservazioni sulla morale cattolica,*" *Rinnovamento* 3, nos. 1, 2 (1909).

12. Galletti, "Le idee morali di Alessandro Manzoni e le *Osservazioni sulla morale cattolica,*" p. 44.

13. Natalino Sapegno, *Compendio di storia della letteratura italiana* (Firenze: La Nuova Italia, 1952), III, 187.

14. As Manacorda (p. 606) points out—and Croce and Momigliano too—Manzoni's political judgment in this essay is frequently in error: Italian "concordance" or the oligarchy of 1861, for example, or, as opposed to his statement that "the temptation to oppress was prevented," the beginning of Italian colonialism in Africa at the same time he was writing these lines.

15. C. De Lollis, p. 132ff. Another "Crocean" position is argued by Niccolini, *Peste e untori nei "Promessi sposi" e nella realtà storica* (Bari: Laterza, 1937), and *Arte e storia nei "Promessi sposi"* (Milano: Hoepli, 1939).

16. Croce, p. 54.

17. Letter to Pagani, Paris, August 31, 1808, *Epistolario*, I, 76–77. From Brusuglio on August 27, 1866, he wrote to Luigi Longoni, the Librarian of the Braidense, asking for documents published by one Mr. Spark relative to various declarations during the years 1765, 1774, 1775, and 1776, and for George Bancroft's *History of America* (August 29, 1866). See also *Lettere inedite*, pp. 146–47.

18. See Manacorda, p. 607.

19. Galletti, *Alessandro Manzoni*, p. 393.

20. Letter to Fauriel, Milan, November 3, 1821, *Epistolario*, I, 219, 218.

21. Letter to Fauriel, Milan, March 6, 1822, *Epistolario*, I, 228.

22. In *Letteratura Italiana: I Maggiori*, II, 979.

23. Eugenio Allegretti, in *Manzoni: tutte le opere*, p. 259. Verri's work, *Osservazioni sulla tortura*, is of the late 1600s, but was not published until 1804 because of censorship.

24. Giancarlo Vigorelli, *Il Manzoni e il silenzio dell'amore* (Roma: Macchia, 1954), p. 77–80.

25. Luigi Russo, in *I classici italiani nella storia della critica* (Firenze: La Nuova Italia, 1955), vol. III, part 1, p. 307.

26. Galletti, p. 497.

27. Momigliano, p. 164.

28. Giovanni Rizzi, in *Epistolario*, II, 339.

29. *Letteratura Italiana: I Maggiori*, II, 939. The *Lettre* takes its place in

a polemic battle waged in Italy among writers over the article they read by Mme. de Staël in the *Biblioteca italiana* (January, 1816), "Sulla maniera e utilità delle traduzioni," in which she urges Italians to renovate the sources of their culture by looking to the new poetics and philosophy in Germany and England. She was attacked by Gherardini, Caleppio, and Leopardi, defended by Di Breme, Borsieri, and Berchet, and the melee was entered also by Visconti, Torti, Pellico, Grossi, Porro, Porta, and Cattaneo. As usual, Manzoni's abstention from literary arguments kept him apart. Though the excited intellectual climate may have encouraged him, this does not mean that the *Lettre* must be "entirely understood and studied in the context of this battle," as Natalino Sapegno says (*Ritratto di Manzoni e altri saggi* [Bari: Laterza, 1961], p. 92). Another questionable—and more seriously so—attitude toward this piece is that of viewing it as fundamental for understanding the genesis of the great novel. Debating the merits or demerits of this critical perspective launched by De Sanctis has become the pastime of many Italian critics (Cestaro, Zottoli, Barbi, Fossi, Russo, Berselli, Bobbio, Forti, Lo Priore, Mazzamuto, etc.), who otherwise have important things to say about the document. Not that the inquiry is vain, but if the answer is affirmative and the *Lettre* is so inescapably central, then we might as well look into any number of possible intellectual sources of Manzoni's thinking in this respect: Schlegel's *Vorlesungen über dramatische Kunst und Literatur,* Sismondi's *Littérature du Midi de l'Europe,* de Staël's *De l'Allemagne,* Le Tourneur's anthology of English critics gathered in preface to his translations of Shakespeare, Lessing's *Hamburgische Dramaturgie,* Batteux's *Principes de la littérature,* etc. (See Lucio Felici, in *Manzoni: tutte le opere,* p. 1057). If the answer is negative, then much ink has been lost. Along these lines, we might recall how many critics signaled the umbilical tie between the *Osservazioni* and the poetry of Manzoni, and how Francesco Flora had to expend an argument to refute it: there is "the same difference we find between a program and a concrete action, or at best between a dramatic motif and the real drama" (III, 225).

30. Letter to Fauriel, Milan, October 17, 1820, *Epistolario,* I, 185.

31. Letter to Fauriel, Brusuglio, July 13, 1813, *Epistolario,* I, 146.

32. Letter to Fauriel, Milan, September 12, 1822, *Epistolario,* I, 257–58.

33. See a discussion of this relationship in Michele Barbi, "*I Promessi sposi* e la critica," *Annali manzoniani* 3 (1942), 163. Barbi opposes the views of Angelandrea Zottoli (*Umili e potenti nella poetica del Manzoni* [Roma: Tumminelli, 1942]), who looks askance at the supposedly integrating role of history which actually deprives poetry of its necessary autonomy.

34. Barbi, p. 167.

35. Momigliano (p. 143) suggests that Manzoni is alluding to the serenity of Greek art, made, however, more "pensive" by the addition of the Christian element.

36. Letter to Fauriel (probably Milan, 1821), *Epistolario*, I, 207.

37. See Sapegno, *Alessandro Manzoni: La "Lettre à M. Chauvet"* (Roma: Ateneo, 1947), p. 20ff. Manzoni often complained that the cult of vagueness or that of form had prevented poetry from expressing ideas along with sentiments, particularly as practiced in Italy: "For a long time Italian poetry was not much used to express what one thinks, and what one feels in real life . . ." (Letter to Fauriel, Milan, January 19, 1821, *Epistolario*, I, p. 201).

38. Momigliano, op. cit., p. 139.

39. This rigid phrase, too rigid for Manzoni, appears in the first version of the *Lettera*. He removed it later, when a number of theoretical writings were gathered under the general heading of *Materiali estetici*.

40. These are interpretations promoted by Galletti.

41. Momigliano, pp. 153–54.

42. Letter to Fauriel, Milan, November 3, 1821, *Epistolario*, I, 214.

43. Letter to Fauriel, Milan, January 19, 1821, *Epistolario*, I, 200.

44. See Lucio Felici, p. 1058.

45. M. Sansone, *Letteratura Italiana: I Maggiori*, II, 947.

46. L. Felici, p. 1058. See also Piero Fossi, *La Lucia del Manzoni* (Firenze: Sansoni, 1937), p. 44, and Febo Allievi, *Testi di poetica romantica (1803–1826)* (Milano: Marzorati, 1960), p. 315–19.

47. Letter to Emilia Luti, Milan, September 5, 1854, *Epistolario*, II, 232.

48. Known as MS XV A^2.

49. See for Giordani, *Biblioteca italiana* 2 (1816), and for Borsieri, "Avventure letterarie di un giorno," in *I manifesti romantici del 1816* (ed. C. Calcaterra).

50. Letter to Giuseppe Borghi, Milan, February 25, 1829, *Epistolario*, I, 395. There is no concensus on the chronological evolution of the development of Manzoni's linguistic thought, since he did not finish the treatise he had planned, possibly because so much of it had already appeared in fragments. Domenico Bulferetti brought out his *Sentir Messa* in 1923 as *Sentir Messa, libro della lingua d'Italia contemporaneo dei Promessi Sposi* (Milano: Bottega di poesia, 1923), Barbara Reynolds (*The Linguistics Writings of A. Manzoni* [Cambridge: Cambridge University Press, 1950]) revealed MS XV A^2 only relatively recently, and Fiorenzo Forti ("L' 'eterno lavoro' e la conversione linguistica di Alessandro Manzoni," *Giornale storico della letteratura italiana* 131 [1954]) further complicated the discussion by suggesting that the Tuscan orientation was not Manzoni's sole one, but indeed that a "European" phase had preceded the "Tuscan" phase. The literature is rich on this subject.

51. Letter to Fauriel, Milan, November 3, 1821, *Epistolario*, I, 214–16.

52. The second part, on the true Italian language, and the third, on the effectiveness and need for such a language, were never written, but their content appears scattered in his other linguistic writings.

53. Momigliano, p. 109. See his discussion also in the subsequent pages, which we have followed here.

54. Momigliano (ibid.) lists the extraordinary number of ancient, Renaissance, and modern grammarians with whom Manzoni was acquainted (p. 115).

55. Letter to Emilia Luti, Milan, September 5, 1854, *Epistolario*, II, 231.

56. Momigliano, p. 112.

57. Letter to Emilia Luti, Milan, September 5, 1854, *Epistolario*, II, 231.

58. Letter to Gaetano Cioni, Milan, February 8, 1836, *Epistolario*, I, 492. See also the Letter to Fruttuoso Becchi, Brusuglio, August 8, 1833, *Epistolario*, I, 470.

59. Letter to Giuseppe Borghi, Milan, February 25, 1829, *Epistolario*, I, 398.

60. In any event, literary vocabulary, Manzoni maintained, was too limited to constitute a dictionary. As a way to disseminate the Florentine-Italian language, he proposed a series of dialect-Italian dictionaries, and a new dictionary of Italian. His first suggestion was not heeded, and the idea would be worth considering even today.

61. Momigliano, pp. 130–31.

Chapter Six

1. The author has not located the records, but the story has been in many a critic's mouth.

2. S. B. Chandler, *Alessandro Manzoni: The Story of a Spiritual Quest* (Edinburgh: Edinburgh University Press, 1974), p. 128.

3. Scholars have juxtaposed the versions quite profitably to arrive at any number of determinations about Manzoni's creative process. Some of the more significant contributions have been made by Pietro Mazzamuto (edition of *I promessi sposi* [Palermo: Palumbo, 1955] and *Poetica e stile in Alessandro Manzoni* [Firenze: Le Monnier, 1957]), A. Momigliano (*Dante, Manzoni, Verga* [Messina-Città di Castello: D'Anna, 1944]), N. Busetto (*La genesi e la formazione dei "Promessi sposi"* [Bologna: Zanichelli, 1921]), Giuseppe De Robertis (*Primi studi manzonian:* [Firenze: Le Monnier, 1949]), F. Flora (pp. 251–53), Giacomo Devoto (*Profili di storia linguistica italiana* [Firenze: La Nuova Italia, 1953]), and most recently Rocco Montano (*Comprendere Manzoni* [Napoli: G. B. Vico Editrice, 1975]).

4. Letter to Fauriel, Milan, May 21, 1823, *Epistolario*, I, 273.

5. Letter to Fauriel, Milan, January 19, 1821, *Epistolario*, I, 202.

6. See Colquhoun, p. x.

7. Quoted from Sarino A. Costa and Giuseppe Mavaro, *L'opera del Manzoni nelle pagine dei critici* (Firenze: Le Monnier, 1962), p. 143.

8. See ibid., re Zaiotti in the first instance, and re Tommaseo in the second, p. 177.

9. Galletti, *Alessandro Manzoni*, pp. 415–426, passim.

10. Helen Cam, *Historical Novels* (London: Historical Association, 1961), p. 19.

11. Georg Lukács, *The Historical Novel* (London: Merlin Press, 1962), p. 70.

12. Ibid.

13. Lion Feuchtwanger, *The House of Desdemona* (Detroit: Wayne State University Press, 1963), p. 62.

14. Luigi Settembrini, *Lezioni di letteratura italiana* (Napoli: Morano, 1894), p. 311.

15. G. Lukács, p. 70.

16. De Sanctis, p. 63.

17. F. D'Ovidio, *Le correzioni ai "Promessi sposi" e la questione della lingua* (Napoli: Guida, 1933), p. 13.

18. Rocco Montano, *Manzoni o del lieto fine* (Napoli: Conte, 1950), quoted from Costa and Mavaro, p. 203.

19. Alberto Moravia, Introduction to *I promessi sposi* (Torino: Einaudi, 1960).

20. See Francesco Ruffini, *La vita religiosa di Alessandro Manzoni* (Bari: Laterza, 1931), especially pp. 460–66.

21. Adolfo Omodeo, *Figura e passioni del Risorgimento italiano* (Palermo: Ciuni, 1932), p. 21.

22. R. Montano, *Lo spirito e le lettere*, 3 Vols. (Milano: Marzorati, 1971), III, 72–79.

23. See L. Russo, *Ritratti e disegni storici*, p. 126.

24. Mazzamuto, *Poetica e stile in Alessandro Manzoni*, pp. 151–55 passim.

25. E. Allegretti, p. 250.

Chapter Seven

1. Taken from Colquhoun, p. xi. Along these lines, a fine discussion of Shakespeare and Manzoni is to be found in Giovanni Getto, *Manzoni europeo* (Milano: U. Mursia & C., 1971), pp. 229–298.

2. Allegretti, p. 254. See L. Russo, *I personaggi dei "Promessi sposi"* (Bari: Laterza, 1952), and "A. Manzoni, Poeta-nume del 1848," *Belfagor* (Firenze, 1948).

3. Ever since De Sanctis noted that Manzoni's was the first novel to have a peasant as protagonist, a chain of critics has held to, and developed, the view that the humble are the central figures: C. De Lollis, A. Zottoli, M. Barbi, N. Sapegno, and A. Moravia, in previously quoted works, as well as Ferruccio Boffi, two articles in *Critica sociale*, 3–4 and 7 (1908), and Antonio Gramsci, *Letteratura e vita nazionale* (Torino: Einaudi, 1953).

4. A. Zottoli, p. 230.

5. See Umberto Colombo, *Manzoni e gli "umili"* (Milano: Edizioni Paoline, 1972), p. 44.

6. Gramsci, p. 105.

7. Moravia, (Introduction).

8. Ibid., p. xxxviii.

9. Montano, *Lo spirito e le lettere*, III, 107.

10. Umberto Calosso's tendency to reduce the perspective and see Renzo as "an honest Italian worker" (*Colloqui col Manzoni* [Bari: Laterza, 1948], p. 86) seems limited to us, as does Cesare Angelini's near identification of him as a Lombard farmer (p. 157).

11. Montano, *Lo spirito e le lettere*, III, 110.

12. De Sanctis, p. 70.

13. Piero Fossi, p. 119.

14. Eugenio Donadoni, *Scritti e discorsi letterari* (Firenze: Sansoni, 1921), p. 338.

15. Ferdinando Giannessi, in *Dizionario letterario Bompiani*, (Milano: V. Bompiani, editore, 1950), VIII, 662.

16. L. Gessi, ed., *I promessi sposi* (Roma: A. Signorelli, 1960), p. 29n.

17. F. Flora, III, 231.

18. L. Russo, in *Dizionario Letterario Bompiani*, VIII, 246.

19. E. Allegretti, p. 254. See, as this critic suggests, A. Zottoli, *Il sistema di Don Abbondio* (Bari: Laterza, 1933), whose thesis seems to derive from F. D'Ovidio's belief that the priest's egoism represents a concrete and reasoned system (*Saggi critici* [Napoli: Morano, 1878]).

20. De Sanctis, p. 3.

21. Sansone, *L'opera poetica di A. Manzoni*, p. 268.

22. Russo, in *Dizionario Letterario Bompiani*, VIII, 262.

23. The term belongs to Filippo Crispolti, *Indagini sul Manzoni* (Milano: Garzanti, 1940), p. 345.

24. Momigliano, p. 219.

25. See M. Sansone, in *Letteratura Italiana: I Maggiori*, II, 290.

26. A. Moravia, p. xxv.

27. He was an historical character, but sources strangely omitted his name, so that Manzoni was easily encouraged to call him as he did, and thereby weave a myth around him.

28. Russo, *I personaggi dei "Promessi sposi,"* p. 45.

29. Ibid., pp. 80–81.

30. The "miracle" thesis is upheld by Achille Pellizzari, "Estetica e religione di A. Manzoni," *Studi manzoniani*, vol. I (Napoli: Perella, 1914); Giuseppe Citanna, *Il romanticismo e la poesia italiana* (Bari: Laterza, 1949); and others, while the contrary is upheld by De Sanctis, *Manzoni*, ed. C. Muscetta & D. Puccini (Torino: Einaudi, 1955); F. D'Ovidio; and others.

31. See Arturo Graf, *Foscolo, Manzoni, Leopardi* (Torino: Chiantore, 1945).

32. Indeed, the Cardinal was a famous, remarkable man—which does not mean that he was exempt from any number of seventeenth-century vices.

33. See Russo, *I personaggi dei "Promessi sposi,"* p. 158. We might note at this point, with S. B. Chandler, that "For Manzoni, as against Locke, Hume, Condillac, and Rousseau, the definition of the individual is not the unifying memory of feelings or perceptions, but the enduring moral personality" (p. 110).

34. L. Russo, in *Dizionario Letterario Bompiani*, VIII, 337.

35. Historically, she was Marianna, the daughter of Martino De Leyva, born in Milan in 1575, who became nun in Monza at sixteen under the name of Sr. Virginia.

36. See, for example, Giovita Scalvini, "Dei *Promessi sposi,*" in Marcazzan, *Foscolo, Manzoni, Goethe* (Torino: Einaudi, 1948), pp. 247–48, and F. D'Ovidio, *Nuovi studi manzoniani* (Caserta: Editrice Moderna, 1928), pp. 461–69.

37. N. Busetto, *La genesi e la formazione dei "Promessi sposi,"* p. 401.

38. This is the very aspect which appeals to Moravia.

39. See Marcella Gorra, *Mito e realtà del Manzoni* (Milano: Gentile, 1945), p. 125.

40. See C. De Lollis, pp. 164–84 passim.

41. G. Petronio, *A. Manzoni: I promessi sposi* (Torino: Paravia, 1946), p. 153n. Note that elsewhere Petronio disputes the notion of predestination again by referring us to a passage in the *Storia della colonna infame* (p. 168n.).

42. Colquhoun, p. xiii.

43. E. Donadoni, in *Dizionario Letterario Bompiani*, VIII, 253.

44. M. Gorra, p. 51.

45. See L. Russo, *I personaggi dei "Promessi sposi,"* pp. 239–40.

46. E. Donadoni, p. 314.

47. Momigliano, *Alessandro Manzoni*, p. 228.

48. Letter to Fauriel, quoted in E. Allegretti, p. 252.

49. Momigliano, *Alessandro Manzoni*, p. 265.

Chapter eight

1. G. Petrocchi, *La tecnica manzoniana del dialogo* (Firenze: Le Monnier, 1959), p. 43.

2. Letter to Alfonso della Valle di Casanova, Milan, March 30, 1871, *Epistolario*, II, 387. For studies of Manzoni's corrections, see Dante Isella, *Postille al Vocabolario della Crusca nell'edizione veronese* (Milano-Napoli: R. Ricciardi, 1964), and Maria Corti, "Uno scrittore in cerca della lingua," and "Il problema della lingua nel Romanticismo italiano," both in *Metodi e fantasmi* (Milano: Feltrinelli, 1969), pp. 145–159 and 163–191 respectively.

3. Momigliano, pp. 219–20.

4. Petrocchi, *La tecnica manzoniana del dialogo*, p. 43.

5. See Angelica Chiavacci, *Il "Parlato" nei "Promessi sposi"* (Firenze: Sansoni, 1961), pp. 27–79.

6. Ibid., p. 228.

7. Momigliano, *Alessandro Manzoni*, p. 255.

8. Ibid., p. 260.

9. Luigi Pirandello, *Saggi*, ed. Manlio Lo Vecchio Lusti (Milano: Mondadori, 1939), p. 158.

10. Galletti, *Alessandro Manzoni*, p. 444.

11. See Russo, *I personaggi dei "Promessi sposi,"* p. 265.

12. See E. Allegretti, p. 251.

Chapter Nine

1. We wish to call attention to the book on Verga by G. Cecchetti, who discusses the "word-symbols" and the "expressive structure" of *I Malavoglia* (*Il Verga maggiore* [Firenze: La Nuova Italia, 1968]; see, for example, p. 113).

2. The basic ingredients of our discussion exist in *Gli sposi promessi*, but without the same sense of cogency and coherence. Manzoni's elaboration of his first version gives greater artistic relevance to some of the details we shall be considering. For instance, "wall" and "devil" are not so much in evidence in the early version; the sun-cloud interplay is almost nonexistent, Don Rodrigo's death does not have the metaphoric analogy of the skull, and in the end Renzo does not state the imprudence of "raising his elbow too much." Note that the division of the subject matter in the early version into four volumes or books is considerably different from its arrangement in the final version and from the aesthetic meaning we give to it.

3. Giuseppe De Robertis, pp. 107, 499. See also Luigi Tonelli, *Manzoni* (Milano: Corbaccio, 1935).

4. A. Pellizzari, p. 199.

5. Giovanni Gentile, *Dante e Manzoni* (Firenze: Vellecchi, 1923), p. 119.

6. M. Sansone, *L'opera poetica di A. Manzoni*, p. 238.

7. In the novel, wine is rarely used in a positive context (as when the tailor's good wife sends some food and "a *fiaschetto* of wine" to a widowed mother). Such incidents are minor—usually illustrative of some of Manzoni's countless human touches—and receive only passing reference. Manzoni's association of bread with good and wine with evil would seem to date back to the years immediately following his conversion. If we check the *Inni sacri* of 1819, we note that the words appear only in the sacrificial poem "La passione":

> In the shadow of the transformed breads,
> The Host alive with peace and love. . . .
>
> (vv. 11–12)

verses relating to the "blessed mysteries" (v. 9) of the transubstantiation
through which bread becomes the body of Christ; in contrast with:

> As the drunkard wishes wine,
> That hatred is vexed in injuries. . . .
> (vv. 53–54)

verses relating to the people's jeering at Christ's supreme sacrifice on the
cross, which resulted from the "foremost of crimes" (v. 55), Judas' betrayal
of the "blood" of Jesus.

8. See, for example, how the word returns at the moment of the invasion and war, when the *lanzichenecchi* become "devils," "anti-Christs,"
"devils in the flesh," "bedeviled," etc.

9. Tolstoy, also a writer conscious of "expressive" style, creates a relationship between an exteriorized aesthetic and an interiorized moral structure. So does Verga: see Cecchetti, pp. 95–96.

10. Mario Marcazzan, "Il paesaggio dei *Promessi sposi*," *Humanitas* no. 3
(1948), 1199.

11. Momigliano, *Alessandro Manzoni*, pp. 212–13.

12. A. Pellizzari, p. 72.

13. Marcazzan, "Il paesaggio dei *Promessi sposi*," p. 104.

14. R. Montano, *Manzoni o del lieto fine*, p. 92.

Chapter Ten

1. See Arturo Pompeati, *Storia della letteratura italiana*, 4 Vols. (Torino: UTET, 1953), IV, 119–22.

2. See Marcazzan, "Il paesaggio dei *Promessi sposi*," pp. 1198–203.

3. See Riccardo Bacchelli's *La cultura illuministica in Italia* (Edizioni
Radio Italiana, 1957), pp. 286–88. In this regard, we call attention again to
E. Gabbuti and De Lollis, cited above, as well as to Gaetano Ragonese,
L'eredità illuministica in Alessandro Manzoni (Milano-Roma: Gastaldi,
1948), in which the author establishes a number of relationships between
Manzoni and De Tracy, Verri, Rollin, Crevier, and Voltaire.

4. A. Graf, p. 38. Let us recall that Manzoni did not participate directly
in the Romantic rebellion (he avoided the polemics of Classicism and
Romanticism, and did not contribute to the reviews *Il Conciliatore* and the
Biblioteca italiana). His participation was indirect, though forceful.

5. Letter to Fauriel, Milan, May 29, 1822, *Epistolario*, I, 242.

6. See G. A. Borgese, *Storia della critica romantica in Italia* (Milano:
Treves, 1920). The author alludes to Manzoni's sense of reserve, of the "not
too much" (p. 205).

7. A. Allegretti, p. 252.

8. S. B. Chandler, p. 115.

9. See the works, alluded to above, by Piemontese, Zottoli, De Rober-

tis, and De Sanctis. A notable exception to this point of view is that of F. Flora.

10. See the works of Momigliano, De Lollis, Faggi (*Giornale storico della letteratura italiana*, 67, 1962), and Angelini.

11. R. Montano, *Lo spirito e le lettere*, III, 101.

12. L. Tonelli, p. 304.

13. L. Russo, *Ritratti e disegni storici*, p. 13.

14. Letter to F. G., in Padova, Brusuglio, May 21, 1872, *Epistolario*, II, 408.

15. A. Moravia, p. xx.

16. Letter to Edmondo De Amicis, Milan, June 15, 1865, *Epistolario*, II, 314.

17. Galletti, *Alessandro Manzoni*, p. 383.

Selected Bibliography

PRIMARY SOURCES

Alessandro Manzoni: Tutte le opere. Edited by Bruno Cagli, a cura di G.
Orioli, E. Allegretti, G. Manacorda, and L. Felici. Romà: Avanzini e
Torraca, 1965.

Tutte le poesie di Alessandro Manzoni. A cura di A. L. Castris. Firenze:
Sansoni, 1965.

Liriche. A cura di Attilio Momigliano. Torino: Einaudi, 1932.

The Sacred Hymns and the Napoleonic Ode. Translated by Reverend Joel
Foote Bingham. London/New York: H. Frowde, 1904.

Alessandro Manzoni: Tragedie. A cura di P. Egidi. Torino: Einaudi, 1921.

Adelchi, tragedia storica. A cura di Giorgio Derzero. Torino: G. B. Paravia,
1947.

Il Conte di Carmagnola. A cura di Alberto Chiari. Firenze: Le Monnier,
1947.

*I promessi sposi: storia milanese del secolo XVII scoperta e rifatta da Ales-
sandro Manzoni.* Torino: Società Editrice Internazionale, 1933.

I promessi sposi. Edited by L. Gessi. Roma: A. Signorelli, 1960.

I promessi sposi. Edited by Pietro Mazzamuto. Palermo: Palumbo, 1955.

I promessi sposi. Edited by Alberto Moravia. Torino: Einaudi, 1960.

I promessi sposi. Edited by Giuseppe Petronio. Torino: Paravia, 1946.

The Betrothed Lovers. With a biographical introduction by G. T. Bettany.
London/New York: Ward, Look, 1889.

The Betrothed. With a critical and biographical introduction by Maurice
Francis Egan. New York: Appleton, 1900.

The Betrothed. With an introduction by James, cardinal Gibbons. New
York: The National Alumni, 1907.

The Betrothed. Edited by Charles W. Eliot. Harvard Classics, vol. 21. New
York: Collier, 1909–1910.

The Betrothed. Translated, with a preface by Archibald Colquhoun. London: J. M. Dent, 1951/New York: E. P. Dutton, 1956, 1959.

The Betrothed. Translated by Archibald Colquhoun. New York: E. P. Dutton, 1961.

Epistolario di Alessandro Manzoni. Edited by Giovanni Sforza. Milano: Paolo Carrara, 1882.

Lettere inedite di Alessandro Manzoni. Edited by Ercole Gnecchi. Milano: L. F. Cogliati, 1900.

Carteggio di Alessandro Manzoni. A cura di Giovanni Sforza e Giuseppe Gallavresi. 2 vols. Milano: U. Hoepli, 1912–1921.

SECONDARY SOURCES

CHANDLER, S. B. *Alessandro Manzoni: The Story of a Spiritual Quest.* Edinbourgh: Edinbourgh University Press, 1974. A general view of Manzoni's works, rich in insights relating to how all of them successively permit a unitary development toward a spiritual view of life.

CHIAVACCI, ANGELICA. *Il "Parlato" nei "Promessi sposi".* Firenze: Sansoni, 1961. A good discussion not only of speech and dialogue but also of how the whole novel is aesthetically and implicitly dialogued.

COLOMBO, UMBERTO. *Manzoni e gli "umili".* Milano: Edizioni Paoline, 1972. Stresses the notion and the meaning of the commoner in the novel, making good use of recent scholarship.

COSTA, SARINO, and MAVARO, GIUSEPPE. *L'opera del Manzoni nelle pagine dei critici.* Firenze: Le Monnier, 1962. A helpful anthology, with introductory notes, of Manzoni criticism.

CROCE, BENEDETTO. *A. Manzoni.* Bari: Laterza, 1930. A seminal study in Manzoni criticism, relating to questions of historiography, language, aesthetics, didacticism, and the oratorical nature of the novel.

DE LOLLIS, CESARE. *Alessandro Manzoni e gli storici liberali francesi della Restaurazione.* Bari: Laterza, 1926. A look into the intellectual formation of Manzoni and the attitude of "deheroization" of history, along with certain ideas of Thierry.

DE SANCTIS, FRANCESCO. *Manzoni.* Edited by C. Muscetta and D. Puccini. Torino: Einaudi, 1955. Fundamental observations, in the historical method, focusing on Manzoni's liberal, democratic inspiration, his dramaturgy, the novel as fictionalization of religious, philosophical ideas, and his psychological perceptiveness.

D'OVIDIO, FRANCESCO. *Nuovi studi manzoniani.* Caserta: Editrice Moderna, 1928. In the lineage of De Sanctis and the historical method, looking into the popular-national character of the novel and its genuine historicity.

GABBUTI, ELENA. *Manzoni e gli ideologi francesi.* Firenze: Sansoni, 1936. Manzoni's analytical mind in contact with the Ideologues and the question of the nature of things relative to truth, knowledge, language, and art.

GALLETTI, ALFREDO. *Alessandro Manzoni.* Milano: A. Corticelli, 1944. A capital study on the total Manzoni in a context of intellectual history and what today would be called comparative literature.

GETTO, GIOVANNI. *Manzoni europeo*. Milano: U. Mursia & C., 1971. An excellent compilation of essays from 1960 to 1970 dealing with Manzoni internationally: the baroque novel, France, Rousseau, Schiller, Shakespeare, and Cervantes.

GOFFIS, CESARE FEDERICO. *La lirica di A. Manzoni*. Bari: Adriatica Editrice, 1967. The maturing continuity of Manzoni's thought, and the possibility of lexical analysis to penetrate the soul of the poet.

GORRA, MARCELLA. *Manzoni*. Palermo: Palumbo, serie Storia della critica, 1959/1962. A valuable review of the avenues and problems of Manzoni criticism.

GRAF, ARTURO. *Foscolo, Manzoni, Leopardi*. Torino: Chiantore, 1945. Manzoni's romanticism, his primacy in historiography, and the psychological dimension measured against the presence of the supernatural.

MARCAZZAN, MARIO. "Il paesaggio dei *Promessi sposi*," *Humanitas*, 1198–1203 no. 3, (1948). The relationship between nature, characters, and the novel's meaning.

MAZZAMUTO, PIETRO. *Poetica e stile in Alessandro Manzoni*. Firenze: Le Monier, 1957. The Chauvet letter background of Manzoni's poetics, a fine appreciation of the relationship between irony and his tragicomic direction, and its influence on his realism.

MOMIGLIANO, ATTILIO. *Alessandro Manzoni*. Milano: Principato, 1966. A loosely discoursed but insightfully penetrating appreciation of the total Manzoni, stressing the notions of musicality and of the essential unity of his works.

MONTANO, ROCCO. *Comprendere Manzoni*. Napoli: G. B. Vico Editrice, 1975. A tightly and clearly argued interpretation of Manzoni's realism with reference to the Absolute, the narrative, the problem of history and art, the happy ending, the role of language, the notion of moralism, and the intellectual background of the novel.

PELLIZZARI, ACHILLE. "Estetica e religione di A. Manzoni," *Studi manzoniani*, edited by G. de Robertis, Vol. 1. Napoli: Perella, 1914. Generally favoring historical criticism over aesthetic approaches to Manzoni, and his tie with Jansenism and its spiritual values.

PETROCCHI, GIORGIO. *La tecnica manzoniana del dialogo*. Firenze: Le Monnier, 1959. An expert exegesis on the realtionship between speech and character (psychological, moral, and otherwise) in the novel.

REYNOLDS, BARBARA. *The Linguistic Writings of A. Manzoni*. Cambridge: Cambridge University Press, 1950. A valuable attempt to direct attention to unedited or insufficiently researched linguistic essays of Manzoni or to the philological problems he raises.

RUSSO, LUIGI. *I personaggi dei "Promessi sposi"*. Bari: Laterza, 1952. A profound, though sometimes too religiously oriented, analysis of the main characters of the novel.

SANSONE, MARIO. *L'opera poetica di A. Manzoni*. Milano-Messina: Principato, 1947. A convincing look into the coherence of Manzoni's lyricism, or the poetic internalization of his most fundamental ethical convictions.

ULIVI, FERRUCCIO. *La lirica del Manzoni*. Bari: Adriatica Editrice, 1967. The intellectual background and the aesthetic experiences of the poetry, before and after the conversion, including the tragedies, considered as poetry.

WALL, BERNARD. *Alessandro Manzoni*. New Haven: Yale University Press, 1954. A rapid—often too rapid—introduction to Manzoni and the major features of his more important works.

ZOTTOLI, ANGELANDREA. *Umili e potenti nella poetica del Manzoni*. Roma: Tumminelli, 1942. An illuminating comparison of Manzoni and Thierry with reference to the historyless "subaltern" classes and the implications for the historical novel.

Index

Abbadie, Jacques, 27
Adrian, Pope, 65, 76
Aesop, 125
Aleardi, Aleardo, 15
Alfieri, conte Vittorio, 13, 16, 23, 27, 40, 44, 57, 58, 77, 89
Antologia, 14
Ariosto, Ludovico, 78
Aristotle, 26, 29, 134
Augustine, St., 95
Austen, Jane, 159

Baggesen, Emanuel, 42
Ballanche, Pierre, 89
Balzac, Honoré de, 36, 102, 118, 128
Barbiera, Raffaello, 33
Beauharnais, Eugène de, 14, 36
Beccaria, Cesare, 15, 23
Beckett, Samuel, 94
Bentham, Jeremy, 88
Berchet, Giovanni, 15, 23, 51, 158
Bergier, Nicolas-Sylvestre, 27
Bonald, Louis-Gabriel vicomte de, 27, 89
Bonghi, Ruggero, 32, 102
Boileau, Nicolas, 26
Borghi, Giuseppe, 102
Borromeo, cardinal Federico, 74
Borsieri, Pietro, 102
Bosco, don Giovanni, 31
Bossuet, Jacques-Bénigne, 49, 97
Botta, Carlo, 90
Bourdaloue, Louis, 26
Brecht, Bertolt, 81
Broglio, Emilio, 32, 102
Büchner, Georg, 81
Bülow, Karl-Eduard von, 30
Burckhardt, Jacob, 95
Byron, George Gordon lord, 14, 27

Cabanis, Charlotte, 17
Cabanis, Pierre-Jean, 17
Caesar, Julius, 78
Calderón de la Barca, Pedro, 56
Capuana, Luigi, 160
Carbonari, the, 14
Carducci, Giosuè, 31, 51, 79, 115, 127
Carena, Giacinto, 32, 102
Carlo Alberto, king of Italy, 36
Carlyle, Thomas, 89
Carmagnola, Francesco Bussone, conte di, 28
Cattaneo, Gaetano, 27
Cavour, Camillo Benso, conte di, 14, 38
Cesarotti, Melchiorre, 105
Charlemagne, emperor, 26, 29, 66
Charles, St., 154
Chateaubriand, François René, vicomte de, 20, 23, 25, 44, 77, 85, 122, 142
Chauvet, Joseph-Joachim Victor, 29, 96, 98
Chekhov, Anton, 124
Cioni, Gaetano, 141
Coen, Marco, 26, 101, 119
Collet, Louise, 34
Conciliatore, Il, 14, 22, 27, 29, 48, 99
Condillac, abbé Etienne Bonnot de, 17, 104, 108
Condorcet, Marie-Jean, marquis de, 17, 18
Condorcet, Sophie de, 17
Constant, Benjamin, 17
Corneille, Pierre, 26, 56, 62, 77
Cousin, Victor, 26, 35, 36, 37, 78, 104, 107, 108
Crébillon père, Prosper Jolyot de, 26
Crevier, Jean-Baptiste, 109
Croce, Benedetto, 54, 76, 82, 90, 161
Cuoco, Vincenzo, 16, 92

Daniel, 45
Dante Alighieri, 27, 31, 32, 39, 40, 45, 46, 88, 102, 137, 160
D'Azeglio, Cesare, 35, 99
D'Azeglio, Massimo, 15, 23, 34
De Amicis, Edmondo, 27
Dègola, padre Eustachio, 20, 85
De Luc, Jean-André, 27
Desaix, général Louis-Charles, 40
De Sanctis, Francesco, 44, 45, 77, 96, 115, 122, 125
Descartes, René, 26, 104, 108, 109
Desiderio, king of the Longobards, 66
Destutt de Tracy, Antoine Louis, 17
Dickens, Charles, 102
Diderot, Denis, 23
Dostoievsky, Fyodor, 118
Du Bellay, Joachim, 32
Ducis, Jean-François, 26

Eckermann, Johann Peter, 31
Eliot, Thomas Stearns, 45

Fauriel, Claude, 17, 18, 19, 22, 25, 26, 27, 28, 29, 31, 32, 34, 42, 66, 76, 102, 103, 107, 112, 131, 140
Ferdinand I, emperor of Austria, 36
Flaubert, Gustave, 133
Foscari, doge Francesco, 58
Foscolo, Ugo, 15, 23, 40, 44, 64

Galiani, abate Ferdinando, 27
Galluppi, Pasquale, 27, 108
Garat, comte Dominique Joseph, 17
Garibaldi, generale Giuseppe, 14
Genovesi, Antonio, 27
Giannone, Pietro, 92
Gioia, Melchiorre, 27, 29, 112
Giordani, Pietro, 30–31, 31, 36, 102
Giudici, padre Gaetano, 85
Giusti, Giuseppe, 15
Giovane Europa, La, 14
Giovane Italia, La, 14
Gladstone, prime minister William Ewart, 27, 36
Goethe, Johann Wolfgang, 26, 27, 31, 36, 43, 45, 48, 51, 56, 57, 65, 81, 100
Gosselin, Jean, 30
Gozzi, Carlo, 41

Grabbe, Christian Dietrich, 81
Grillparzer, Franz, 81
Grossi, Tommaso, 15, 23, 31, 112
Guénée, Antoine, 26
Guerrazzi, Francesco Domenico, 15
Guizot, François-Pierre, 17

Hegewisch, Dietrich Hermann, 26
Hebbel, Friedrich, 81
Hegel, Georg Wilhelm, 107
Helvétius, Anne-Catherine, 17
Helvétius, Claude-Adrien, 17, 18
Herder, Johann Gottfried von, 95, 102, 105
Hofmannsthal, Hugo von, 139
Holbach, Paul Henri, baron d', 18
Horace, 24, 27
Hugo, Victor, 13, 15, 23, 27, 44, 81, 89, 114, 127

Imbonati, Carlo, 16, 18, 41, 42
Isaiah, 45

Job, 45, 82
John, St., 45
John of the Cross, St., 48
Jonson, Ben, 118

Kant, Immanuel, 26
Keats, John, 157
Keller, Gottfried, 102, 159
Kleist, Heinrich von, 52, 81
Koerner, Theodor, 50

La Bruyère, Jean de, 118
Lamartine, Alphonse de, 23, 27, 31, 36, 91
Lambruschini, Raffaello, 32–33, 102
Lamennais, Hugues-Félicité de, 23, 85
Lebrun, Pyndare, 17
Leonardo da Vinci, 122
Leopardi, Giacomo, 15, 31, 36, 50
Leroux, Pierre, 89
Lessing, Gotthold, Ephraim, 26, 97
Lessmann, Daniel L., 30
Le Tourneur, Pierre, 26
Littleton, Edward, 26
Locke, John, 26, 104, 108
Longfellow, Henry Wadsworth, 36

Lombroso, Cesare, 15
Lorenzo de' Medici, 46
Louis-Philippe, king of France, 36
Ludwig, Otto, 81
Luigina, 16
Luke, St., 45, 50
Luti, Emilia, 105, 141

Machiavelli, Niccolo, 27, 78, 82, 92, 115
Maffei, contessa Clara, 36
Maine de Biran, Marie François, 17, 104
Maistre, Joseph-Marie, comte de, 89
Manzoni, Alessandro: *Biography:* birth
and early years, 15; Italy at his birth,
13–14; formative years, 16–19; marriage to Enrichetta, 19; conversion,
19–21, 23; intellectual development,
26–27, 34–35; travels in Italy, 22, 31,
103; friends, 25, 29, 31; recognition,
36; health, 34; death, 36–37. *Topics:*
agriculture, 26, 167; attitudes, 25–26,
28, 33, 37–38, 84; criticism (literary),
95–102; history, 28, 29, 30, 35, *89–95*,
99; language (philology), 31–33, *102–
107*, 140, 141, 143–144, 147, 159; patriotism, 28, 36; philosophy, 88, *107–
109*, 160; poetry, 24, 34, *39–54*, 96,
98–99; realism, 157, 158–159, 160–
161; religion, 23–24, *84–89*; romanticism, 25, 29, 32, 35, 58, 63, 99–100,
110, 157; style, *140–47*; symbolism
(and imagery), *148–56*; tragedy,
56–83; utilitarianism, 88, 108

WORKS:
*Abozzo di un Capitolo sull'-
Utilitarismo*, 85, 86
"Adda, L'," 16
Adelchi, 29, 33, 56, *65–80*, 81, 82, 83,
92, 117, 162; Notizie Storiche, 67
"Ascenzione, L'," 24
"Assunzione, L'," 24
"Cattedra di San Pietro, La," 24
"Cinque maggio, Il," 27, *51–54*, 56,
63, 117
"Contro i poetastri," 41, 44
Conte di Carmagnola, Il, 28–29, 55,
56, *57–65*, 66, 67, 80, 95, 117; Pref-
ace, 85, 95

"Corpo del Signore, Il," 24
"Delia, A," 41
*Discorso sopra alcuni punti della
storia longobardica in Italia*, 29, 67,
91–93
"Epifania, L'," 24
Fermo e Lucia, 30, 92, 112, 131, 140,
141
"Francesco Lomonaco, A," 16, 40
Inni sacri, 24, *43–50*, 51, 56, 77, 94,
99, 117
Indipendenza dell'Italia, Dell', 91
Intorno al vocabolario, 32, 102, 106
Invenzione, Dell', 35, *108–109*
*Lettera ad A. de Lamartine sulla causa
della indipendenza e dell'unità
italiana*, 91
*Lettre à M. C*** (Chauvet) sur l'unité
de temps et de lieu dans la tragédie*,
29, 56, *96–99*, 100, 118
Lettre à Victor Cousin, 35, 104, *107–
108*
Lingua italiana, Della, 32
Lingua italiana, Sulla, 32, 102, 106
"Marzo 1821," 27, 29, 50–51, 56
"Morte di Carlo Imbonati, In,"
Carme, 17, 40, 41–42, 43, 44, 98
"Morti, I," 24
"Musa, Alla," 40
"Natale, Il," 24, 45, *46–47*, 50
"Nome di Maria, In," 24, *46*
"Ognissanti," 24
Osservazioni sulla morale cattolica,
23, 24, 34, *84–89*, 98, 108, 116, 161
"Pagani, A G. B.," 41
"Panegirico a Trimalciano," 41
"Pateneide, A," 42–43
"Passione, La," 24, 45, *47–48*
"Pentecoste, La," 24, *48–50*, 56, 117
"Proclama di Rimini, Il," 28
Promessi sposi, I, 20, 30–31, 32, 33,
34, 35, 38, 43, 47, 77, 78, 79, 86,
87, 92, 97, 99, 100, 101, 110, *111–
63*; characters, 118–39; deter-
minism (and Jansenism), 116–17;
historicity, 114–15; (the) humble,
119–120, 135, 142, 144, 147, 159–
160, 162–63 (also 47 and 94);
humor, 125, 144–47; irony, 125,

144–47, 158; oratory, 115–16; psychology, 138–39, 141, 145; realism, 117, 157–61; romanticism, 157–61; story, 113–14; versions (and influences), 111–13, 114
"Qual su le cinzie cime," 40–41
"Risurrezione, La," 24, *45–46*
Romanticismo, Lettera sul, 35, *99–100*
Romanzo storico, Del, 30, *100–102*
Saggio comparativo sulla rivoluzione francese del 1789 e la rivoluzione italiana del 1859, 35, *89–90*
Sentir Messa, 32, 102, 105, 106
Sermoni, I, 16, 41, 44
Sistema che fonde la morale dell'utilità, Del, 34
Sposi promessi, Gli, 30, 112, 140, 147, 148
Storia della colonna infame, 35, 91, 92, *93–95*, 99, 143
"Trionfo della liberta, Il," 16, 40
Unità della lingua e dei mezzi di diffonderla, Dell', 32, 102, 106; Appendix, 102
"Urania," 17, 42, 43
Vulgari eloquio, De, 102
CHARACTERS: See *Index of Manzoni's Characters*
FAMILY:
Blondel, Henriette or Enrichetta (first wife), 19, 20, 22, 29, 33, 77, 122
Manzoni, Clara (daughter), 34
Manzoni, Cristina (daughter), 34
Manzoni, Enrico (son), 33
Manzoni, Filippo (son), 34
Manzoni, Giulia Beccaria (mother), 15, 20, 41
Manzoni, Giulia Claudia (daughter), 20, 31, 34
Manzoni, Luigia M. Vittorina (daughter), 34
Manzoni, Matilde (daughter), 34
Manzoni, count Pietro (father), 15
Manzoni, Pietro (son), 34, 36
Manzoni, Sofia (daughter), 34
Manzoni, Teresa Borri Stampa (second wife), 34
Manzoni, Vittoria (daughter), 19, 33
Stampa, Stefano (stepson), 19

Marie-Louise of Austria, empress of France, 19
Marx, Karl, 81, 120, 160
Matthew, St., 45
Maximilian, archduke of Austria, 36
Mazzini, Giuseppe, 14, 15
Metastasio, Pietro, 56
Metternich, count Clemens Lothar, 14, 115
Michelangelo Buonarroti, 79
Molière (Jean-Baptiste Poquelin), 26, 118, 134
Montesquieu, Charles-Louis de Secondat, baron de, 23
Montgolfier, Adélaïde de, 43
Monti, Vincenzo, 15, 16, 40, 42, 44, 63
Montrand, Maxime de, 30
Morbio, Carlo, 27
Murat, Gioacchino, 28, 66
Muratori, Lodovico Antonio, 29, 92
Musset, Alfred de, 56

Napoleon(e) B(u)onaparte, 13, 14, 17, 19, 20, 27, 28, 51–54, 63, 78
Newman, John H., 36
Niccolini, Giovanni Battista, 31, 141
Nicole, Pierre, 26, 47
Nietzsche, Friedrich, 129
Nievo, Ippolito, 15
Novalis (Friedrich von Hardenberg), 25, 77, 142

Ovid, 39

Pagani, Goivambattista, 16, 41
Parini, Giuseppe, 16, 27, 40, 41, 44
Paroletti, Luigi, 66
Pascal, Blaise, 20, 21, 84, 88, 116, 129, 162
Paschoud, Martin, 27
Paul, St., 20, 45, 78
Pedro II, emperor of Brazil, 36
Pellico, Silvio, 15, 23, 51, 63, 64
Pérez Galdós, Benito, 102
Petrarca, Francesco, 40, 46, 50
Petronius, 41
Plato, 26, 86, 107, 108
Plutarch, 26
Poe, Edgar Allan, 31, 141
Praga, Emilio, 15

Quinet, Edgar, 89, 90

Rabelais, François, 26
Racine, Jean, 26, 56, 58, 77
Ranke, Leopold von, 94
Reid, Thomas, 107
Rey-Dusseuil, Antoine-François, 30
Ripamonti, Giuseppe, 29, 112
Risorgimento, the, 14–15, 65, 102
Rollin, Charles, 109
Romagnosi, Gian Domenico, 27
Romanticism, 14–15, 22, 25–26, 29, 32, 35, 76–77, 80–81, 98, 99–100, 101, 102, 104, 110, 128, 138, 142, 158
Rosmini, Antonio, 27, 34, 35, 94, 107, 108, 109
Rossari, Luigi, 31, 102
Rossini, Gioacchino, 36
Rousseau, Jean-Jacques, 23, 26, 97

Sainte-Beuve, Charles-Augustin de, 81
Sartre, Jean Paul, 129
Say, Jean-Baptiste, 27
Schelling, Friedrich Wilhelm, 107
Schiller, Johann Christoph, 26, 56, 57, 77
Schlegel, August Wilhelm, 26
Scott, sir Walter, 26, 29, 31, 100, 101, 112, 113, 114, 118
Senancour, Etienne Pivert de, 25
Seneca, 56
Serre, Olivier de, 26
Settembrini, Luigi, 15, 31, 115
Shakespeare, William, 26, 56, 57, 74, 77, 78, 79, 81, 96, 97, 118, 134
Sismondi, Jean-Charles, 24, 31, 57, 85
Soave, padre, 105
Sophocles, 77
Staël-Holstein, Anne-Louise-Germaine, baronne de, 17, 23, 26

Stendhal (Henri Beyle), 14, 27, 31
Sterne, Laurence, 26
Stewart, Dugald, 107

Taine, Hippolyte-Adolphe, 89
Tasso, Torquato, 50
Theophrastus, 118
Thierry, Augustin, 76, 82, 92, 119
Togliatti, Palmiro, 38
Tolstoy, Lev, 102, 133, 162
Tommaseo, Niccolò, 22, 49
Torti, Giovanni, 31
Tosi, padre Luigi, 20, 24, 30, 34, 85, 131

Valle de Casanova, Alfonso della, 102
Van Gogh, Vincent, 149
Varano, Alfonso, 40
Verdi, Giuseppe, 36
Verga, Giovanni, 102, 160
Verri, Giovanni, 27, 93
Vico, Giambattista, 27, 92, 100, 104, 105
Vida, Marco Girolamo, 27
Vieusseux, Giovan Pietro, 31
Vigny, Alfred de, 114
Villers, Charles François de, 26
Virgil, 27, 39, 41, 45, 122
Visconti, Ermes, 31, 112
Visconti, duca Filippo Maria, 57
Vittorio Emanuele II, king of Italy, 36
Volney, Constantin-François de, 17
Voltaire (François-Marie Arouet), de, 16, 23, 26, 40, 97

Wackenroder, Wilhelm Heinrich, 25
Wergeland, Henrik, 52, 141
Wordsworth, William, 142

Zola, Emile, 102

Index of Manzoni's Characters

Abbondio, don, 113, 121, *123–25*, 126, 131, 135, 139, 144, 146, 150, 151, 161, 162
Adelchi, 67–76, *76–77*, 78, 79, 82
Adriano, papa, 67, 68

Agnese, *123*, 144, 145, 148, 150
Anfrido, 71
(Anonymous Chronicler), 130, 138, 139, 140, 144, 157
Ansberga, 72

Antonietta, 61, 62
Attilio, conte, 136
Azzeccagarbugli, 113, 123, *134*, 135, 139, 145

Bettina, 137
Borromeo, cardinale, 77, 113, 123, 124, 125, *130–31*, 135, 136, 137, 139, 140, 144, 146, 152, 161, 162

Carlomagno, imperatore, 67, 68, 69, 70, 71, 72, 75, *78*, 82, 83
Carmagnola, conte, 57–63, *62–63*
Cecilia, 137, 143
Conte Zio, 136
Cristoforo, fra, 77, 113, 116, 121, 122, *126–28*, 135, 137, 139, 143, 149, 150, 151, 153–54, 157, 158, 161

Desiderio, re, 67, 68, 69, 74, 75, *78*, 82

Egidio, conte, 123
Ermengarda, 33, 67, 68, 70, 72, 73, 76, *77–78*, 79, 82, 83, 122

Farvallo, 71
Fazio, fra, 135
Ferrante, don, 114, *134–35*, 145
Foscari, doge, 58, 59, 61

Galdino, fra, 135
Gerberga, 67
Gertrude, suor, 31, 113, 122, *131–34*, 139, 148, 150, 162
Gervasio, 135
Gonzaga, 61, 62
Griso, il, 113, 126, 136, 137, 150
Guntigi, 71, 74, *78–79*

Ildechi, 71
Indolfo, 71
Innominato, l' (the Unnamed), 113, 116, 121, 122, 124, 126, *128–30*, 131, 135, 136, 139, 140, 141, 146, 148, 149, 152, 155, 158

Lucia, 33, 78, 113, 114, 120, *121–23*, 126, 128, 129, 131, 134, 135, 136, 137, 139, 141, 142, 143, 144, 145, 149, 150, 151, 152, 153, 154, 161, 163

Malatesti, 59
Marco, 59, 60, 61, *63*
Marino, 59, 60
Martino, 70, 80, 82
Matilde, 61, 62
Menico, 137
Mora, 93

Nibbio, il, 122, 129, 136

Padilla, 94
Padre Provinciale, 136
Padre Superiore, 135
Pergola, 59
Perpetua, 113, *123–24*, 139, 143, 145
Piazza, 93
Piccinino, 59
Prassede, donna, 114, 122, *134–35*, 139

Renzo, 113, 114, *120–21*, 122, 123, 124, 126, 128, 134, 135, 137, 139, 141, 143, 145, 148, 149, 150, 151, 152, 153, 154, 157, 159, 163
Rodrigo, don, 113, 121, 122, 124, *125–26*, 127, 128, 129, 135, 136, 137, 139, 141, 144, 146, 148, 149, 151, 153, 154, 161
Rutlando, 71, 83

Sforza, 59
Svarto, 69, *78–79*, 82, 83

Tonio, 135, 137
Torello, 59
Trimalchio, 41

Visconti, duca, 57, 58, 63